LITERARY LANDSCAPE
TURNER AND CONSTABLE

LITERARY LANDSCAPE
TURNER AND CONSTABLE

Ronald Paulson

YALE UNIVERSITY PRESS   NEW HAVEN AND LONDON

Published with assistance from
the Louis Stern Memorial Fund.

Chapters 11–17, on Constable, originally delivered as the Brown
and Haley Lectures, are published by arrangement with the University of Puget Sound.

Designed by Nancy Ovedovitz
and set in VIP Garamond type.
Printed in the United States of America by
Murray Printing Co., Westford, Mass.

Library of Congress Cataloging in Publication Data

Paulson, Ronald.
    Literary landscapes, Turner and Constable.
    "Chapters on Constable originally delivered
as the Brown and Haley Lectures at the University of
Puget Sound in November 1979"—Pref.
    Includes bibliographical references and index.
    1. Turner, J. M. W. (Joseph Mallord William),
1775–1851.   2. Constable, John, 1776–1837.
3. Landscape painting—19th century—England.
4. England in art.   I. Title.
ND497.T8P3   758'.1'0942   81-16185
ISBN 0-300-02804-0   AACR2

10 9 8 7 6 5 4 3 2 1

CONTENTS

LIST OF ILLUSTRATIONS

All illustrations follow page 201.

PREFACE   This book is a historical account of the
two great English landscape painters,
J. M. W. Turner (1775–1851) and
John Constable (1776–1837). They were
contemporaries and by all odds the two greatest painters England has produced.
They both painted landscapes at a time when landscape painting was becoming, through their efforts as much as anyone else's, the great genre (replacing
history painting) and the most viable one for an Englishman (replacing
portraiture).

This is also an attempt to relate landscape painting to verbal discourse—to
explore the kinds of verbal formulation that can be, or must be, applied to
landscape. But since my subject is English landscape painting, the literary
formulation is the most obvious, at least on the surface. It seems to have been
almost impossible for the painters in the English tradition to avoid the
verbal-conceptual as a mediator between them and the natural world, though
formulation is often too strong a term for the complex interplay they derived
from their literary sources. English literature, even in the eighteenth century, pulls against formulation off into irony and disparity. My procedure has
been to ascertain what purpose the literary (or its converse, the reaction
against the literary) served for these painters. I should add that Turner and
Constable are of interest to me precisely because they are not essentially
literary landscapists. The essence of their landscapes seems to defy verbal
formulation—even when the artist himself read literary texts into them.

By "literary landscape" I mean the tradition of landscape painting that
legitimated itself by using the landscape as a backdrop for human activity.
The landscape, as A. Richard Turner says, "is not seen for itself, but as a
commentary upon the human condition, as a speculation upon the tension
between order and disorder in the world."[1] For Bellini or Titian, Leonardo or
Raphael, the landscape was harmoniously related (subordinated) to the
Madonna or some other principle of order in the foreground. When landscape
began to predominate, however, the relationship between it and the human
element became more arbitrary. Claude Lorrain was the chief model for this
sense of "literary": his painting is obviously *about* the prospect, the wonderful glow of the horizon, which he frames and to which he leads the eye; but
he still places unobtrusively in the foreground, over to one side, a few small
figures: Narcissus and Echo from the Ovidian story (fig. 2, to cite one
painting available to English artists in Sir George Beaumont's collection, and
a favorite of Constable's).[2] We shall see that in the 1830s and 1840s both
Turner and Constable, in order to elevate their landscapes to the level of
history painting, still retained human, moral, and literary traces, even
though sometimes they were expressed by no more than a tiny emblematic
rabbit almost invisible on the periphery (see Turner's *Rain, Steam, and Speed*
and Constable's *Stonehenge,* figs. 30, 51).

In the landscape surrounding the emblem, however, we can see the basic
difference between the two great exemplars of English landscape painting.

Turner is the Romantic of James Thomson's *Winter* and *Summer,* of the oppressive and cataclysmic. His paintings are basically mythopoeic, analogous to Blake's prophetic books and derived from Gibbon's *Decline and Fall,* the Ossianic poems, the poems of Byron, and Turner's own poetic fragments, *The Fallacies of Hope.* Although he could portray a particular time and place almost as accurately as Constable, and sometimes did so in his sketches, Turner at his most ambitious (as opposed to Constable at *his,* in the six-foot paintings of the 1820s) depicted those two most fluid of subjects, sky and sea, and so freed himself to carry on a formal play that was finally as obsessive and capricious as Gainsborough's had been in his stylized valleys and ponds. Almost every picture of Turner's that tends toward the "poetic" resolves itself into a vortex freely arrived at through the medium of sky, sea, and mist. Mountains are crumbling or engulfed in snow or clouds, and land is seen through a physical haze or a haze of memory or nostalgia, but still in some way disintegrated (as in the Petworth interiors) and reconstituted as sea or sky.

My underlying assumption is that landscape painting, insofar as it is not strictly descriptive (topographical), lends itself by the fluidity of its subject matter to a personal, even private expression, to a regressive representation of primal materials, to projective identification, substitute formation, and part-object displacement onto natural terrain. Turner is only a peculiarly extreme example of this process. Both he and Constable in their different ways demonstrate this fact about landscape painting.

I must admit, however, that I have come to believe that Constable does this in a more complex way than Turner, and I find his method intellectually more rigorous, in part at least because his medium is more refractory. There is no obvious form like Turner's vortex (or obvious symbol like Turner's sun) that dominates his compositions, because the only free or fluid element in his landscape is the sky, and even this has to reflect (or correspond to) the light pattern on the ground. And so the relationship of nature to imagination, of imitation (or representation) to formal play, of patient recreation to powerful personal associations, is itself to a large extent Constable's subject. I hope that the resulting discussion has tested and qualified these prejudices.

The chapters on Constable were originally delivered as the Brown and Haley Lectures at the University of Puget Sound in November 1979. I have filled out the book version of the lectures with the chapters on the English landscape and topographical tradition and on Turner. These chapters draw upon essays that were originally published in *Eighteenth-Century Studies,* vols. 8 and 10 (1974, 1976), and in *Images of Romanticism,* edited by Karl Kroeber and William Walling (New Haven, 1978).

New Haven, Connecticut
March 1981

INTRODUCTION

          . . . I was smitten
Abruptly, with the view (a sight not rare)
Of a blind Beggar, who, with upright face,
Stood, propped against a wall, upon his chest
Wearing a written paper, to explain
His story, whence he came, and who he was.
Caught by the spectacle my mind turned round
As with the might of waters; an apt type
This label seemed of the utmost we can know,
Both of ourselves and of the universe.

Wordsworth, The Prelude, 7. 637–46

LANDSCAPE AS THE CONTROL OF NATURE

In Wordsworth's confrontation with the blind beggar, the "label" or "emblem" is so inadequate against the actual "spectacle" of the man (whose blindness simply emphasizes the absence of any direct communication with him) that the poet feels his "mind turned round / As with the might of waters." This experience is what any scholarly analyst feels when confronted by a visual image he is trying to come to terms with: there is, of course, *no* way in which words can convey its reality. But though inadequate, the words are *something* to keep us from losing ourselves in the unfathomable depths of the visual image, especially so long as we continue to be aware of the fact that they *are* only words, inadequate labels. We cannot simply say nothing about the picture or just look at it, or measure it and talk about its purely formal elements. If we are humans in society we have to do more, even though conscious of inadequacy, as we know that any translation from one language into another will be only a conventionalizing equivalent, and no doubt one of several possible ones.[1]

We like to think of a painting as a *virgo intacta,* unsullied by verbal attention. E. H. Gombrich, for example, fears that once something too strong has been said about a painting no one will ever again be able to look at it innocently.[2] But the weakest word about the painting sullies it as much as (or more than) the strongest, and I must sadly report that there are few virgins among the great paintings. Once we begin to think or speak about a painting, once we have moved it out of the realm of private fantasy into social and human converse, there is no turning back.

To what extent does a picture itself conceptualize? The one-point perspective system within a frame, which suggests a single person and an unmoving eye, is a conceptualizing of nature and of the painted image. At the extreme limit, a picture in which every detail is a variation on a moral theme— dissoluteness or avarice—is conceptualized. A picture that offers a moral admonition (Beware of avarice!) or an affirmation (O Liberty!); one that is informational, like a de Hooch interior with every window open, every wall covered, and every dress patterned; one that illustrates a literary text; or one that is itself expandable with every detail either into a social or literary code or into a chapter revelatory of an aspect of a character—all of these are conceptual structures. Perhaps the line of separation lies between the work of the eye and that of speech. This is the point at which what is seen has to be described, therefore put into words: as Virginia Woolf said of Sickert's paintings, "I'd like to possess them for the purpose of describing them."[3]

In my own case, I began my contact with graphic art as a literary scholar studying the work of William Hogarth—art which is far along a spectrum of the readable and verbalizable. Hogarth produced a kind of art that requires us to talk about its social setting, its structure as language, and its connections to related literary and social as well as graphic forms. This is an art that intends to make percept and precept (or concept) interchangeable, and so, more than most art, exists as an act of social exchange. Hogarth's "modern moral subjects" offer us an initial model for a work of art, from which we can then work our way (up or down) to more purely and exclusively graphic representations.

The most visual or graphic object in the Hogarthian series, by virtue of its relatively unmediated colors, forms, and textures, is the painting; but even here, Hogarth's rococo forms (for which Robert Wark has called him the most rococo of English painters),[4] far from serving as a total architectonic structure, break into local units that only direct the eye from one part of the picture to another, producing a pattern for reading a complex moral plot. The painting is followed in time by an engraved copy with more clearly denotative structures, which include a title and often verses that assist the translation of images into words. The engraving is then prefaced by an engraved subscription ticket with a programmatic design and inscriptions which explain Hogarth's artistic or political or moral intentions in the print itself. Publication is followed in many cases by a written commentary, explaining the print's meaning, at first for French readers and later for English as well. Hogarth authorized these (as he did cheap copies for buyers who could not afford the subscription price); but after his death other commentators appeared to carry on a conversation about the meaning of his designs that has continued to the present.

The model I am describing is a visual object constructed so as to project a verbal text (the reverse of an illustration for *Paradise Lost* or *King Lear*), which is materialized in various kinds of commentary, becoming ever more verbal as it moves out from the visual image. The verbal text is also, of course, translatable back into a prior verbal text (a story) in the mind of the artist before he put his first brushstroke on the canvas. But from Hogarth's own words posterior to the design we can discern an interpretive bias, carried on in the written commentaries of Trusler, Nichols, Stephens, and the rest; Hogarth has set the vocabulary of discourse which we have all followed ever since, and it is a moral vocabulary. At every stage he attempts to close or *en*close the visual image with something we have to call "meaning"; though this "meaning" itself may exfoliate luxuriantly and ambiguously, it is still conceptual meaning. Without this verbal exchange, which may in fact represent a process of repression as well as elucidation, Hogarth's work of art does not in any significant sense exist. It would take something on the order of Hercules in the Augean stables to return Hogarth's original painted image to the way it looked still wet on his easel.

My approach to graphic art has been determined, I suppose, by my involvement with Hogarth. I have not sought analogies between the arts of poetry and painting; I have attempted to employ where appropriate the methodologies of literary criticism to graphic materials, which means essentially the same sort of translation of visual into verbal (or social or humanly viable) structures that Hogarth initiated in his own art. Admittedly, this approach is less useful with Reynolds, Gainsborough, Constable, and Turner, whose major contributions lie in portraiture and landscape; but Reynolds and even Turner—great as Turner is as an artist—are strange and anomalous figures, and what is strange can only be explained in terms of the tradition of literature as well as of art. Turner's is a visual imagination on which is superimposed a literary structure. Gainsborough and Constable, whose imaginations remained purely visual, nevertheless in their historical context have to be seen as reacting against the literary tradition, and ultimately as conditioned by it. Gainsborough is conditioned in significant ways by Hogarth's graphic and yet literary (formal yet moral) assumptions in *The Analysis of Beauty* (1753); and Constable, by the need to infuse his later landscapes with symbols, graphic forms to be sure, but of a sort we may be inclined to call literary. The questions raised by a Chardin, a Watteau, or even a David are not comparable; they are *visual* questions. The art of Turner and Constable, however visual at the core (or in its most important aspect), persists in asking verbal questions, and is incomprehensible without a consideration of its verbal aspect.[5]

Landscape painting is undeniably a far more difficult case than Hogarth's "modern moral subjects" (as he called them). These chapters follow directly from my earlier book *Emblem and Expression: Meaning in English Art of the Eighteenth Century;* but they differ in important ways.[6] I dealt in that book with the Hogarth tradition of subject painting, and I can see in retrospect a failure to make clear in my final chapter on Gainsborough that his landscape painting raises issues far too large and determining to be passed over so cursorily. Since then I have been thinking about the large issues of how one responds to a primarily nonverbal image like landscape painting. Martin Price's suggestion (in a review of *Emblem and Expression*) that landscape painting is "victimized by the claims of verbal meaning" is a good way to state the pitfall of moving directly from figure painting to landscape without investigating the intermediate stages in the landscape tradition such as the work of Richard Wilson, or the ultimate stages of Turner and Constable.[7]

We cannot verbalize a landscape as we can a Hogarth "modern moral subject," but if the painting is to become a human and social event and not merely serve as an over-door or decorate a chimney-piece, we do have to use words in some way. We have to resort to other technical (and so metaphorical or allegorical) vocabularies, equally dependent on linguistic if not literary structures. I mean the vocabularies of aesthetic theory (the beautiful, picturesque, and sublime), of biology/physiology (habitat theory, prospect-refuge theory), of psychology (part- and whole-object, or breasts and buttocks), or of cultural (biblical or classical) reference in which a garden is Arcadia or Eden, a tree the Tree of Life or Knowledge or the cross, and a mountain Pisgah, Sinai, or Ararat. These are all metaphors created by man in order to make understandable or to control the existent natural landscape. For human purposes, landscape does not exist without them. As the word *landscape* suggests, it is a formulation of nature into a scene beginning as an arrangement of the ground into fields, farms, and gardens, and then proceeding (in representations of ·it) to paintings and the words which artist and spectator need to understand the painting.

The first of these categories, the aesthetic, is fairly obvious; it classifies landscapes by formal properties, by genres, and by psychological effects of a very general sort. It consists at bottom of art-nature oppositions, and therefore one model for landscape painting is the garden, man's physical attempt to order nature, which is unformulable, "a chaos, indiscriminately clamoring for attention,"[8] into some humanly acceptable order based on art. One form the art-nature contrasts take is the classification of landscapes (or gardens) according to style. They can be, like history paintings, baroque or rococo or neoclassical. They can be Italian, French, or Dutch, a form associated with a national tradition of art; style and national topography can be mutually influencing. But underneath remains the contrast of art and nature, for an Italian or a Dutch landscape also may be divided into an ideal and a local landscape, and these, in turn, into a landscape that emphasizes the horizontal or vertical axes or diagonals, and into a landscape that can be called classical or baroque.

The physiological and psychological vocabularies require some preliminary explanation. In *The Experience of Landscape,* Jay Appleton lays out the possibilities of habitat theory and prospect-refuge theory as ways of understanding the effect of landscape.[9] Habitat theory says "that aesthetic pleasure in landscape derives from the observer experiencing an environment favourable to the satisfaction of his biological needs"—that is, behavior of a sexual, exploratory, ingesting, shelter-seeking, agonistic, allelomimetic, nurturing, and eleminative kind. Prospect-refuge theory narrows this idea to the assumption "that, because the ability to see without being seen is an intermediate step in the satisfaction of many of those needs, the capacity of our environment to ensure the achievement of *this* becomes a more immediate source of aesthetic satisfaction." Thus he argues that "landscape which affords both a good opportunity to see and a good opportunity to hide is aesthetically more satisfying than one which affords neither; however, weakness in prospect or in refuge may be compensated for by strength in the other." And, as one finds in explaining the ritual origins of satire or tragedy, he concludes that when the "strategic value ceases to be essential to survival it continues to be apprehended aesthetically."

There is an example among the paintings in the Queen's Collection of which I am sure Appleton would approve.[10] This is Robert Streeter's representation of the landscape seen by Charles II from the oak tree in which he hid after the defeat of the royal forces at Worcester. Although one can make out the king in the branches of a tree at far right in the foreground, the scene has to be regarded as essentially a Charles-eye view of the terrain. Here indeed is the viewer (Charles's surrogate) seeing without being seen, his eye ranging warily, and yet in retrospect with as much aesthetic appreciation as animal cunning, over both prospect and refuge.

Appleton describes what he calls the symbolism of prospect, refuge, and hazard, dependent not only on the object itself, which as symbol may function by merely "suggesting environmental situations which are not actually realized" in the landscape, but dependent also on its position, whether seen in shadow or sunlight, blocked or exposed, in closed forest or open countryside or on the edge of a wood, or in relation to another object. The significant, perhaps symbolic, relationship of objects in nature leads to further distinctions "between those features which have been disposed by nature and those whose origin has involved also the rule of man"—i.e., again nature or art. An example of a man-made object in nature is a church spire on the horizon, of which Appleton says:

> A distant church spire, for instance, is certainly a common form of indirect prospect symbol. . . . But it also suggests 'refuge' in a number of senses. It implies the presence of a large building which provides physical shelter against meteorological hazards. It symbolizes, through historical association, the idea of 'sanctuary' provided by ecclesiastical authority against hostile powers, both temporal and spiritual. It generally indicates the whereabouts of a settlement, often concealed from view, by trees, for instance, or by the lie of the land, and thus it symbolizes the comfort of civilization within an open landscape which may be still largely possessed and dominated by the forces of nature.

Another example is the mill, which as a windmill is an ambiguous symbol, possibly of refuge but dominated by the "sense of exposure" because it has to be "exposed to nature as a source of power . . . [and] is functionally required to reach upwards into the moving air."[11] A watermill, by contrast, finds its source of power in a low-lying site, sheltered by trees and often other buildings, and is a strong refuge symbol.

What Appleton draws our attention to is the human need to organize nature into refuges or enclosures, as well as escape routes—partly by formal patterns, partly by the association of ideas. A landscape by Philips Koninck is almost all formal pattern, a representational and flattened Mondrian, in which the represented fields, gardens, canals, and rivers tend to draw one ever farther into a distant, shallow labyrinth, seeking a refuge among the flat fields and canals. Gainsborough's landscapes, on the other hand, are strongly dominated by symbols of refuge; they have almost no prospect, and what there is usually leads into a refuge structure. Courbet's rocky landscapes often present an impenetrable wall of foliage and cliff with one escape route— which is also a refuge—a cave or river-source that draws us into the depths of the picture. Koninck's use of the unprotected horizon, stretching unbroken

from one edge of the canvas to the other, or Gainsborough's or Courbet's use
of the vortical refuge, is as much a mode of communication as Richard
Wilson's use of a composition that recalls Claude's ideal Campagna Romana,
pastoral retirement, and assorted literary texts.

Appleton's theory, I believe, is limited in that he gives the physiological
explanation priority over all others, declining to acknowledge that it is only
another metaphor which may indeed postdate them. His model does, however, offer an explanation for the use of figures within the landscape, as
surrogates (or sometimes hazards) to the spectator, and also for the use of
cultural signs within nature—the churches, mills, and bridges that relate
different parts of the landscape to each other. His categories also relate at
various points to those of eighteenth-century aesthetic theory, most obviously the picturesque, which seeks intricacy, connection, roughness, quick
alternations of prospect and refuge, safe movement through (down into) a
landscape or other labyrinthlike structure. I would not be surprised if the
pleasure we feel in looking at most cityscapes, or even at Hogarth's complicated interiors crowded with cultural objects and figures, is an extension of
this picturesque theory. The city is only a more organized version of
haphazard enclosure patterns and curious natural juxtapositions.

What Appleton only hints at—in his discussion of driving a car through a
landscape, down highways and through tunnels, or "driving" a golf ball
across a course—is the cultural aspect of prospect-refuge theory: the *mastery*
one seeks in a landscape. This takes the form of our translating the
landscape—or the wilderness for that matter—into cognitive structures,
patterns of knowledge, or information. There is another sense in which we go
into a landscape: to find our way around, to gain what London cabbies refer
to as "the knowledge"—the infinite series of routes from one place to
another, which not only are something to hold onto (for example, in the face
of shifting human relationships) but allow for surprises that would not emerge
except out of a mastery of the terrain.

The "knowledge" also carries Appleton's atavistic landscape forward to a
socioeconomic formulation. Mastery as walking, driving, or surveying may
become mastery as possession and ownership, either directly of the land or
indirectly of representations of the land. John Berger has argued that oil
paintings were possessions that were representations of possessions, and in
these terms, landscape was a relatively undesirable genre—unless it showed
one's house or could be turned into a moral emblem.[12] In England, at any
rate, where religious painting was felt to be dangerously close to idolatry, the
only flourishing genres before the eighteenth century were portraits and
topographical views of houses and estates. Both were primarily portraits that
retain order, presence, and possession through representation. Pure landscape
was another matter. Berger is right to notice that in Holland in the seventeenth century "pure" landscape meant the ordering of natural scenery with-

out literary or emblematic superstructures—landscape which "answered no direct social need." As a result, he adds, Ruisdael and Hobbema starved, but also landscape painting became the genre to look to for artistic innovation: "each time the tradition of oil painting was significantly modified, the first initiative came from landscape painting." The reference is to something like Rembrandt's or Turner's use of light. "Furthermore," Berger concludes, "their innovations led progressively away from the substantial and tangible towards the indeterminate and intangible."

According to this interpretation, the history of landscape painting is a movement from description to self-expression, from either topography or emblematization toward "landscapes of the mind." It is this postliterary phase of landscape painting that yields most from Appleton's conceptual model based on survival, feeding, self-preservation, and nesting. There is, after all, a conscious atavism in much of the landscape painting that can be called postclassical. But the biological-physiological landscape model has to be supplemented by the sexual-psychological landscape of desire. This is a landscape that is shaped toward the recovery of primal scenes, toward the symbolizing of natural objects as extensions of the human body, as we project ourselves onto nature at a deeper level than prospect and refuge (though "deeper" may be a culturally determined judgment in this case). Landscape is probably the most powerfully cathected of objects, recreated in the mind as a displacement from the viewer's body to the suggestive shapes of trees, ravines, hills, and above all points of intersection that recall the originary areas of the female body. The sex of the viewer hardly matters, of course, since it is the mother to whom the landscape of desire refers. Nevertheless, the male possessor (in Berger's sense) of a portrait of a lady, or better still of a nude, will perhaps bear a different relation than his wife and daughters to the landscape of his hereditary estate.

Symbolization, the most basic linguistic activity, always refers to body-ego. The formation of symbols occurs around bodily experiences of pleasure and pain, around the senses and organic functions, by a displacement from the body or an object associated in some way with the body to a less impor-tant object.[13] One of the earliest of landscape-painters, Giorgione, makes the equation explicit. In his *Sleeping Venus* (fig. 1) he gives us the natural landscape itself in the background, a nude female body extended parallel below it in the foreground, and at the bottom a third element, the drapery that is not covering her body. These are the three kinds of form out of which fantasies can be made without unduly distorting representation. Landscape, like drapery, is pliable, open to manipulation into body-suggestive shapes. Among other things, Giorgione's painting shows the human figure in har-mony with nature, a secularized version of the relationship also seen in Bellini's *Madonna of the Meadow* (National Gallery, London), where, how-ever, the harmony and not the parallel is emphasized. Giorgione makes the hills intersect parallel to the woman's pubic area, and just at that point he adds a strange phallic stump for emphasis. Human body, landscape, and drapery become three patterns that are both abstract and cathected. Giorgione helps along the virtual equation of the three by the moisture-laden atmosphere he paints intervening between us and the scene but unifying the figure, drapery, and landscape—pointing ultimately toward the Turner "medium" and the Constable "fresh dew" (or "whitewash").[14]

In our own time Willem de Kooning's two chief representational referents are women and landscapes. They are often interchangeable: he turns a woman he has begun to paint on her side and develops a landscape out of her shape—or vice versa. The femininity of landscape was a convention of landscape poetry, something a painter also would have breathed in with the air: for example, in eighteenth-century England, from Thomson's reference to "The negligence of Nature wide and wild / Where . . . she spreads / Unbounded beauty to the roving eye." Or from Pope's lines in *Windsor Forest:*

> Here waving groves a checquered scene display,
> And part admit, and part exclude the day;
> As some coy nymph her lover's warm address
> Nor quite indulges, nor can quite repress.

Or from Pope's remark that in gardens one must "penetrate into the Recesses of those sacred Shades," in which was usually to be found a naked goddess or nymph.[15] What some landscapes suggest is the advisability of going beyond prospect-refuge theory to the need to master in the sexual sense, that is, to know completely—to "interrogate,"[16] to see as well as feel and explore the ways in, out, and around the landscape, which give knowledge of the structure that is only implied by the dressed woman—whether as one's own body or the body of the Other, whether as part-object or as whole-object. Then, of course, with this knowledge comes the power to order and control, perhaps, in Berger's terms, to possess.[17]

In short, far more than the adaptability of shapes for the painter is at stake here. The visual tropes may be based originally on verbal ones—or the verbal on visual ones; but they are mutually supporting. If we can go along with the Frenchman who, speaking to Sterne's Parson Yorick, equated the experience of the nakedness of the land with the nakedness of women, suggesting that Yorick would be affected equally by the "prospect" of either,[18] we can also accept the analogies in religious and secular writings between the human soul and its body, the divine soul and nature, the nation and the body politic, and the body politic and the natural landscape.[19] At its most general, this formulation (a literary equivalent of the psychological) says that mind or soul uses nature as its means of self-expression and as its means of communication. Nature is the personification of the human body and its political analogues.

It is also, of course, a metaphor of life as a journey or pilgrimage. Thus, as Everyman, one wants to find a way through the wilderness to the clearing—metaphorically, to light and vision—as in Appleton's terms one wants to find a refuge or an escape route, or in psychoanalytic terms one wants to find a womblike hole to climb (back) into.

The biological and sexual categories can also be related to the aesthetic. Edmund Burke's point, in his *Philosophical Enquiry into the Origin of Our Ideas of the Sublime and Beautiful* (1757), is that the beautiful landscape renders the mother available, easy, emphasizing her breasts and nourishing aspect, but allowing an exploration of the "cross-valley" intersection. In prospect-refuge terms, the beautiful landscape is one that reduces hazard symbols to a very low level, balancing prospect and refuge, with shadows under richly inviting foliage against long, open views in which the "most menacing animals are browsing sheep."[20] There is not even an apprehension of oncoming darkness. If in aesthetic terms this scene is beautiful, or in stylistic terms ideal, in generic terms it is pastoral. The sublime landscape, on the other hand, blocks the "cross-valley" intersection—or access to the sunlit valley—with large, threatening, generally male shapes, or makes the intersection a horrifying chasm.

The American Thomas Cole's *Sunny Morning on the Hudson River* (fig. 3), which Bryan Wolf has analyzed in terms of a "sublime" mountain mass contrasted with an isolated promontory in the foreground for the spectator and a "beautiful" sunny river valley in the distance, poses the problem of how to get from the foreground around the obstructive shape of the mountain to the beautiful spot of rest.[21] The problem is usually solved, as in this case, by wisps of mist that lead the eye over the impassable areas to the distant valley. It would seem that Cole has translated the infrastructure of psychological landscape into Burke's aesthetic categories, or vice versa. But he has also, without a doubt, translated these into their cultural equivalents. On the foreground promontory is an altar, and this induces a reading of the promontory position, the sublime mountain, the impossible gap between, and the beautiful valley as Covenant (a crucial concept for any American painter), Wilderness, and Promised Land.[22]

In the minor key of late eighteenth-century literature, in the works most read by the writers and artists coming of age in the 1790s, landscape was represented as follows.

Emily St. Aubert (in Ann Radcliffe's *Mysteries of Udolpho,* 1794) returns to the castle in which she is being held a virtual prisoner: "Its massy and gloomy walls gave her terrible ideas of imprisonment and suffering: yet, as she advanced, some degree of hope mingled with her terror; for, though this was certainly the residence of Montoni, it was possibly, also, that of Valancourt."[23] Montoni is her villainous oppressor, Valancourt her lover, and the castle, and in particular the suite of rooms in which she is confined, establishes an identification first felt by Emily, and then by the reader, as the imaginary projection of the female occupant's body. Her painful task is to undergo the siege of a conflict—sexual arousal and threat—which amounts to her sexual initiation. This pattern explains, perhaps better than anything else, the popularity of the genre of the gothic novel.[24] The same projection and association take place in the natural landscape through which Emily travels to reach or escape from the castle.

As she approaches the castle her first response, as we have seen, is to emblematize the castle as a prison with both keeper and possible rescuer. More practically, however, her approach becomes a series of apprehensive glances around her for prospects or paths of escape and refuges in which she can hide, and for signs of the enemy's presence. She is the frail female approaching the castle in which Count Montoni lives and is surrounded by his noisy, roistering, threatening followers. When she reaches the hall door, and the guide has left her, "while she waited for admittance, Emily considered how she might avoid seeing Montoni, and retire unnoticed to her former apartment, for she shrunk from the thought of encountering either him, or any of his party, at this hour." The noise of the reveling soldiers reaches her ears and terrifies her; she is afraid they will hear and be attracted to her, and she takes time "to deliberate on the means of retiring unobserved: for, though she might, perhaps, pass up the great stair-case unseen, it was impossible she could find the way to her chamber, without a light, the difficulty of procuring which, and the danger of wandering about the castle, without one, immediately struck her."

The drama is based on Emily's need to know the routes of escape, to see, to hear, and to detect sounds but not be seen or heard herself—all as protection against a male threat. When she is seen, she is of course pursued down those labyrinthine passages of the castle and, when caught, deposited in one of those rooms which have locks only on the outside of the door.

The external landscape, seen from a closed room within the castle, from the battlements, or from traveling beyond the castle, elicits responses that derive from the categories with which we are now familiar. It need only be said that the moral-conceptual and the aesthetic are the covering categories that sanction the subconscious fears and desires.

Tortuous gothic plot aside, *The Mysteries of Udolpho* is structured on contrasting responses of the good and evil, the sensitive and insensitive characters in whom moral and aesthetic sensibilities are equated. Their responses are to people, to social situations, to the St. Aubert estate, and then most extravagantly to the landscapes through which they pass. The basic contrast between Emily and her aunt, Mme. Cheron-Montoni, emerges in the ever more sublime landscapes to which they are exposed on their way to Udolpho.

Mme. Montoni "only shuddered as she looked down precipices"—precipices "from which Emily too recoiled; but with her fears were mingled such various emotions of delight, such admiration, astonishment, and awe, as she had never experienced before."

As the party crosses the Alps Montoni's thoughts turn to Hannibal, and he falls into argument with Cavigni about which route Hannibal followed. While Mme. Montoni can only contemplate "in imagination the splendour of palaces and the grandeur of castles, such as she believed she was going to be mistress of in Venice and in the Apennine" (having married Montoni for this purpose), Emily has a different response, one which Turner may have read before he undertook his *Hannibal Crossing the Alps* (1812):

> The subject brought to Emily's imagination the disasters he [Hannibal] had suffered in this bold and perilous adventure. She saw his vast armies winding among the defiles, and over the tremendous cliffs of the mountains, which at night were lighted up by his fires, or by the torches which he caused to be carried when he pursued his indefatigable march. In the eye of fancy, she perceived the gleam of arms through the duskiness of night, the glitter of spears on helmets, and the banners floating dimly on the twilight; while now and then the blast of a distant trumpet echoed along the defile, and the signal was answered by a momentary clash of arms. She looked with horror upon the mountaineers, perched on the higher cliffs, assailing the troops below with broken fragments of the mountain; on soldiers and elephants tumbling head-long down the precipices; and, as she listened to the rebounding rocks, that followed their fall, the terrors of fancy yielded to those of reality, and she shuddered to behold herself on the dizzy height, whence she had pictured the descent of others. [p. 166]

Montoni feels a self-identification with the conquering Hannibal. Emily identifies herself with all the elements of the sublime. She imagines Hannibal's "vast armies" among the "tremendous cliffs of the mountains," "at night . . . lighted up by his fires." She imagines them attacked not only by natural forces but by partisans, and in their confusion and death she notes that "the terrors of fancy yielded to those of reality, and she shuddered to behold *herself* on the dizzy height, whence she had *pictured* the descent of *others*" (emphasis mine). She is, of course, about to be threatened herself, and we can sense the foreshadowing of her own condition (as also Montoni's in the ultimate fate of Hannibal). She populates the landscape with the figures of Hannibal's army; she shows her ability to respond (as opposed to Mme. Montoni, who is merely "exceedingly rejoiced to be once more on level ground") to sublime scenery; and she is projecting on the landscape her apprehensions about the future.

I have spoken elsewhere of the eighteenth-century novel from Defoe through Fielding and Richardson as being structured on a conflict between metaphors of life as journey (or pilgrimage) and as theater.[25] Radcliffe's first novel, *The Castles of Athlin and Dunbayne* (1789), shows its heritage near the beginning:

> When first we enter on the theatre of the world, and begin to notice the objects that surround us, young imagination heightens every scene, and the warm heart expands to all around it. . . . As we advance in life, imagination is compelled to relinquish a part of her sweet delirium; we are led reluctantly to truth through the paths of experience; and the objects of our fond attention are viewed with a severer eye. Here an altered scene appears;—frowns where later were smiles. . . . [pp. 4–5]

After this series of theatrical responses, Radcliffe concludes: "We turn indignant from a prospect so miserable, and court again the sweet illusions of our early days." The passage sums up the Radcliffe gothic in one aspect. The reader of the novel, as well as the characters within the novel, are spectators of theatrical extravaganzas *and* of journeys. The "theatre of the world" and "scene" become an "advance in life" "led . . . through the paths of experience," and the two strands join in the words *viewed* and *prospect,* which apply to both theatrical and touristic travel. As the metaphors suggest, the immediate progenitors of this sort of fiction were Sterne's *Sentimental Journey,* Mackenzie's *Man of Feeling,* and Smollett's *Humphry Clinker,* in which the theatrical (involving spectators and response as well as elaborate acting out of roles) was wedded to a journey and the reading of landscape as a screen on which to project oneself.

Radcliffe's landscape is used very differently from that of a slightly later form of the gothic, M. G. Lewis's *The Monk* (1795), where the only sublime landscape is that which kills Ambrosio at the end. It is actually present, as an actor and a nemesis rather than as scenery into which the "imagination" can project ideas of freedom and aspiration that lift one out of present captivity into the role of Burke's spectator at sublime events, whether human or natural.

Emily's experience is, however, of two kinds: comforting and unsettling. One of her earliest experiences of the Alpine landscape sums up the simplest relationship between the sublime and the beautiful:

> The solitary grandeur of the objects that immediately surrounded her, the mountain-region towering above, the deep precipices that fell beneath, the waving blackness of the forests of pine and oak, which skirted their feet, or hung within their recesses, the headlong torrents that, dashing among their cliffs, sometimes appeared like a cloud of mist, at others like a sheet of ice— these were features which received a higher character of sublimity from the reposing beauty of the Italian landscape below, stretching to the wide horizon, where the same melting blue tint seemed to unite earth and sky. [pp. 165–66]

The sublimity of the mountains is heightened by—is finally established in perspective by—the "repose of the beauty" below. From the beautiful "Italian landscape below" Emily learns the value of sensibility: it is a way of discovering the latent good in an evil-seeming world.

In the upper area both the placement and the nature of objects are uncertain. One moment the forests are at Emily's feet, the next hanging "within their recesses." The torrents are here insubstantial mist, there solid ice. Things are undefined, spaces open, and the depth of the precipice and "blackness" of the forest defy limitation and perspective. Yet this same sublime landscape seems to enclose Emily, *surround* her, in *falling, waving, dashing* things that press toward her to crush and to suffocate. Openness (in a melting horizon) is beauty in this landscape, as it is freedom. Elsewhere the forest moans, the torrent roars, and the "sulphureous crimson" surrounds her in the air (p. 406). If she opens her emotional eyes to this world, she runs the risk of being overwhelmed by the magnitude and power of natural forces that correspond to her reading of the human forces of Montoni.

The landscape consists of the sublime mountains, the beautiful valleys, and the imprisoning castle. The last in particular upsets the ordinary aesthetic categories Emily attempts to impose. The castle is a labyrinth in which the aesthetic categories no longer apply in the same way and are replaced by the terminology of prospect, refuge, and hazard. The psychosexual is never far off: "the thought of sleeping in this remote room alone, with a door opening she knew not whither, and which could not be perfectly fastened on the inside" is constantly with her (p. 235). But the landscape is present outside to raise or oppress her thoughts, to lift her out of her depression or sometimes further depress her.

Radcliffe presents in words the elements—including the "cloud of mist"—which also make up the Thomas Cole landscape, and such descriptions may indeed have served as the precedent for Cole, who so far as we know had no graphic models that contained all the elements of his sublime-beautiful compositions. These elements were to be the desiderata of the great English landscapes of the period: the wild, sublime area of undifferentiation, open and unassimilable, a wilderness onto which one's worst fears can be projected; the closed *locus amoenus* in which one seeks refuge, a beautiful sunlit meadow unaccountably lodged somewhere in the sublime landscape; and the prison cell which is the false *locus amoenus,* in some sense the immediate enclosure of one's own body, out of which views and glimpses can be taken of the natural landscape of prospect/refuge and desire or affection.

As the example of Emily may suggest, landscape does raise one important issue that is present but less acute in other types of painting. And therefore these chapters are going to differ from *Emblem and Expression* in the important respect that "meaning"—the verbal, linguistic, symbolic order—is no longer given a privileged position.

Meaning in history painting was essentially manifest content—meaning in the sense of what an artist *thought* he was doing. I did not really, except perhaps in the case of Gainsborough's landscapes, get into the question of what an artist did not *know* he was doing. In Hogarth's case, for example, intention was fixed by the programmatic statements of subscription tickets and authorized commentaries. Hogarth regarded meaning as the be-all and end-all of the work of art—even though that meaning might in some cases bifurcate into complementary, even contradictory, meanings for different audiences or into some degree of private significance (as in his *Industry and Idleness* or Zoffany's *Tribuna*). Since writing *Emblem and Expression* and moving into the later part of the century, I have found artists who more obviously and single-mindedly used meaning as a way to authenticate something that was not meaning. In Freud's terms, the present indicative "It is," or even the imperative "You shall," may be used to conceal or repress the optative "I wish."

Landscape painting, above all, offered the painter a way out of all "literary" structures of meaning into pure representation or pure form, and therefore into some degree of subjectivity. The major shift in eighteenth-century English art was from history painting to landscape as the norm of artistic expression. This transformation began with the displacement of portraiture (the real mode practiced) disguised as history painting to landscape disguised as history, and moved in the direction of pure landscape painting. The function of a picture tended to change from acting "as an object embodying normative values" to acting as "a medium expressing and arousing subjective fantasy; an object whose interest is centered in form and texture, to which the viewer has less an intellectual or moral response than a sensuous and emotional one."[26] It is then only a question of whether the scholar tries to analyze the landscape from the point of view of the spectator or of the artist.

Some art historians, whose most distinguished spokesman is Gombrich (whose philosophical authority is Karl Popper and literary authority E. D. Hirsch), take history to mean only *wie es eigentlich gewesen war*. The painting's (or painter's) intention is therefore limited to the evidence of his patron's program—or, less satisfactorily, to the artist's own description of what he did. The latter is felt to be less satisfactory because the artist may deceive himself more easily than he can his hardheaded patron. I find the dialectic of the painter's verbal intention and the phenomenological evidence of the painting more useful, as also the contemporary comments which show how much of what the artist intended—or did not intend—got through. Most of those who saw, of course, did not commit their thoughts to paper; and often those who did were precisely the ones who should not have. Nevertheless, this sort of evidence can be extremely valuable, as John Barrell shows in his discussion of George Morland.[27] He uses contemporary criticism to show what was disapproved of or completely repressed by viewers of Morland's work. Leo Steinberg has explored the same approach in engraved (or painted) copies of paintings that correct or suppress details which bothered such viewers, and are therefore probably significant.[28] If I tend to settle on the artist himself, it is because the two principal landscape painters I am concerned with have left us the evidence for such an investigation.

A second assumption of some art historians who accept the view of history mentioned is that only categories available in the artist's lifetime can now legitimately be used by the critic. Freud was not born in the time of Turner and Constable, therefore condensation, displacement, and repression are not to be found in their paintings. Some art historians also distrust the application of nonaesthetic categories such as the psychological or the philosophical to an art object. I believe that a truth may be arrived at only much later, when critical or experiential categories have been created which were not available to the artist or his audience. An extreme case exists in the stories of Edgar Allan Poe, which could be enjoyed but not seriously written about— their peculiar quality described and valued—until after readers had absorbed Borges's type of fiction and could read it back into Poe's. The categories used to analyze Poe's work did exist, even though they were not yet formulated; they existed at some level of preverbal awareness in the viewer's mind, or more likely in the artist, the person who creates the answers for which critics have to find the questions—and so, of course, in the object, lying there in wait for the unwary critic. We have almost reached the time when most historians will agree that new generations can find previously unthought-of ways to interpret works of art. The philosopher Richard Wollheim has written: "Whole ranges of fact, previously unnoticed or dismissed as irrelevant, can suddenly be seen to pertain to the work of art. . . . The spectator will always understand more than the artist intended, and the artist will always have intended more than any single spectator understands."[29]

Finally, these historians assume that a statement is either true or false, that a picture can mean only one thing. Popper's principle of falsifiability holds sway: if one contrary example can be adduced, the hypothesis fails. I come from a less optimistic discipline that has long since given up the hope of establishing an either/or when in most cases the answer has to be both/and.

If these generalizations are true (as I believe they are) of the more literary genres such as history painting, they are even more true of landscape, that late-blooming genre which emerged hesitantly triumphant at the beginning of the nineteenth century (though some of the best had appeared in the seventeenth). The visual structure of a landscape painting is the place to look for subtexts, for "plots of desire," struggles for power, and needs for prospect or refuge, escape or protection. These are all visual phenomena which the artist who has created them may then try to understand by verbalizing, by translating them into structures of meaning with which he is more consciously familiar, such as the literary or conceptual structures of Virgil or Milton, the graphic structures of Claude or Gaspar. With landscapes the question of meaning can be phrased thus: Does meaning become more a mode of repression than in other kinds of painting? Is the cultural component in fact as insistent—or originary—in landscape painting as in history painting? Does landscape painting perhaps *require* other than natural signs to complete itself? Does landscape reveal to us better than other genres the unconscious, socially determined ways of seeing that require, for example, the repression of the laboring poor from a pastoral scene (as John Barrell has argued)?

Is the whole process of landscape painting one of secondary-revision? To control something that seems uncontrollable, whether one is an artist or a farmer or a gardener, one must package, label, verbalize, and humanize it. But certainly parallel to the attempt to control there is a realization that no landscape *can* be completely controlled. If one knows he cannot successfully order nature—which becomes a metaphor for mortality itself—by pruning and planting, by geometry and mathematics, that is, by a strictly formal ordering, then he orders by literary or symbolic references to Aeneas and the New Troy, or by aesthetic categories like the "beautiful" and "sublime"—or by anthropomorphizing the landscape or by making it all part-whole symbols, or by an atavistic act of reverting to biological categories of perception such as prospects, refuges, and hazards. With the increasing anxiety of knowing that nothing can be controlled, one maps, fences, improves, and mythologizes (or makes literary) all the more.

The Blind Beggar passage with which I began, like the other "spots of time," resolves feelings of prospect, refuge, and hazard, those urban senses of disorientation and fears in dissolution, in an assertion of the power of the controlling imagination. Stated in another way, the emptiness of urban objects that has been threatening Wordsworth in London now appears as an opportunity to infuse them with his own meanings and organize them with his own structures. But Wordsworth is also implicitly identifying the blind man with that other poet, John Milton, and he borrows the structure of *Paradise Lost,* Book 7, Raphael's description of God's creation of the world, to serve as the framework for his own recreation of the city in Book 7 of *The Prelude.* The strategy of writing (which includes literary allusion) becomes the act of controlling as far as control is possible.

PART I
LITERARY AND TOPOGRAPHICAL LANDSCAPE IN ENGLAND

CHAPTER 1 🔯
ANTI-LANDSCAPE

The most basic cultural interpretation of a landscape is to relate the wilderness to that which is not wilderness. This can be done by adding a bridge, building, or some other human trace, some reference to the city. Carl O. Sauer has written: "geography is based on the reality of the union of physical and cultural elements of the landscape. The content of landscape is found therefore in the physical qualities of area that are significant to man and in the forms of his use of the area, in facts of physical background and facts of human culture."[1] Nature consists of the site-qualities of terrain, which are beyond man's "power to add to them; he may 'develop' them, ignore them in part, or subtract from them by exploitation." These "developments" add up to the landscape's cultural expression, "the impress of the works of man upon the area," which set going the formal or thematic interplay of art and nature.

The wilderness may be turned into garden by defining it as a scene in which something significant has taken place—perhaps in history or perhaps only in some private, domestic sense—or in which something significant is taking place at the moment, such as the shooting of a stag, the building of a bridge, or the acting out of a myth. For the humanizing of a landscape can be carried out either through resemblance, as in the Giorgione *Sleeping Venus,* or through reference to something that appears elsewhere in another context or dimension—that is, by adding an emblem, like the foreground altar in *Sunny Morning on the Hudson River.* There is, accordingly, a large difference between portraying an action in a landscape and portraying a place where an action is known to have taken place but few signs of it remain, or alien signs appear (once a meadow, now a housing development). The contrary of this emblematic landscape or landscape of association (with Welsh nationalism, with a *genius loci,* with the artist's childhood) is, once again, the wilderness portrayed "as a thing taking place in itself," as simply the growth of natural forms, which draws us back to prospect-refuge and psychoanalytic categories. But natural growth, too, is likely to be anthropomorphized into humanly suggestive shapes, into positive and negative forces, past and future, left and right, up and down, and so on. It is not exaggerating to say that every landscape, by the very fact that it is painted, is about culture or art as well as nature.

As wilderness becomes "cultivated," it is divided into fields or ordered into a garden, covered with buildings, populated, and emblematized by a poetic painter. The process, however, can be narrowed down when we consider the particular case of England. The symbolic point of origin is the fact that Turner donated Hogarth's palette to the Royal Academy in response to Constable's donation of Reynolds's palette. Any discussion of English landscape painting as a literary-conceptual form has to begin with these two urban artists, whom Turner and Constable recognized as their founding fathers.

Of Reynolds it need only be said that some of the most beautiful passages

21

SAINT PETER'S COLLEGE LIBRARY
JERSEY CITY, NEW JERSEY 07306

in his paintings are the landscape backgrounds. They never merge with the figures as they do in Gainsborough's late portraits, but Reynolds's women, especially when accompanied by children, sit or stand placidly beside a tree, looking like the Raphael (or Leonardo) Madonnas who derive from the same Tellus / earth figures that may have inspired Giorgione's *Sleeping Venus.* Some of his men, though distinct from the landscapes behind them, make a single androgynous form with their horse and a tree. Many of Reynolds's figures, however, seem so self-contained as to be hugging themselves; their domestic or ceremonial accoutrements of culture and art are part of them, while the natural landscape is only glimpsed between or behind curtains or pediments, which block access to the Edenic prospect.

Reynolds also painted Cupid as a London linkboy and Mercury as a pickpocket—urban versions of mythological figures in which their shapes relate in vaguely comic ways to the implements they carry and the chimneys and tenements in their background. These travesties derive from the frame of mind that led Turner to designate Hogarth and that stimulated Hogarth's one excursion into the genre of landscape in his *Four Times of the Day* (1738, figs. 4–7).

My feeling that Hogarth tested the landscape genre in this series is based partly on observation of the paintings themselves and partly on the fact that he uses the didactic *Boys Peeping at Nature* as his subscription ticket for the engraved versions. In this series he fulfills the model I have outlined: he begins with four of his loveliest, most sensuous paintings, which represent London street scenes; then engraves them, adds a subscription ticket outlining his program, and publishes advertisements in the newspapers. In this case the ticket was one he had already used for *A Harlot's Progress* (1732), which had made clear his intention to correct the outworn ideas of history painting in his time by turning to contemporary London life. He used this ticket two other times, in each case broaching a new area of subject matter in his art. The first use was for comic history painting; the second was for the pastoral-georgic mode in the *Four Times of the Day;* and the third was for the sublime history based on a religious subject, in *Paul before Felix,* for which he revised the design of *Boys Peeping* itself. The idea of Hogarth considering the landscape mode—or even producing a travesty of it—at first seems strange; but of course in these years he was making a series of statements about art as it seemed possible in England in his time.

Like other English painters, Hogarth's models were literary—in this case I have no doubt that he again drew on that mediating genius between the generations of Pope/Swift and Fielding, John Gay. Hogarth had begun his painting career, setting up the assumptions he would explore fully in *A Harlot's Progress,* by painting and repainting Gay's *Beggar's Opera.* The other relevant works were *The Shepherd's Week* and *Trivia,* Gay's mock pastoral and mock georgic. In the first, Gay placed real, more or less contemporary, farmers in Virgil's Arcadia; and in the second—closer to Hogarth's own intention in the *Harlot's Progress*—he showed that cityscape was the form of landscape most appropriate to poetry at that moment.

It is said that Hogarth's *Times of the Day* paintings were originally made to decorate Jonathan Tyers's Vauxhall Gardens, where they would have suggested to the diners the tension between this "garden" and the crowded city just up the river from which these pleasure-seekers had come. If there is any truth to this story, the paintings would have served only as modelli for designs painted by other artists.[2] But Vauxhall Gardens did represent the sort of transitional state between art and nature, between history painting and landscape, that Hogarth was exploring in his early paintings. It also, as a repository of Roubiliac's statue of Handel *en déshabillé,* was the place where accommodations were being worked out between the Italian and the local English traditions in music and art.

Hogarth's pictures require both verbal and visual traditions, however, to explain his intention. When a medieval or Renaissance artist painted landscape, he ordinarily did so within conceptualizing forms such as the "Four Times of the Day," the "Seasons," "Winds," "Ages of Man," or even "Saints." The traditional design presented an allegorical figure hovering above and a landscape or townscape with farmers, hunters, and shepherds below. Such allegorical figures legitimated the landscape and the human activity beneath it. Among the works of Dirck Barendtsz (1534–92), for example, there are many series of prints showing an allegorical figure dominating, or giving meaning to, a set of landscapes (see figs. 9, 10).[3] In conjunction with landscape, the usual allegory was one of time. As Kenneth Clark has shown, the calendar was a way to join symbolic and factual landscape: "Now calendars, with the occupations of the months are, throughout the middle ages, the best illustrations of everyday life; and the new profane art of the fifteenth century fastened on these as an available form in which to explore its new interests."[4] Such works as the *Très Riches Heures* of the duke of Berry were structured on the correspondence between the month, the appropriate human activities, and particular kinds of landscape. Though some scenes show Arcadian retirement in a verdant spring landscape, many represent the work done in woods and fields—sowing, hunting, and reaping. Single plates of the seven days of the week were often tiered in days, months, and seasons, making a compendium of calendrical, astrological, psychological, and astronomical wisdom—all in terms of different landscape settings.

With the coming of the Renaissance and the emergence of the single, detached, sculptural figure, the model for these landscapes became the Michelangelo figures of the times of the day in the Medici Chapel. Along with the two-level design we also find, carried over from the earlier seven-day series, divisions of left versus right (which survive in Hogarth's prints as, for example, in the divided street of *Noon*). The "Times of the Day" are some-

times further structured by borrowings from the "Ages of Man," which add
the dimension of history, usually by imposing a movement in a declining
direction, from the Age of Gold to the Iron Age. Biblical echoes could also
be added, as well as implicit contrasts and comparisons between the allegorical figures above and the humans below.[5]

The "Times of the Day" is an example of how landscape in its early forms
(as an independent or semi-independent genre) emerged from such allegorical
legitimizing. As the landscape grew more particularized and contemporary,
the contrast between the figures in the landscape and the allegorical figure
reclining on a cloud overlooking the scene became incongruous. Eventually
the allegorical figure shrank in size and prominence until it disappeared, or
reappeared in an inset scene within the landscape. By 1600 the secularization
of the tradition was well under way. What survived was the landscape (or
genre) scene alone. Well into the seventeenth century, however, random
landscapes (by Berchem, even by Claude) were linked as if they were still
"Times of the Day," "Seasons," or "Ages of Man." All of these stages of
development survived, jumbled together in the printshops of London, where
Hogarth could have seen them.

The "Four Times of the Day" was the particular series Hogarth chose,
with its divisions of morning, noon, evening, and night. Although he was
making a statement about genres—landscape, pastoral, and georgic—in
painting and poetry, he was not, as the landscape artist would be, interested
in the peculiar light or atmosphere of these different times of day, but only in
their moral overtones. He did not let go of the "wisdom" of the allegorical
series. He therefore disposed in two ways of the allegorical elements that now
seemed outmoded. He reduced the gods and goddesses in their rural ambience to a contemporary servant girl or a drunken magistrate in an urban
setting; and he took the gods and goddesses themselves, with their costumes
and poses, and transposed them to an accompanying plate where they are
more appropriately shown as actresses playing these roles in a country setting, inside a barn. For as well as the *Boys Peeping at Nature* subscription
ticket, with its sense of "nature" as harlotry, Hogarth also added to the four
plates of the *Times of the Day* a fifth plate, *Strolling Actresses Dressing in a Barn*
(fig. 8), a repository of what no longer seemed to fit into the *Times of the Day*.

The usual verbal surround of the visual image was also augmented before
publication by a piece of writing published in a newspaper. Hogarth's
"Britophil" essay, which attacks picture-collectors and jobbers of so-called
dark masters, appeared in the same issue of the *St. James's Evening Post* (7–9
June 1737) that carried an early announcement of his proposals for the
subscription of *Four Times of the Day* and *Strolling Actresses*.[6] In one passage,
for example, Hogarth addresses himself to a stupid connoisseur who is com-
mending an antique statue: "Mr. Bubbleman," he says, "that Grand Venus
(as you are pleased to call it) has not Beauty enough for the character of an
English Cook-Maid." This passage anticipates the better-known one in *The*

Analysis of Beauty: "Who but a bigot, even to the antiques, will say that he has not seen faces and necks, hands and arms in living women, that even the Grecian Venus doth but coarsely imitate?"[7] It also draws our attention to the fact that the handsome cook-maid who appears in *Noon* is thus a "London Venus," and alerts us to the kind of game Hogarth is playing in the dual context of Gay's "town georgic" and of the declining graphic genre of the rural "Times of the Day." Hogarth is saying that the only appropriate application of the "Times of the Day" in the 1730s, whether it is considered decline or ascent, is to urban landscape.

This "Venus" is accompanied, as she sometimes is in the "Times of the Day" series, by a Cupid, in this case a weeping little boy who has spilled his pie. What was traditionally a dining scene, with men and women around a table, becomes a scene in which food flies out a window, a pie spills, and a little girl gorges in the gutter not far from the corpse of a dead cat; and this contrast with the abundance of food in the country is also set off against the "spiritual" nourishment dispensed by the Huguenot chapel on the other side of the street. The gutter that divides physical from spiritual hunger is only a suggestion of a country rivulet; the kite caught on the church roof recalls its more usual perch in a tree; and the cityscape evokes its absent opposite, country landscape.

The other three plates operate in the same way. In the "Morning" of graphic tradition, the figure of Aurora or Cephalus usually appears above, accompanied below by human hunters and gardeners. Hogarth substitutes for the panoramic country scenes with vistas to the horizon a city square with buildings rising against the sky, as closed and oppressive as one of his *Harlot's Progress* interiors. Only through a pun is a "garden" present: this is Covent Garden, London's greengrocery, with a few unappetizing carrots and turnips lying about. Not shepherds and shepherdesses at their labors but city beggars, market girls, hucksters, and whores are shown. Instead of the sun in the sky, there is only a clock over the portal of St. Paul's church, and the icy old woman is all that remains in this setting of the young Aurora, the dawn, accompanied by Eosphoros the dawn-bearer, here represented by a shivering page trailing behind rather than preceding his "goddess."[8]

Diana or Hesperus ordinarily appears on the upper level in "Evening," and in "Night," Proserpina, Nox, Cerebus, or perhaps Pluto himself. On the lower level, figures with shepherds' crooks appear in "Evening" and with torches in "Night"; they are shepherding or walking around in the one and sleeping in the other. Hogarth shows, instead of lovers strolling across a landscape, a weary married couple: a tiny, cuckolded husband and a huge, forbidding wife. She is a formidable Diana; the horns of her husband (the cow's horns are attached to his head by an optical illusion) recall the fate of Actaeon. Or perhaps in eighteenth-century London Actaeon is merely considered a cuckold, as Hogarth shows him to be in *Marriage à la Mode,* plate 4. The couple does attempt a stroll in the country, but they are frustrated by the heat and the encroaching London suburbs. There is no escape from the city because the countryside is now built over and the distant hills are remote and inaccessible (as they are in *Southwark Fair* and other prints that introduce bits of country glimpsed in the distance). The stream running beside the couple is wider than the gutter in *Noon,* but it is a man-made canal, the "New River" which brought to London its water supply from the country. The country itself remains a remote ideal, lost to contemporary Londoners.

Whereas in "Night" sleep was traditionally represented by a recumbent figure (Pluto) and by images of sleeping figures and Saturnalian revelers in a landscape, Hogarth represents Hesperus as a linkboy, indigent couples asleep on the street, and Proserpina's chariot overturned, out of which she herself gapes in bewilderment. In the center is Justice Thomas de Veil, a modern Pluto as lord of the London underworld, familiar with criminals and a harsh enforcer of the Gin Act, but here transformed into an urban equivalent of the Saturnalian reveler.[9]

In terms of the "Times of the Day" tradition, the pendant *Strolling Actresses Dressing in a Barn* reclaims the goddesses and gods that were formerly suspended above scenes of contemporary or pastoral life and puts them in their proper surrounding, a backstage dressing-room. The extra plate is, so to speak, made up of the supernatural detritus of the upper level of the "Times of the Day": Aurora, a black woman, kills lice on the Siren's costume; and Diana, the central figure, returns from "Evening" revealed as human—all-too-human—beneath her costume, as her own Actaeon ogles her through a hole in the roof. (Contrast this with Gainsborough's *Diana and Actaeon* in its accustomed natural setting, fig. 24.) Other miscellaneous gods and godlings are present: Apollo the sun-god has to hang his (or her, since all are women) socks on a stage cloud to dry, and Ganymede, in a reversal of his role as cupbearer to the gods, is not dispensing but receiving, not nectar but gin. The only way the Arcadian past can enter now, Hogarth says, is through actresses "dressing in a barn"; for this is a country performance by town actresses, bringing together the antipastoral and antimythological strains of the "Times of the Day" in a country setting in which no country is visible— and (as the document in the left foreground shows) this is the last performance.

The theme of art from the *Boys Peeping at Nature* subscription ticket is represented in the painter's materials (including a chamber pot for mixing paints) associated with scene-painting, the best an English painter could hope for at the time if he wanted to paint either history or landscape. The monkey appears in this context as an emblem of artistic imitation; but our eyes move from his cloaked and wigged figure up to the actresses, who also imitate the characters of superior beings. Hogarth is not, I think, here satirizing men's and women's attempts to become gods and goddesses so much as the aesthetic (academic) and social assumptions that set up such inappropriate ideals to which ordinary artists and citizens were therefore supposed to aspire. The enemy is Mr. Bubbleman of the "Britophil" essay, whose cry is, "O L—d, Sir, I find you are no *Connoisseur.*"

This is an important point, because Hogarth's assumption about figural art is appropriated by other English painters as well. His common sense still informs Walter Sickert's well-known passage about the artist's model he calls Tilly Pullen. She is of no interest dressed as a lady, turned this way or that, posed or elevated to a goddess. The artist puts a curtain or a mirror behind her: "But it is always Tilly Pullen. . . ."

> But now let us strip Tilly Pullen of her lendings and tell her to put her own things on again. Let her leave the studio and climb the first dirty little staircase in the first shabby little house. Tilly Pullen becomes interesting at once. She is in surroundings that mean something. She becomes stuff for a picture. Follow her into the kitchen, or, better still—for the artist has the divine privilege of omnipresence—into her bedroom; and Tilly Pullen is become the stuff of which the Parthenon was made, or Dürer, or any Rembrandt. She is become a Degas or Renoir and stuff for the draughtsman.[10]

Like Hogarth, however, Sickert cannot see Tilly without the notion of what she is *not.* Her ordinariness is defined in terms of her roles as artist's model, fine lady, or goddess standing in front of a curtain. English landscape painters also avoid the simple rejection of ideal forms and allusions that distinguished Dutch landscape. There is the native landscape and *something else.*

Hogarth's five pictures of 1738 raise other issues about landscape painting. While he is clearly drawing on a graphic tradition, his use of that tradition derives directly from a local literary one: Swift's "Description of a Morning" and "Description of a Shower" of 1709 and 1710, and their elaboration in Gay's *Trivia* of 1714. Hogarth's series could almost be said to "illustrate" these poems, particularly *Trivia,* accompanied as it is by allusions to Oedipus, Regulus, and Julius Caesar.[11] I have no doubt that his contemporaries read his prints more in the context of Swift's and Gay's poems than in that of the graphic tradition. And yet the acerbic tone of Swift's view of landscape—

> Here elements have lost their uses,
> Air ripens not, nor earth produces:
> In vain we make poor Shellah toil,
> Fire will not roast, nor water boil.[12]

—does not carry over into the pictures. Hogarth replaces the traditional setting of "Morning" in spring with winter, the traditional abundance of flowers and fruits with a few scrawny vegetables, only to suggest another of the deprivations the city-dweller knows so well. Fire still warms and—to judge by the voluptuous young women—air ripens among these people who are doing their best to endure and come to terms with city life. Some sense remains of Gay's stroller in *Trivia,* who fends off the hazards of London streets, and the artist is commenting on the inhuman London these people are trying to protect themselves against and live and survive within, as he is on the chilly gods and goddesses who have no place in this setting which makes more sense in terms of prospect and refuge. In literary terms, I suspect that Hogarth is aspiring to the greater, more general "nature" of the preeminent English model, Shakespeare.[13]

In any case, it was difficult for an English landscape painter, with the great tradition of English and continental literature at hand, to paint a landscape without some awareness of the irony underlying the genre. In poetry the irony had its *locus classicus* in Horace's *Epode* "Beatus ille qui procul negotiis," the origin of the topos of retirement which is at the heart of the century's love of poetry and painting depicting country life. Horace has this praise of the country life spoken by a city usurer. The irony persisted in the city-based painter who represented nature for his city-based clients, the Henry Hoares and William Beckfords who were the equivalents of Horace's usurer.

Those painters and poets who failed to admit the irony exposed themselves to the charge of repressing certain aspects of their subject. John Barrell argues that something like this happened in England because society, and the painter as society's spokesman, did not want to acknowledge the existence of labor and the social oppression that produced the demi-Eden of the poetic, pastoral, Claudian landscape.[14] A Hogarth-influenced painter like George Lambert or Samuel Scott could make a gesture in the direction of Horace's irony or contemporary reality either by adding Hogarth's figures in the rural setting or by painting a cityscape.

But there is the further fact that the city-based poet traditionally used the country as a metaphor for court, city, and state.[15] Landscape poetry was almost always about something besides landscape. Pastoral, of course, was about art itself: the young poet who cannot yet write out of personal experience tries out his wings on the subject of his art, constructed from the conventions of pastoral poetry. The Claude tradition of landscape painting operated in a similar way, building less on observation of nature than on the conventions of a kind of elegant picture-making. In painting, however, natural observation of some sort was necessary in a way it was not in poetry. The relationship between sign and object was to some extent based on resemblance, not wholly on linguistic convention. The contradictions of art-nature were probably recognized by all intelligent artists, but in England the paradox was writ large: the fountainhead was a city-bred artist who brought to bear a naturally skeptical provincialism as well as a wide knowledge of the satiric poetry, the mock-pastorals' and mock-georgics of the time.

CHAPTER 2 ❦
FIGURES IN
THE LANDSCAPE

Distant figures like notes of colour. Portraits to which the landscape is a background. Mythological figures, goddesses and so on, with which nature interweaves to 'dance to the music of time.' Dramatic figures, whose passions nature reflects and illustrates. The visitor or solitary onlooker who surveys the scene, an *alter ego* for the spectator himself.

In this passage John Berger outlines most of the possibilities for the use of figures in a landscape (a subject on which A. Richard Turner also has interesting comments).[1] Berger's categories can be traced back to the three-layered structure of the "Times of the Day," as the figures develop from intellectual justification for the landscape to "notes of colour" that are necessary to balance the composition.

Somewhere between these extremes fall the Hogarthians of the 1730s and 1740s, the generation that preceded Richard Wilson. George Lambert painted "classical landscapes" in the manner of Claude and Gaspar Dughet, with Roman shapes in a pastoral setting. But he also—and this was his distinctive contribution to English painting—painted local scenes with local figures, often added by Hogarth himself, which furnish an anecdotal rather than a poetic dimension.

There is a remarkable pair of paintings, originally executed for the duke of Bedford, now divided between the Tate Gallery and the Yale Center for British Art: *Extensive Landscape with Four Gentlemen on a Hillside* and *Hilly Landscape with a Cornfield* (1733, figs. 11, 12). The paintings, though one is two inches longer than the other, were painted as a pair; one represents spring and a haymaking scene, the other autumn and wheat-harvesting; one is a close-up of a hillside, probably the same that is prominent in the distance in the more panoramic view of the second, the panoramic spread being emphasized by the extra width. Both, as Elizabeth Einberg has said, reduce "the remnants of the classical wings of trees into insignificance."[2] The "spring" landscape, which moves the viewer up onto the hillside, employs a vertiginous composition based on one, long diagonal sloping from upper left to lower right with no closure whatever at the bottom—leading down into the second canvas and "autumn."

The contemporary figures, which were probably painted by Hogarth, fall into contrasting groups within each landscape. In *Hilly Landscape* some figures are reaping and others resting, and these laborers are complemented by some gentlemen lounging about, including one sketching the landscape itself. In *Extensive Landscape with Four Gentlemen* the hillside is pocked with excavations of some sort, perhaps chalk, which is being handed up out of a pit in the foreground to a woman assisting at ground level. The artist is again present, sketching the scene, and his friends are picnicking—a cloth is spread with food on it and bottles nearby.[3] At the lower end of the slope a couple is embracing on a hay-wagon in the roadway. In the distant field the hay is being cut and gathered by other workers.

There is a great deal of activity, including those who are working and those who are not. The contrast between the two groups is not, however, stressed; the principle of arrangement is by different categories, with no sign of moral structuring or even schematic social structuring. The informing principle would seem to be a spectrum of art and nature, as was common in a Hogarthian conversation picture taking place in a natural setting. Within this portrait-group genre Hogarth always included heterogeneous elements—a dog, the family's children behaving like children, and perhaps some surrogate of the artist himself. Here he and Lambert include with the laborers at work and play some gentlemen at leisure, in particular one drawing the landscape.

John Barrell argues that landscapes like these, or better, Gainsborough's Suffolk landscapes of the 1750s, represent "the ideal rural life, as a blend of work and play."[4] But then he allegorizes the landscape into "the image of a society divided between those who must, and those who need not work" (p. 41). He even suggests that in Gainsborough's *Woodcutter Courting a Milkmaid* (Lord Tavistock Collection) the woodcutter and the milkmaid, leisurely flirting, are not of the same class as the busy ploughman. His point is that these landscapes "proclaim" the ideal of Britannia as "a rich, happy, harmonious land, in which all men work together and all consume the fruits of that common industry," but they "portray," perhaps unconsciously, "the repressive [and repressed] actuality, that the sweets of life are reserved for the rich, the sweat for the poor; and their success is to conceal this contradiction, by a careful handling of iconography and structure" (p. 52).

Barrell's argument is that labor entered landscape through contrasts of work and idleness, which in some sense conveyed the contrast of the laboring and the proprietorial classes. If so, the source for this interpretation would have been Hogarth's *Industry and Idleness* (1747) or even *The Rake's Progress* (1735), where Tom Rakewell's indolent rakishness was set off by Sarah Young's pious labors. Were this the case, landscapes would have been structured on a contrast or discrepancy; industry would be pitted against idleness. What we do *not* find in landscape painting of this period is the social awareness that would logically have derived from Hogarth's modern moral subjects. When Gainsborough includes a ploughman and a resting woodcutter chatting with a milkmaid, he is coming as close as he ever does to direct observation of the Suffolk scene, but basically his strategy is to play off one sort of activity against another: work and leisure, perhaps even georgic and pastoral, are the categories. The one landscape in which he quotes Hogarth—borrowing the slab-tomb and the loiterers from *Industry and Idleness,* plate 2—omits the essential element of contrast: there is no example of industry (unless we are to suppose a lost pendant).[5]

The only convincing example Barrell adduces is George Morland: a Hogarth-ian subject-painter who carried the practice of Lambert to the point where he was painting modern moral subjects in rural rather than urban settings. That he separates different class groups represented in his pictures and turns them away from each other means that "he is unconvinced of the assump-tions about society implicit in notions of pictorial organization" which we associate with the Renaissance tradition and he would have associated in his own day with the Royal Academy and its president's *Discourses*. Barrell is able to demonstrate this fact about Morland's paintings not only from inter-nal evidence but by quoting the words of his friends, patrons, and critics: "where his admirers wish to see the image of a unified society, he shows them a divided one; where they wish to see the poor as cheerful and industrious, he shows them as discontented, desperate, contemptuous, or defiantly idle" (p. 128).

This should surprise no one, given Morland's and Hogarth's assumptions about their figurative, moral, and subversive genre. The landscape painter is quite a different matter. And yet it is important to follow Barrell's lead and see how the figures *are* used. Earlier landscapes, we have seen, were often structured according to topoi such as the "Ages of Man," the "Senses," the "Seasons," and the "Times of the Day." I have no doubt that there were also landscapes structured on binary oppositions of abundance and dearth, corre-sponding to the seasons of spring and autumn or winter. The topos of Hercules at the Crossroads projected a kind of landscape in which alternative paths were offered the spectator on his spiritual pilgrimage to the Palace of Wisdom. The elaborate engraving accompanying some editions of the *Tabula Cebetis*, which also took the form of a journey through life, shows an extensive landscape of contrasting paths, with numerous people trying them out. In the 1750s and 1760s, Henry Hoare's garden at Stourhead was con-structed on contrasts between Flora and Ceres, pastoral and georgic, war and peace, and war and commerce, and the contrasting motifs were supported by branching paths that took the visitor on alternate routes through the garden. The general idea of easy and difficult paths visually supported the use of industry and idleness, or virtue and vice, as the basic pattern of choice. On a somewhat more polite level, the industry-and-idleness contrast was em-ployed in Pope's later imitations of Horace, Pomfret's "The Choice," and countless other poems that contrasted the active and retiring life, the *via activa* and the *via contemplativa*.

Barrell makes the point that landscapists like Lambert habitually paint the scene in a polarity of light and shade, so that "the rich and their habitations must be illuminated, and the poor and theirs be left in the shadow of the 'dark side of the landscape'" (p. 22). But this misses the fact that the picture can also be read as the rich man's house standing out in the open, exposed in a prospect, as the great by definition *are*, while the poor man's (and there is nothing concrete, of course, to indicate "poor") is a refuge, more significant for its position among trees than for being in the dark. This was precisely the argument of the poets of retirement who wrote so copiously in the middle part of the eighteenth century.

Richard Wilson's two large landscapes, *Dinas Bran* and *View near Wynnstay*, painted for Sir Watkin Williams Wynn (R.A. 1771, figs. 13, 14), are balanced. The first is a close-up of the river Dee with workmen removing a fallen tree and fishermen pulling in their nets, and Dinas Bran looming over them. The second is a panorama of the whole valley, with Dinas Bran small on the horizon, and the shepherdlike figures relaxing on the high terrain in the foreground, taking in the scene stretched out before them. The workmen of the first scene are now invisible, subordinated to (or absorbed by) the rich panorama. The relaxed figures in the foreground are surrogates for Williams Wynn or any genteel spectator outside the painting.

Wilson's paintings are examples of the landscape mode that prevailed. He juxtaposes not only two levels of involvement—one down inside and the other above and detached—but two genres, the picturesque detail of twisted tree trunks and laborers versus the pastoral overview with shepherds—and two perspectives on a single scene, two "landscapes" out of a single geo-graphical area. The presence of representatives of labor and leisure remains one structuring agency, but as a unity, a relation of pastoral and georgic, not as a contrast or a moral choice.

The landscape painter ordinarily seeks ways to unify his diverse materials, to order nature into something intelligible and beautiful, or at its most diverse, picturesque. He inevitably employs binary relationships, which tend to be aspects of nature or of art and nature. These can be intimated through natural forms and forces or through alternative kinds of human activity in nature: on the level of laborers, between work and rest; on the level of the landowner, between active and contemplative life; on the level of the poet, between art and nature, pastoral and georgic, or ideal and real. Wright of Derby sometimes constructs his landscape, as he does his genre scenes, around a human source of light—in a factory or a cottage, or perhaps a fire—and a natural source of light in the sun or moon. His antinomy is of nature and culture or science, and whether he intends them as unity or as disjunction is for each viewer to decide.

Wilson closes his spectrum of nature and art with the figure we have already encountered in the Lambert-Hogarth landscapes: the artist. One of the versions of *Carnarvon Castle* (fig. 15) includes the artist in the foreground drawing the landscape. The painting itself (with its rich painterly surface) shows a painted castle, its reflection in the water, and the artist at work on its representation.

I have not mentioned one figure in that strange landscape, Lambert's *Extensive Landscape with Four Gentlemen*, namely the central figure running down the hillside accompanied by a dog. No eighteenth-century farmer would have gone bare-legged and bare-footed in a skirt of this sort, wearing such a headdress. The figure is lifted straight out of a Gaspar landscape—a conventional piece of "classical" staffage. Is he a joke, a figure painted by Lambert himself to contrast with the contemporary, Hogarthian figures on either side? Is the juxtaposition of him running down the hillside and the lovers on the hay-wagon (toward which he appears to be running) a Hogarthian visual joke of the sort he employed in the *Analysis of Beauty* plates? The simplest explanation is that he follows in some sense from the presence of the artist, as a materialized aspect of the spectrum of art and nature that seems to be so persistent an intention of the landscape school in England. A very particular place is represented, with contemporary figures, perhaps even portraits; but also shown is a spectrum of the degrees of art, including the painter himself and, in this case, a fugitive from the artist's classicized representations of so many other landscapes. This idea is, of course, sheer speculation, but it will do until a better explanation offers itself.

Barrell's thesis is useful in a second way. The landscape painter had quite different aims than Hogarth or Morland, and yet there is no denying that a social dimension exists in many of these paintings. The pastoral-georgic alternatives do carry political overtones, and for a brief spell Gainsborough does convey information about the social relations in rural Suffolk of the 1750s (before he moves to Bath and London and his form becomes formula). It is possible to trace a change in attitudes toward perceiving landscape— from an emblematic, spiritualized landscape to a secularized, socialized, perhaps personalized one—which also reveals political tensions.

For a man of John Dyer's generation, all nature was a subject for emblematic interpretation. In his *Grongar Hill* (1726) he describes the view from the hill:

>   And see the Rivers how they run,
>   Thro' Woods and Meads, in Shade and Sun,
>   Sometimes swift, and sometimes slow,
>   Wave succeeding Wave they go
>   A various Journey to the deep,
>   Like human Life to endless Sleep!
>   Thus is Nature's Vesture wrought,
>   To instruct our wand'ring Thought;
>   Thus she dresses green and gay
>   To disperse our Cares away.
>
> [ll. 93–102]

The alternation of description and its emblematic interpretation is also the model for much landscape painting, in particular the earlier works of Wilson. But, as Jay Appleton has noted of *Grongar Hill*, Dyer also describes the panorama in prospect-refuge terms, creating contrasts in his references to

woods and shade against meadows and sunlight, swiftly running rivers
against a "Journey to the deep." What Appleton has described as an alternation of prospect and refuge was also, seen in cultural terms, a version of the
topos of *concordia discors*, summed up in Denham's famous lines, "Though
deep, yet clear, though gentle, yet not dull, / Strong without rage, without o'er-flowing full."[6] I have already quoted part of the well-known passage
from the opening of Pope's *Windsor Forest* (1713) in which natural description is based on contraries that are resolved in a *concordia discors*. *Concordia
discors* is still an operative principle for Wilson in, for example, the relating
of the beautiful and rugged parts of the Dinas Bran landscapes, as of the
close-up and distant prospect. But his treatment of light and natural forms
suggests that he is also a contemporary of Gilbert White, the tireless
classifier of natural forms who looked beneath emblematic analogies in nature
to establish precise relationships of cause and effect.

It was also White who recorded, in his *Natural History of Selborne* (1789),
the actual social tensions he observed beneath the surface of the hunting
which Pope described in *Windsor Forest* as a *concordia discors* of the active and
retired, a sublimation of warlike instincts. "Our old race of deer-stealers are
hardly extinct," he remarks, discussing the Black Laws: "it was but a little
while ago that, over their ale, they used to recount the exploits of their
youth." His frank appraisal expresses the "dark side of the landscape" which
is not often exposed in the poetry, and never in the painting of landscape:
"At present the deer of the Holt are much thinned and reduced by the
night-hunters, who perpetually harass them in spite of the efforts of numerous keepers, and the severe penalties that have been put in force against them
as often as they have been detected, and rendered liable to the lash of the
law."[7] He mentions General Emanuel Scroope Howe's attempt to stock the
area with wildlife for his own sport: "General Howe turned out some German
wild boars and sows in his forests, to the great terror of the neighbourhood;
and, at one time, a wild bull or buffalo: but the country rose upon them and
destroyed them."[8]

It then only remained for William Cobbett to visit White's Selborne,
having enjoyed reading his *Natural History*. Though Cobbett found the place
"very beautiful," he noted that "As I was coming into this village, I observed
to a farmer who was standing at his gateway, that people ought to be happy
here, for that God had done every thing for them. His answer was, that he
did not believe there was a more unhappy place in England: for that there
were always quarrels of some sort or other going on." This remark led
Cobbett to recall seeing that a reward had been posted "for discovering the
person who had recently *shot at the parson of this village*." This parson was
Gilbert White's own successor, a tithe-grabbing litigant whom the rural folk
had risen up against, as they had against General Howe.[9]

Of course, the French Revolution (begun the year White's *Natural History* was published) had intervened to establish the unbridgeable gaps between rulers and ruled, rich and poor, free and unfree. Thereafter it was easy enough to read these dichotomies back into the landscapes of Wilson, Lambert, and Gainsborough. The milieu of Constable and Turner was, however, very different from that of prerevolutionary landscapists.

CHAPTER 3 ⚐
CITYSCAPE AND
LANDSCAPE-ENCLOSURE

Hogarth's other landscapist friend, Samuel Scott, focused his attention on the city of London and on the Thames. In his *Westminster Bridge* (fig. 16) he individualizes the people, who resemble the figures in a Hogarth room or street (in contrast to the unidentifiable blobs which his model, Canaletto, sometimes made them). Perhaps the simplest analogue is the Hogarth room with certain kinds of information on the walls and in the inset pictures, and other kinds seen through a window or a door. Scott builds his picture around striking demarcations. He conveys a variety of information through the apertures and divisions of the bridge, creating something like a cross-section of London. We see the massive masonry of the bridge itself; the workmen on the scaffold atop the still unfinished bridge, revealing the process and method of construction; the water in the immediate foreground, with bargemen as well as swimmers representing different kinds of activities and uses made of the river; and, seen through one arch of the bridge, the shoreline of the city itself stretching from Westminster to the Fire Monument and, through the other arch, buildings along the Southwark side. The confluence of river, bridge across the river, barges, and the London buildings served by river and bridge produces an interaction of forms and areas of human experience in their man-made setting. It is also important that Scott shows the bridge at the moment of construction, with men still working on the balustrade. This is a moment of transition, not stasis and permanence, as one would expect of a country-house portrait.

Scott's cityscapes offer a very different view of London from the standard Renaissance one, which began with the "Antwerp View" of A. V. D. Wyngaerde (1543), known through the engraving of C. J. Visscher (1616). This view looked north from a point below Southwark Cathedral and displayed the city's spires, labeled such points of interest as the Globe Theater, and presumed an external, linear sense of the aggregate. The overall effect closely resembled a line of stalls in a marketplace. In the succeeding centuries, artists varied the scheme but continued to place London Bridge in a prominent role and continued to offer a linear inspection of the city's contents. (Hogarth includes London Bridge framed by a window in the last scene of

Marriage à la Mode.) Scott, however, in painting after painting takes up
London's peculiar double focus on the City and Westminster, building his
scene around such significant lines of demarcation as Westminster Bridge.
He connects the City and Westminster (the East and West Ends) by the
curving river, which reflects the organism's social structure and is its chief
channel of communication.

Scott draws, of course, upon Canaletto, who came to England in 1746
(staying until 1750 and then returning again from 1751–53 and 1754–55)
and left an indelible impression on English topographical painting.[1] He
brought his own native perception to the city's workings in a series of
dramatic river scenes which lend to the northern city not merely the splendor
of Venice's Grand Canal but its sense of curvatures and striking juxtapositions (fig. 17). He also applied these configurations to the country house and
its environs.

Canaletto established a viewpoint for the whole school of English topographical artists. Scott and William Marlow are his immediate heirs, but he
established the perspective for writers as well, including Wordsworth, who
chose the precise subject of some of Canaletto's finest paintings for his sonnet
"On Westminster Bridge," with its implicit contrasts of city and country,
organic and inorganic life. Although anti-city positions were taken by the
Romantic landscape painters, as by the poets, the cityscape remained an
orienting point of reference. Constable looked down from the north, with the
villeggiatura of Hampstead as foreground and the shadowy city relegated to a
dim background; even when he looked north to Harrow there is a sense of the
city at his back; and it is significant that he painted his six-foot canvases of
the Stour Valley in a studio on Charlotte Street in London.

Canaletto's cityscape is as closely related to the conversation picture, that
characteristic English portrait genre of the 1730s and 1740s, as to a landscape. He shows that with a slight tilt, interest can shift from the figures to
their surroundings. First of all, the drama of demarcation is his contribution
to the English landscape tradition. He divides his space for purposes of
information rather than to make moral distinctions, contrasting map space
with perceptual space in his representations of buildings related to shoreline,
bridge, river, and boats. His waterless views of Whitehall from Richmond
House show a street of hardly any inherent interest, architectural or otherwise, divided in a labyrinthine way into patterns of enclosure and openness,
of inner and outer—all seen in relation to the viewpoint of Richmond House,
which made the view part of that great house and its owners. Paul Sandby's
views from Windsor Castle and other country seats work in the same way,
ordering the landscape in relation to demarcations like those of the architectural foreground. It is salutary to remember Gainsborough's dismissive remarks on Sandby-like topography, but also Constable's opinion that Sandby
was "the only man of genius" who painted "real views from Nature in this

country," by which he meant that Sandby both avoided the trappings of the landscape tradition and was devoted to conveying a sense of a particular place, to delineating not large contrasts and effects but a description of the specific "contours and lineaments of a subject."[2]

Second, Canaletto bequeathed a tension between map and perceptual space, achieved by the remarkable stereopticon effect which suggests that the buildings do not—as in the Claude composition or the topographical views of another Venetian like Carlevarijs—recede or withdraw, but actively fill space, approaching the viewer as if to make physical contact with him. To achieve this stereoscopic view, Canaletto used the sun—not as subject but as a method of eliciting and defining relationships between things and man in his environment. This was a function of the sun which, while of no use to Turner, was essential to Richard Wilson and later to Constable, both in their topographical phases and in their attempts toward personal recovery of a landscape out of the past.

Finally, Canaletto's basic divisions are street, house, and water, linked by boats and bridges; the river is also divided from its nearest equivalent, the sky, by different textures and lights. Sometimes, as in his English and Italian paintings on terra firma, the distinctions extend to man-made structures and grass and trees. The effect on the viewer is to make him a participant in the scene without destroying his analytic detachment from it. The spectator must follow and explore, and learn from, the relationships implied between each part and the whole, while mentally mapping and reconstructing the complex of divided spaces.

My argument is analogous to Mark Girouard's, in *Life in the English Country House,* that the development of country-house architecture followed the practice of town-house architecture in London.[3] I believe that something similar is true of the landscape tradition. First, London embodies the paradox of a natural expanse that is organized and ordered and yet beyond the comprehension of man. Hollar's *Long View from Bankside* (1643–46) is a narrow rectangle over six feet long; it is a map that presents a bird's-eye view, in three dimensions, seen at an angle instead of from straight above. Like the "Times of the Day," it is accompanied by allegorical figures on either side, in this case angels flying over London as protectors. Among other things, Hollar's map signifies that London cannot be taken in at a single glance. In 1746, just before Canaletto arrived, Jean Rocque's huge map appeared (twenty-four sheets with a total area of over 70 square feet). Although it is literally a map, it outlines virtually every house in London. And yet it abandons altogether the idea of fitting London into a perceivable frame.

Views like Hollar's were followed by the cityscapes of Kip, Bowles, and Bucks (a 13-foot view); Boydell's prints were also appearing just as Canaletto arrived in England. If the point of Bucks's 13-foot view was that London cannot be framed, broken down, and simplified, the point of Boydell's series was that Englishmen have a right to views of certain public and semipublic buildings in and around their capital city—and that these multiple views correspond to the long panorama of Visscher-Wyngraede or Bucks.[4]

Accompanying these maps and views were the written and illustrated surveys. Going back to Stow and Strype, and following in the eighteenth century in the wake of Defoe's *Tour* (1724–26), these surveys offered brief descriptions of every London street and square. This London is compared with previous Londons in order to account for the London of the present at the moment of change. For each square and street a description in social and economic, historical, and antiquarian terms is provided. The device is a trip through the city, or in the case of Defoe's *Tour,* out into the countryside—an itinerary, a succession of places, and the same place seen from different perspectives and distances. London becomes only one of many city and country scenes, and as the century draws to a close, the interest is intense in the relationship between past and present in villages and hamlets. But in every case the author returns to London to start again; London is the center and heart, the context in which the rest of England is seen.[5]

The country can be, and in England often is, seen as the unpopulated, uncultivated city. The city waits in the wings as the final capability of the English countryside—as has been all too well proved. Much of the mystery of a country landscape lies in this fact, especially as signs of human habitation grow. We begin with the fact that the founding of the city in the country— the first stage of turning nature into culture—is based on divination, relic-burial, limitation (boundary-marking), orientation, and quartering. Divination is based on the sacrifice of a body. As Joseph Rykwert puts it, "There seems to have been some sort of direct link between details of a landscape, such as the surroundings of a besieged town, and part of the sacrificial victim's entrails."[6] The analogy between body and landscape thus draws also upon the division of that land into civilized areas. Boundaries are the essential point of contact between city and country. Rykwert recalls the "Romano-Etruscan belief in the sacredness of land titles and boundaries . . . the terrible penalties Roman law imposed on boundary-breakers as well as the cult of the god Terminus with its repeated blood-sacrifices."[7]

The first need is to integrate one's own body into the city, the most stirring example being Curtius plunging into the gap to save Rome. The second need is to organize that human area into a constant, uniform pattern—not only the town but the countryside. What the traditions of Hogarth and Canaletto show us as we move into landscape art is how highly charged a genre it is, whether because of its repressed sexual (or maternal) overtones or because of its magic origins, and also how close the city generally is when the artist is painting the country.

The garden, too, as it developed from Bridgeman to Kent to Capability Brown, enclosed clearly delineated parcels of ground with artfully posi-

tioned, discreetly concealed fences. Carole Fabricant, in a brilliant sociopolit-
ical analysis, has shown how, in a society with death penalties for stealing
and rigorous punishments for poaching on a gentleman's land, the garden
could symbolize the fragmentation and personal possessiveness implicit in a
system founded on private property.[8] Pope's garden, whose motto was "Se-
cretum Iter," was described as an enclosure: "Near the Bounds of the Garden, the Trees unite themselves more closely together, and cover the Hedges
with a thick Shade, which prevents all prying from without, and preserves
the Privacy of the Interior Parts."[9] Henry Hoare's motto, on the face of his
Temple of Ceres at Stourhead, was the warning of the Sibyl to Aeneas's
comrades: "Beware, ye uninitiated, stay away." But as Pope put it in his
verses to Burlington on the true landscape garden, "He gains all points, who
pleasingly confounds, / Surprises, varies, and conceals the bounds." His
verses expressed the principle of the ha-ha, which served as a fence to keep
the cattle and other intruders out and to demarcate one area of the
property from another, while appearing to be nonexistent—until the spectator was too close to be deceived (and supposedly uttered the exclamation,
"Ah-ha!").

Clear demarcations, discreetly concealed fences, and the use of hidden
retreats—the uniting of enclosure and exclusion—were summed up by
Stephen Switzer as the need to "preserve some private Walks and Cabinets of
Retirement, some select Places of Recess for Reading and Contemplation,
where the mind may privately exult." Even the immense expanse of Stowe
was divided into larger and smaller spaces, clearly delimited. Sir Thomas
Whately writes of the enclosed temple settings at Stowe, that "all external
views are excluded: even the opening into the lawn is but an opening into an
enclosure."[10]

Whately omits the complementary view outward; Switzer accompanies his
advocacy for private walks with the need for expansive prospects outward as
well. Walls and other enclosures "by which the Eye is as it were imprisoned"
are to be avoided. This is, of course, from the single-point perspective of the
spectator within the garden looking out; he needs both the security of
enclosure and the freedom of seeming geographical boundlessness. The landscape painter's aim, drawing on the precedent of Claude and his other prede-
cessors, was to separate the disorderly foreground from the more easily man-
aged prospect. The importance of this separation of the painter or the poet
from the landscape he represents is reflected in the poetic vocabulary of the
eighteenth century, and particularly in those words which were more or less
interchangeable with the word *landscape* itself—*view, prospect, scene*—all of
which make the land something *out there*, something to be looked at from a
distance, and in one direction only, something which could be ordered,
parceled, and possessed.[11] Like the painter, Pope in his *Epistle to Burlington*
satirizes the garden in which "On every side you look, behold the Wall" (ll.
113–14), but he opposes it not to open spaces but to a garden in which the

gardener "conceals the Bounds" and spreads "Spontaneous beauties all around" (ll. 56, 67).

The painting or the poetry is formulated from the point of view of the patron, that is, of the property-owner. Hogarth's concern with boundaries and enclosures is quite a different matter. Based on an awareness of the repressive power of art, the enclosure is seen from the point of view of the prisoner, the malefactor who is locked up and has only a glimpse of the other man's property through a window. Hogarth's vision leads to the gothic image of the prison cell through which Emily St. Aubert glimpses a sublime or beautiful landscape. Landscape painters, without Hogarth's political bias, wished to enjoy the unruly seductiveness of nature without sacrificing the artist's control. They still recognized the power of the poet or the landscapist to enclose and immobilize, to impose clearly outlined shapes and vigorously delineated boundaries on all within his field of vision, which is thereby rendered a passive object, a kind of still-life. The eighteenth century was also, of course, simply a time when the natural human desire to master one's environment—to know, order, and control it—was particularly urgent but uncertain enough of itself to require the "bounds concealed" and at least the appearance of distant expanses.

CHAPTER 4 ❦

THE HOUSE IN
THE LANDSCAPE

The most obvious fact about English landscape painting is that it emerged as a distinct tradition out of topographical painting. Local English landscape begins as portraiture of country houses, sometimes with genre interest added. This sort of landscape is an image of ownership, property, and self as embodied in property. It can be seen in the portraits of Zoffany and others which depict the master standing in front of his country house, in the midst of his park, with his family, horses, and servants around him. The other portrait tradition was that of Reynolds, in which self is embodied in class, status, and personal magnetism, and is represented by formal and iconographical allusions to gods, goddesses, and heroes as painted by Michelangelo, Raphael, and the other artists of the High Renaissance (the opposite of Hogarth's suppression of gods and goddesses from *The Four Times of the Day*). The portrait of the house by itself, painted as if by Claude as an analogue to Cicero's or Horace's villa, was a topographical version of the Reynolds portrait of the owner alone.

The country-house portrait as a genre, however, began with the aim of giving information, recovering and retaining an image of a particular place. The process from which landscape painting in England emerged was, in John

Harris's terms, one of "destroying" the descriptive value of the image. By the 1760s, he writes,

> Wilson was beginning to destroy the country house as a clearly identifiable object. . . . In all of these the house becomes subsumed into the atmospherics of the landscape, and in the painting of Minchenden House [Lord Leigh of Stoneleigh] the destructive process is absolute. The oppression of the landscape has completely eliminated the house as an identifiable object.[1]

Of course, Harris is referring to the descriptive usefulness of the image for someone like himself who is writing a book on the English country house; but he also means a loss of the sense of a thing that can be *owned*, and so perhaps explains some of the difficulties with commissions that Wilson complained of. One need only compare Wilson's Syon House (1761? fig. 18) with Canaletto's version (1749, Duke of Northumberland, Syon House): Canaletto's house is centered, while Wilson's is off to the right and nearly invisible. In the tondos he painted for the Court Room of the Foundling Hospital in the late 1740s, before he left for Italy, the urban buildings are in a landscape; in *St. George's Hospital,* the familiar Wilson pond is already present, as well as the tree that is too far in toward the center from the right to serve as the Claude coulisse but is becoming a subject of equal interest with the building. The "destruction" of the country house was, as these examples suggest, the making of the landscape tradition.

It can also be argued that the suppression of the country house owed as much to the development of the concept of the park—the Capability Brown landscaped garden—as to the divagations of a landscape painter. For the object owned was, by the 1760s, no longer thought of as merely a house; and the gardens were no longer immediate adjuncts to the house as in the views of Siberichts, Knyffe, and Kip; instead there was a wide-ranging landscape which included the house—often far-distant and tiny—as in Wilson's *Minchenden House* (1774–75).

At the same time it is possible to argue that the English garden of Capability Brown merely offered a ready subject to the soi-disant landscape painter who was inspired by the call of Hogarth, Hayman, Highmore, and others in the 1740s for an indigenous English art. The equivalent of turning to English history for your subject matter for the great genre of history painting—or to English history as depicted by Shakespeare and the English writers—was to paint the English countryside, including representative English people. The topographical tradition connects directly with the basic Englishness of English landscape painting, and so with "the love of locality and portraiture" which Wilson attempted to develop and (as Edward Dayes wrote) "may be said strongly to mark the *amor patriae*" of the Englishman.[2] Horace Walpole urged English painters to stop painting Italianate landscapes and turn to their own "ever-verdant lawns, rich values, fields of haycocks, and hop-grounds."[3]

Both the desire of patrons for portraits of their estates as of themselves, and the viable and flourishing tradition of georgic poems, led to the depiction of precise spots and particular rural employments. If the poetry of *Grongar Hill* and *The Fleece* could contribute to the Wilson and Turner kind of emblematic history-landscape, it might also contribute to the needs filled by topographical painting and the depiction of the "nature of the place." In the air, in agricultural writings at least, was opposition to the artist's imposition of his artistic structures or general rules, such as the beautiful and picturesque, onto a particular English place: "do not sacrifice its native beauties," writes William Marshall, "to the arbitrary laws of landscape painting." And, he adds, "the nature of the place" is *"sacred."*[4] And this can mean either its historical associations (or even literary, as with an English poet like Pope) or a specifically topographical exactness which equates utility with beauty—not a lovely forest dell but a field ready for harvest.

Again, such landscape tended to be painted in the same way as history: local, immediate English subjects were seen in the light of the great tradition of High Renaissance art. What in the private sphere was the poetic evocation of a landscape in order to heighten the status of a house and park through creating echoes of Roman villas, in the public sphere was the desire to raise the national consciousness by representing public buildings and landscapes where British history had taken place.

I should also mention in passing that the topographical tradition (as John Harris has noted) was much more extensive in England than abroad; and that accuracy of representation remained, even after the so-called depredations of the landscapists who "destroyed" the country house, a goal of high priority for many painters. Part of the sense of accuracy involved the attempt to capture both house and park in their different aspects by means of a series of views. We have seen Lambert and Wilson paint pendants of the same landscape seen close up and from afar. Lambert also painted four views of Westcombe House, Blackheath (1732, Earl of Pembroke), each a different aspect. In one the house itself, sliced off on one side, becomes a stage wing and the landscape prospect a backdrop to the small figures promenading through the estate. The motivation may indeed have been theatrical. A painter like Lambert, who worked for the theaters, would have seen the structure he carried over to some of his country-house paintings as a borrowing from an English stage, with flats flanked by coulisses or wings (and only secondarily an echo of Claude and the ideal landscape). He was painting in the context of Hogarth's wry comment on landscape painters in *Strolling Actresses* and his progresses of six or eight scenes that filled out the reality of a story. He was also recalling Hogarth's words in the *Analysis:* "The eye is rejoiced to see the object turn'd, and shifted, so as to vary these uniform appearances." With Lambert this became a reflection of the idea that the experience of the house and its garden involves a physical movement through space and a series of stops for different perspectives of the same object.[5]

Wilson, too, painted five views of Wilton House (ca. 1758–59, Earl of Pembroke), which show different aspects of the estate, the house serving as a perspective closure, an eye-catcher, a stage wing, and so forth. In *Wilton House, Looking East,* by an odd use of the house and the Palladian bridge as the coulisse elements, he made the empty lawn that stretches between them the subject. *Wilton from the Southeast* is about the lake, and reduces the house itself to one element off to the right in the distance. Wilson's Wilton views are perspectival, in that different prospects are made and complemented by others from a higher point of view, showing the overall layout of the estate. They may also have been intended to complement Lambert's views of Westcombe House, which had been commissioned by the previous Earl of Pembroke.

Wilson's work, however, represents all aspects of the topographical situation and should be followed chronologically. In his valuable thesis on Wilson, David Solkin shows that the painter returned to England and, after executing a few Italianate historical landscapes, chose native English locales that had been given associations with antiquity by contemporary poets like Pope and Thomson and by the architects who built houses on the model of Palladian villas.[6] Wilson evoked these places through topographical paintings which, however, find their equivalents to Pope's or Thomson's poetry in the graphic equivalents of Claude and Gaspar. The same eclecticism caused him, when he painted Hounslow Heath, to adopt the conventions of the Dutch school. Wilson plays with landscape painting styles to fit contemporary English topographical landscape in a way related to but not, of course, including the satiric irony of Hogarth's mimicry of a Carracci *Procession of Bacchus and Ariadne* in his depiction of *Hudibras Confronting a Skimmington* in a rural English community.

Wilson was not at this point representing places where English history took place, but places where classical connotations had been imposed by his own contemporaries—primarily in the vicinity of Windsor Forest and Twickenham. Nor are the associations strictly classical: the villas along the Thames at Twickenham were being referred to at the time as an English Brenta, with the emphasis on Palladio's own villas rather than his allusions back to Roman temples. But whether classical or Renaissance, Wilson used the graphic idiom of Italian models in order to bring out an element of continuity between native English scenes and the ideal past of Italy, much as Pope did in *Windsor Forest.* He also celebrated what is native English, and at this stage had to do so by making it acceptable in a Roman shape—as Walpole's jowlish face was made acceptable by Rysbrack's sculpting him as a Roman senator. He was also merely producing a saleable object, or, in higher terms, making his landscapes respectable (or all landscape painting, since like Hogarth he painted to advance English art as well as his own career, which he regarded as merely paradigmatic) by choosing well-known local places and then painting them as if they were in the great continental tradition of ideal landscape painting.

The next stage in Wilson's career was to depict sites that had their own national associations and did not *need* the structures of Italianate or ideal landscape. He did not, however, abandon those structures, but worked out the loosened Claude structure which is in fact a Gaspar landscape. But in the early 1760s he painted three views of the borderland between English Cheshire and Welsh Flintshire, an area no painter is known to have represented before him. His choice is explained by the fact that this countryside carried personal as well as public associations for him. His own family lived in Flintshire, and this cannot be discounted as an element in his choice. But the area he painted was also one that had been treated by the English poets.

It seems clear that Wilson painted his *View on the River Dee near Eaton Hall* (ca. 1760, Barber Institute) because of the English-poetic associations of the river and because it was on the border of Cheshire and Wales. Spenser wrote of it in *The Faerie Queene:* "And following Dee, which Britons long ygone / Did call 'divine,' that doth by Chester tend"; and Drayton wrote in *Polyolbion* (fourth song) of "the Holy Dee"

> whose prayers were highly priz'd
> As one in heavenly things devoutly exercis'd
> Who, changing of his fords, by divination had
> Foretold the neighbouring folk of fortune good or bad.

The divinity of the Dee, also connected in Milton's "Lycidas" with Druidic bards, derived from its supposed capacity to inspire prophecy of future glories or disasters for the English and Welsh whose territories it divided.[7] The literary echoes of the area also draw on Gray's "Bard" and are documented in Joseph Warton's *Essay on the Genius and Writings of Pope* (1756), in which Warton advises poets that "the mention of places remarkably romantic, the supposed habitation of Druids, bards, and wizards, is far more pleasing to the imagination, than the obvious introduction of Cam and Isis"—the classicized images of Cambridge and Oxford and its learned imitators of Virgil and Horace.[8] There are various other references in English poems, but the phenomenon to take note of is the attempt by Gray, Mason, and others in the 1750s to find a specifically British form, rather than a Virgilian, Claudian, or Italianate one, to suit a British subject.

Welshmen were Britons because the present British dynasty derived from the Tudors, whose origins were Welsh. But they were also British subjects who in the 1760s and 1770s carried around thoughts of political liberty smoldering under years of servitude to an English crown. Wales and liberty were associative links. In the sixth edition of Defoe's *Tour* (1761), the reviser who brings Defoe up to date describes Wales as "the Country of that brave

People who had an original Right to the whole Island, and made so noble a
stand in Defence of their Liberties and Independence; and, at last, rather than
submit to a foreign yoke, chose to be free in this remote and almost inaccessible Part of it."[9]

The two large Denbighshire scenes of 1771 commissioned by Sir Watkin
Williams Wynn (see figs. 13 and 14) focus on a single pair of dominating
features in the Wynnstay area—the River Dee and Castle Dinas Bran. In
Denbighshire the Dee's historical associations recalled Owen Glendower's
revolt against Henry IV, and the area where Llewelyn the Great, the last
native Prince of Wales, routed the English invaders in a number of battles.[10]
Dinas Bran was a castle that dated back to a time before the English invasions, before the fortresses built by the English to control their Welsh
subjects. It was therefore a symbol of an ancient and free Wales, and Wilson
enlarges and emphasizes it in his paintings of the area.

Between the River Dee paintings of 1760 and 1771, Wilson painted a
series of six major Welsh landscapes, all engraved in the same format and
published together. They all dealt with the subject of Welsh nationalism,
and the relation between ancient and modern Wales was their primary concern. While they depict no historic event, they do refer in various ways to the
English-Welsh relationship. (1) *Carnarvon Castle* (S.A. 1766; South African
private collection) shows one of the castles built by the conquering English to
keep down Welsh resistance. In this painting Wilson follows the topographical reality closely. (2) *Mt. Snowden from Llyn Nantlle* (S.A. 1766,
Walker Art Gallery, Liverpool), in the context of the total series, raises the
associations of this mountain with Gray's Bard, who cursed King Edward of
England and his army from its heights and then leaped to his death. (3)
Cader Idris (the Tate version was probably the basis for the print of not later
than 1768) pairs with Mount Snowden in its portrayal of the native British
mountains and lake that starkly contrast with the ideal landscapes of Italy.
Wilson has blunted the contours of Snowden as if to suggest its elemental
form and its permanence beyond historical time. Cader Idris offers a similarly
elemental English version of Lake Nemi, Lake Avernus, and other Italian
volcanic lakes familiar through the work of J. R. Cozens and Wilson himself.

(4) *Pembroke Castle and Town* (Cardiff) presents a ruined castle and a prosperous modern town, in effect contrasting the decaying past of English
domination, now a mere memory, with a flourishing present. (5) *Cilgarren
Castle* (Magdalen College, Oxford; engr. 1766), the pendant to *Pembroke
Castle and Town,* was another castle built by the English to control the Welsh
countryside but which by Wilson's time lay in ruins. Wilson restores Cilgarren Castle to its pristine power and glory, and the reason is an ironic one. By
returning it to its former reality, he pushes time back to the historic moment
when Prince Llewelyn's Welsh troops defeated the English near this spot.
The Cilgarren bards had, moreover, instructed Henry II where to find King

Arthur's tomb at Glastonbury, thus suggesting a yet more ancient lineage for English liberty.[11]

(6) Finally, *The Great Bridge over the River Taafe* (which survives only in the engraving of P. C. Canot, who exhibited it at the Society of Artists in 1766), shows a modern bridge, constructed as recently as 1756. It was a single arch stretching over 140 feet, and was considered in its time a marvel of engineering, said to be the "widest arch in Europe, if not in the world." Its architect was a simple Welsh mason and Methodist preacher, William Edwards. His first three attempts had collapsed and met with ridicule, but he succeeded on his fourth try. A writer in *The Gentleman's Magazine* at about the time of Wilson's painting wrote: the bridge "has now stood eight or nine years, and it is supposed that it may stand for ages to come, a monument of the strong natural parts, and bold attempts of an *Ancient Briton.*"[12]

These paintings, though engraved as a series and clearly programmatic, are as personal as they are public. They are as much a statement about landscape painting as about English politics, as much about Wilson as about Englishmen in general.[13] The landscapes dealing with ancient history and monuments of a specifically Welsh national character probably express his own feelings of beleagueredness as a Welshman and an unappreciated landscape painter. And he himself, like the Welsh patriots, did eventually retreat into the rough mountain fastnesses of his country, where he could live in harmony with nature rather than submit to English rule in the form of the Royal Academy in London.

The concept of "liberty" is artistic as well as political. I suppose Wilson connects his liberty with the "liberty" of the Opposition politicians of the 1730s, Gray's "British Liberty," and this relatively conservative sense of "liberty and property." I do not see him as a supporter of "Wilkes and Liberty" in the 1760s and 1770s. And yet the gardening "liberty" of the Stowe circle of "patriots" does not relate very closely to the "mountain nymph sweet liberty" of Wilson's Welsh landscapes. The mountain, whatever Wilson may have intended, is beginning to stir up associations that cannot even be controlled by Wilkes, let alone by Burke's aesthetic categories in his *Philosophical Enquiry into the Sublime and Beautiful.* Indeed, in the context of Wilson's Welsh landscapes the suspicion arises that Burke intends to make safe by his categorization something that is already beginning to be associated with a political subject, Welsh freedom—which could be used either as a reference to staunch ancient Britons, the original breed now lost, or to a need for greater liberty in the present for artist and for citizen.

CHAPTER 5 ❦
POETIC LANDSCAPE

At the end of the eighteenth century, Heinrich Fuseli distinguished between two kinds of landscape painting: "views," "the tame delineation of a given spot," a "kind of map work"; and landscapes that express large general concepts such as "height, depth, solitude, [which] strike, terrify, absorb, bewilder, in their scenery."[1] This contrast corresponds to Fuseli's distinction between history painting (by which he meant the factual recounting of events) and dramatic and epic painting. James Barry, also an academic painter seeking sublimity, saw as the importance of the second, preferred group its "unity, graceful simplicity, or ethical association."[2]

Fuseli was using an idiosyncratic vocabulary, but his ideas correspond to Barry's, and Barry's ideas echo the fountainhead of official doctrine on the arts, Sir Joshua Reynolds, who praised Claude for being "convinced, that taking nature as he found it seldom produced beauty. . . . His pictures are a composition of the various drafts which he had previously made from various beautiful scenes and prospects."[3] This composite landscape, analogous to the ideal of Appelles's composite painting of Helen drawn from the different perfections of several models, was preferable to the representation of "accidents"—by which Reynolds meant particular places and effects such as those found in the landscapes of the Dutch and Flemish schools.

As in history painting or the illustration of literary texts, there was an Italianate tradition, based on the models of the High Renaissance, in this case filtered through the models of Claude and Gaspar Dughet, with Salvator Rosa serving some other functions; and there was a native English tradition, based on local topography and largely modeled on northern European landscape painting. The native English landscape tradition, which was beginning to flutter to life in the 1730s in the work of Wootton and Lambert, coexisted with (and was sometimes indistinguishable from) imitations of Claude and Gaspar. Lambert's Claude landscapes began as a cross between Claudian theater-set painting and the rural equivalent of Hogarth's histories of contemporary Englishmen (one of these in the Mellon Collection has oddly Italianate mountains behind a scene of Hogarthian harvesters). Though Hogarth bridges the genres, painting the English figures in some of Lambert's English landscapes, his precedent also supports the possibility of a classical, emblematic, or historical landscape that has been secularized, stripped, or urbanized, as in his *Four Times of the Day*.

The landscape tradition in painting corresponded in important ways to the tradition in gardening. In both the emblems were removed, leaving only formal relationships that could be called beautiful or picturesque. Capability Brown simply opened up the closed vistas required to focus on a statue or temple, and removed the emblematic art objects themselves, which narrowed the associations of the scene. Topographical landscape, also under the influence of Brown's landscape gardening, reduced the country house to an aspect of the park, and often a peripheral one at that.

English gardeners and painters of landscape followed, more or less closely, the models of Claude, Poussin, and Gaspar. When they traveled to Italy (as Richard Wilson and Turner did) they brought back Italian sunlight to the English countryside. As they journeyed in the historic Campagna Romana, they saw landscapes divided into the prototypes of Claude and Gaspar: landscapes seen looking into the sun and landscapes seen with the sun behind them, picking out the highlights of a dark hillside—in both cases with the sun fairly low in the sky. They saw the scene framed by coulisses, as if it were a Serlian stage set or a segment of a Renaissance garden. A large tree on one side would be balanced by a smaller one on the other.

The Claude landscape, framed in this way, is essentially a pure prospect structured with alternating bands of shade and sunlight, which are, however, subordinated to the prospect (fig. 2). The eye always moves unimpeded to the horizon and the source of light and then returns to see in a more leisurely fashion how it got there. The whole gradation from foreground to far distance is sunlight and draws the viewer to the sky, while the areas in the distance are not so clearly demarcated as to force him to want to know them in detail. Without too much exaggeration, it can be said that Claude's painting is *about* the prospect, the wonderful glow of the horizon, the sunlight itself, which he frames and to which he leads the eye. But he places unobtrusively in the foreground, over to one side or beneath, and seldom blocking the prospect, a few figures that moralize or mythologize it.[4] It is fair to say that most of Claude's landscapes offer an interplay of horizon and foreground, of natural and human elements and relationships, extending to the mediating shapes of trees and other natural objects. In Poussin's history paintings, by contrast, the prospect is blocked; though the setting is often landscape, the foreground and middle distance are structured by people, who are his subject.

For the English landscape painter the most obvious problem in the Claude model was the middle distance, which in Wilson became a large, defined space quite unlike the continuum of uninterruptedly flowing shapes receding to the originary sunlight of the horizon. The Claude elements were precisely what Wilson, the topographical painter, the portrayer of English country houses, had to modify, reduce, or discard. As we have seen, he did not keep his country house in the center, but tended to replace the hollowed-out interior of a stage set with a carefully defined middle distance. When this was not the house, it was a body of water in relation to the house.

Wilson's well-known words were "Claude for air and Gaspar for composition and sentiment."[5] He takes from Claude his light but not ordinarily his central empty space. Rather, he adapts the more serviceable composition of Gaspar, which offers a compromise between the prospect-centered paintings of Claude and the human-centered histories of Poussin. Gaspar (fig. 19) fills in, if he does not block, the middle distance with an open area—often a body of water—and a building on its edge or above it. This proved an ideal model

for English country-house painting. Rather than allowing for the eye's unimpeded rush to the horizon, it provided a middle distance to linger over,
made of enclosed, fairly stable areas, with paths or roads leading the eye
around them. But to this Wilson adds something essentially English: the
practice of Hogarth and Reynolds of playing with allusions to the past. His
allusions are graphic, on the models of Claude and Gaspar; but they are
literary in that they use these artists for their associations with ancient Rome,
classical myth, and ideal pastoral landscape. The forms evoke the associations, whether the landscape is simply Cicero at his villa or an English villa
along the Thames that is seen in the context of Cicero's villa, or Horace's or
Virgil's.

The interest in light which comes, as Wilson tells us, from Claude, may
be the dominent aspect of his landscape. Perhaps he demonstrates once and
for all—also based on the precedent of the Dutch landscapes of Cuyp—that
landscape can be about light: light on this or that substance, foliage or water;
but essentially *about* light, as history painting is about the heroic actions of
men. (In this sense, Turner's great insight was that, in history-painting
terms, this meant that landscape painting was about the sun, a history of—to
use Thomson's words, which Turner quoted—"King Sun." And Hogarth, in
his ironic way, was exactly on target when he chose as his parody-landscape
the four times of the day.)

The country house, its lake and park are all incidental to the drama of
light in Wilson's landscapes. Light and color (and love of paint texture) set
him apart, in principle at least, from the emblematic garden of his time,
which sought permanent forms, universal meanings, by reducing color and
the incidentals of blooming flowers to a monochrome that emphasized the
meaning of its symbols. They also set him apart from the emblematic tradition of landscape painting, which he practiced in his most ambitious
academy pieces.[6]

Gaspar's occasional mythological subject is treated in a more organic
manner than Claude's. An example known to English painters is the *Eurydice*
that still hangs in Henry Hoare's Stourhead (fig. 20). Gaspar based his
figures on Ovid's version of the story of Eurydice's accidental death from
snakebite: "for as the bride went walking / Across the lawn, attended by her
naiads, / A serpent bit her ankle, and she was gone."[7] But he has also included, resting and observing on a distant hillside, the shepherd Aristaeus,
who (according to Virgil's account in his fourth *Georgic*) was responsible for
Eurydice's death: his pursuit, with rape in mind, led to her treading on the
poisonous snake. Aristaeus's presence, as so distant and passive an observer,
has the effect of diffusing—literally stretching thin—the tension of the
human story, the human relationships, and so of preventing the viewer's
attention from concentrating too heavily on the human plot.

The fact is that Gaspar unites, in a way Claude seldom does, the human and the natural elements. What we notice primarily is that the shape of Eurydice's gesture of recoil is paralleled in the lines of the mountain ranges behind her and reversed in the dark declivity before her, from which she is in effect recoiling—which doubtless prefigures the story of her descent into, and failed ascent out of, the underworld. Gaspar is using the Ovidian rather than the *Georgic* version of the story, in that Eurydice and the landscape are hallucinatorily interrelated. Ovid's story is about the equivalence of human passion and nature, whereas in the fourth *Georgic* the story is, rather, about the overcoming of this pathetic fallacy through labor and the rejuvenation of the depleted beehive.

Gaspar raises the question of which comes first, the human plot or the natural landscape? Which carries more weight? Does a human plot necessarily outweigh the natural setting, and so must Gaspar attenuate it as he does in order to save his landscape? In a sense never true of still-life painting, let alone of history, we have to decide whether this or that aspect is the figure, or simply another part of the ground. At its simplest, this is a question of staffage: Is the landscape about the human figures or about the landscape? Is the latter subject or setting? In Giorgione's *Sleeping Venus,* the Bellini *Madonna of the Meadow,* and perhaps in the Gaspar *Eurydice,* there is a harmony if not a union of man and nature. In many landscapes by Claude or Gaspar, however, we may well ask about figure and ground, seeing them as shifting gestalts.

As a question of figure and ground, Pieter Brueghel's *Fall of Icarus* (Royal Museum, Brussels) is surely *about* the Flemish peasant ploughing the field; but it offers a sidelong glimpse of the tiny figure of Icarus plummeting into the sea unnoticed by the farmer (or anyone but an alert viewer outside the picture) as an alternative center. The picture shows the mythological to be a peripheral, transient element in the panorama of nature. The picture, then, may be said to be about the secularizing or demythologizing of the sacred in nature, an example of how painters gradually reduced the mythological figure or lost it in the texture of the landscape, as the landscape came to predominate.

Or *The Fall of Icarus* may be a georgic in the Virgilian sense, in which the heroic-mythological is absorbed into the round of the seasons. The detail dissociates or makes the mythical peripheral to the routine of everyday life, which is the subject of georgic poetry. Were Brueghel's landscape to reflect Icarus's state of mind, it would be romantic, stormy, tragic; instead, it corresponds to the musing farmer's mind, and so is ordered, totally under control. Still, it has the small element of romantic uncontrol off to one side, bearing no apparent relation to it but perhaps admonitory, a memento mori of the sort contained in Virgil's *Georgics,* which recall the Civil War that is just past and may return again to disrupt this man-made order.

The prototypical landscapes of Claude and Gaspar turn our attention to the basic literary plots or myths that inform landscape painting in England. As one might expect, in the eighteenth century the myths came from three sources: the Bible or Milton's *Paradise Lost;* Virgil's *Pastorals* and *Georgics;* and Ovid's *Metamorphoses*—Eden, Arcadia, the Campagna Romana, and Ovid's dense, mysterious forests.

I suppose that, for the English poets and painters, Ovid was the essential mythographer, because landscape seems to have needed the myth of metamorphosis to link the human and the natural, the staffage and the landscape proper, and so to keep landscape in the ambience of history painting. Metamorphosis was the alternative to "story" (say, of *The Aeneid*), but because it was concerned with a transformation of the human into nature and nature into art, it is not surprising that many landscape painters, even when they did not include mythological figures, saw landscape through Ovid's eyes. In the landscapes of Gainsborough and Turner, where the Ovidian element is strongest, the metamorphosis relates to the idea of beauty (or art) emerging from rape, pain, and violent overturn. The sense of waste and loss (Daphne's and Syrinx's death, at least in human terms) is acknowledged along with the gain. But of course the georgic carried with it the same sense of loss and gain in the fallen garden that becomes precarious farmland. The threat of order slipping back into disorder extends to that tension between the textures of the paint and the illusion of the landscape. The Narcissus myth, for example, emphasizes the contrast between the reflected scene and the real one, with the drowned human figure as mediator.

Insofar as Gaspar (or in some cases Salvator Rosa) dominated English landscape painting, the mode was Ovidian; and insofar as Claude dominated, the mode was pastoral-georgic. One way of viewing Claude's landscapes is to say that the higher the viewpoint, the more coherent and organized the landscape—the Claudian prospect; whereas the lower the viewpoint, the more foreground muddle and particularity. It is in this sense that Brueghel gives us a wide, coherent overview and then smudges it with the tiny figure of Icarus. Claude may be thought to have included the ideal figures of myth in his foreground as much as a way of organizing that area as of mythologizing the landscape.

In Eden itself Milton offers us the georgic and Ovidian alternatives in Adam, who stands upright and names the animals and plants around him, and in Eve who, Narcissus-like, "crouches over her own reflection" in the pool and wants to lose herself in the landscape. These are, as James Turner has said, the "two tendencies—one structuring and objectifying, one blurring and falsifying,"[8]; but they are two ways of ordering experience which are equally falsifying. Adam's classification is scientific, possessive, hegemonic, and not necessarily to be preferred to Eve's; it is certainly no less personally oriented. Both offer a symbolization of what is, in the landscape itself, representation.

The pastoral is only a classical version of Eden, but without the religious overtones it may more narrowly signify a nature that can be controlled without work on the part of laboring people. Politically it can become the fantasy of a ruling class or, under the right circumstances, of the ruled, who look back or forward to a situation in which they will no longer have to work.[9] It is an image, depending on who looks at it, of the ideal or of illusion. The georgic, on the other hand, places human intelligence and labor in relation to a wilderness and describes the tension, the teetering back and forth, the paradoxes and ironies involved in maintaining the process of cultivation.

By the 1760s Gainsborough was turning from his Cuyp-like landscapes of Suffolk to *capricci,* imaginary scenes constructed of a few basic and inter-changeable shapes, textures, and colors. He was the artist who removed the emblems from a charged landscape (as charged in its way as a Hogarth *Time of the Day*), retaining the exciting plunge of the composition and the numinous quality of the landscape through the evocation of what is absent—the nymphs, gods, and swains—and through psychological resonances of a sort set off by the body-echoes in his ravines and gently sloping hillsides.

If Gainsborough represents the metamorphic tradition of landscape-history painting, then the other, the additive or emblematic tradition, is represented by Wilson. The simple structure employed in these early Wilson landscapes is similar to the relationship of foreground to background as human to nature in the English garden of the 1740s and 1750s and in topographical poetry. The Niobe story is like the Cave of Dido in relation to the larger natural setting around it at Stowe, or like the emblematic interpretation that infiltrates the natural descriptions of Dyer's *Grongar Hill* or Thomson's *The Seasons*.[10]

Luke Hermann, who writes with sensitivity of Wilson, notes his procedure of drawing the middle and far distance from life and then (perhaps in the studio) adding the "traditional *staffage* elements of figures and masonry" in the foreground to close the stage set. He goes on to say that, as in the early Roman landscape, *Pastoral Scene in the Campagna* (Ashmolean, Oxford), "It is the freely painted distant landscape that makes the greatest impact, while the carefully posed figures, sheep and ruin [in the foreground] play a secondary role despite their apparent prominence."[11]

Precisely what we notice in Gaspar's best landscapes, the preoccupations that separate him from Claude and Nicolas Poussin, are the soft, palpable, painterly renderings of the distance, which seems to reach out toward the spectator. The drama of the Gaspar landscape lies in its expressiveness of itself. Not light, perhaps (as with Claude), but the painting of distance and distant objects is his subject; or rather, the tension between perspective and the painting of it, between the illusionistic space behind the canvas and the space on its surface. The rich paint dares the viewer to deny the illusionistic reality of its representation. This tension Wilson inherits from Gaspar, and with it the fact that the sun is usually behind the painter or off to the side, and thus draws out the surfaces of the distant or middle-distant buildings or hills as if they were in the foreground.

But Hermann's insight also stresses the afterthought of Wilson's staffage, which indicates the ostensible (or official or complicating) subject and meaning of the Wilson landscapes. In the foreground he tends to paint symbolic objects and figures, the conventional world, and then devotes his painterly attention to the middle and far distance. (The figures are sometimes painted in by other artists, as they were for Lambert.) This is, I presume, the point Reynolds was making about Wilson's *Destruction of Niobe's Children* (fig. 21) when he commented that Wilson was guilty "of introducing gods and goddesses, ideal beings, into scenes which were by no means prepared to receive such personages. His landscapes were in reality too near common nature to admit supernatural objects."[12] It was not the principle of figures elevating landscape to which Reynolds objected, but Wilson's incongruous wedding of mythological figures and meteorological accuracy.

The emblematic Wilson was the early Wilson, just back from Italy. *The Destruction of Niobe's Children* was the culmination of a series of Ovidian landscapes in which the human figures in the foreground (Meleager or merely a group of banditti in the act of murdering travelers) served as an emblem to humanize or give meaning to the natural action, a storm in a distant, rugged landscape of mountains or seacoast.[13] His model was neither Claude nor Salvator Rosa, but a Gaspar painting like the *Dido and Aeneas* (London, National Gallery). The difference is that the violence of nature in the Gaspar bears all sorts of ironic relations to the soft, passionate, but tragically doomed meeting of Dido and Aeneas when they take shelter in the cave. In Wilson's words about Claude and Gaspar, "sentiment" meant the Gaspar story element—the mythological figures—reflected in the landscape, as opposed to Claude's stories, which have certain formal echoes, and which perhaps in a subtle way anthropomorphize nature, but in general leave the elements of myth and landscape separate. Wilson has also moved the storm-tossed tree inward from the edge of the picture, where it would have closed a Claude composition, to reveal in that crucial position the god shooting his arrows downward into Niobe's children. Though an illustration of Ovid's *Metamorphoses,* this avoids the Ovidian metamorphosis (Niobe changed into a weeping stone), showing only the killing that precedes it. It focuses on the older, more animistic metamorphosis, the changing of a tree into a god or of natural into human forces that will eventuate in Niobe's nemesis. The violent action therefore leads the eye back into the violence of nature, and (though the construction is generally planar) into the sky, which opens to make a hole into the infinite distance, a first adumbration of the vortex that will open into the background of Turner's history-landscapes.

There are, however, various ways in which Wilson eliminates the basic disjunction of emblem and natural setting, producing a more personal and characteristic painting. In the *White Monk* paintings (see fig. 22), one of his favorite subjects, the young people bask in the sunlight in the foreground (in at least two versions holding a parasol against the sun), and a hermit is seen in solitary devotion with his cross on a distant hilltop. The staffage transforms this landscape into a kind of *vanitas* scene, conveying a message to the effect that "the physical beauty of the universe is not the whole purpose of life."[14] But the parasol blocks sight of the hermit as well as the sunlight from the young people, and the ravine and distance separate them from an unpleasant truth. The division is itself the subject, the life of seclusion versus the life of play, and the total landscape, not merely a natural object allegorized by some human details, embodies the emblem. This has to do with the relationship between two areas, spatial and experiential, which amount to (in aesthetic terms) the beautiful and the sublime, held in the tension of the traditional *concordia discors* expressed in Dyer's poem.

Looking for a characteristic personal form in Wilson's landscape, I first notice the long, lazy stretch of river in his country-house paintings, the inordinate spaces between the trees, and the refusal consistently to close to left and right with coulisses. This can be regarded as Wilson's attenuation of the Claude stage-set structure to the point of annihilation, or it can be seen as the influence of the Gaspar model of landscape. It is this form we are aware of in the garden of Stourhead, in its second phase of the 1760s, when the reflecting pool that ran between the Pantheon and the grotto and the Temple of Ceres was enlarged into the lake we know today. The effect of this sort of garden should be contrasted with that of Stowe and Rousham of the 1730s and 1740s, which contain subordinate bodies of water, the emphasis falling on the great stretches of lawn and on separate framed pictures or emblematic scenes. The basic landscape structure is now a garden around a body of water, but as at Stourhead, Wilson's landscapes suggest echoes of a particular lake: Avernus.[15]

Wilson's model is Gaspar, who sometimes replaces the planar structure of the Claude stage set with open ends and recessions, but retains a curving line intended to unite the foreground and the background. This is, however, usually a C-curve, taking the form of a lake or some enclosed body of water which fills the empty center of the Claude landscape. Having followed Gaspar in placing a house in the middle distance near the body of water, Wilson begins to push the house back into the far distance (where it sometimes is found in Gaspar), or off to the side, and to fill the middle distance with his favorite form, the empty, sometimes reflecting space of a lake or river. The Gaspar pond, a gentle movement downward (sometimes assisted by the familiar Gaspar waterfall), serves a stabilizing function in Wilson. It is a perfectly flat, horizontal figure, except in some of the river views where it picks up the loosening structure that is another characteristic of Gaspar's landscape.

The Gaspar model is a graphic source for Gainsborough also, though it hardly explains the connotations with which he endows the slight downward movement and the darkness of Gaspar's ponds (fig. 23). Finding in Gaspar's composition the rococo forms and sentiment of his own time, he exaggerates them in order to give the houses on the hillside, the slope, and the pond a meaning all his own.

Gainsborough's structure is quite unlike Wilson's version of Gaspar. Whereas Gainsborough's characteristic curve, a long, loose S (or pair of intersecting Ss),[16] completely destroys and replaces the whole pattern of foreground, middle distance, and background, leading the viewer down into a hazy watery region that disappears off the canvas (and artistically into Turner's scenes, which the critics complained often lacked foreground), Wilson's tends to maintain the compartmentalization and shifts the attention onto this middle area, in which the C is constantly striving to close itself into an O. Even when a river is represented, the foreground configuration is often arranged to make a C-shape out of the middle distance.

Perhaps this is only to say that Wilson paints somewhere between the Hogarth and the Gainsborough generations of closed and open forms; or that he represents a painted version of the Capability Brown park, based on a lake making a C or serpentine but closed figure in the middle distance and around it open grass areas alternating with neat clumps of trees, in which context the country house itself is a subordinate element. At any rate, Wilson likes to paint a hole in the ground in the middle distance that separates foreground and background. This neatness is different from the picturesque disorder and impingement that is always taking place in a Gainsborough landscape, around and within his pond.

To judge by the number of versions of it, Lake Avernus was a favorite subject, and Wilson was especially drawn to volcanic lakes that resemble craters and have smooth, rounded edges, like Gaspar's Albano and Nemi in the Campagna and his own Cader Idris in Wales—well-defined shorelines rather than the relatively indeterminate banks of an ordinary river or lake of the sort Gainsborough preferred. Of course, we cannot know whether Wilson painted Avernus and Cader Idris so often because he saw landscape through the eyes of Gaspar; or because he could not shake the memories of the Snowdonian lakes of his childhood, which have this form; or only because they were "good breeders," as he called his more popular designs. Volcanic lakes and Lake Avernus with its entrance to the underworld are places to fall into, and yet, unlike Gainsborough's potholes, they never lead us off but remain sealed surfaces, firmly controlled and enclosed. A lake or a more or less closed part of a river, as centerpiece, either implies unseen depths or reflects a prominent landscape or architectural feature in the distance, pre-

senting a surface that relates foreground and background—the human and
the natural elements, the happy youths and the isolated White Monk on his
mountaintop. Water is a crucial element for both Gainsborough and Wilson,
but for the former it is a substance to be lured down into, a substance that
blurs into others, natural and human undifferentiated; and for the latter it is
either a carefully delimited surface which gives back an accurate reflection, or
nothing, an area of mediation between this and that (art and reality, or the
ideal and life?)—a mirror or a blank slate, but a substance quite clearly
different from the grass on this side, the rock on that.

While in Wilson's *Narcissus* (Father D. J. Lucey) the water is unconfined,
disappearing off the edge of the canvas, the effect is nevertheless very un-
Gainsboroughlike, for the shoreline is roughly horizontal to the bottom of
the picture, and the trees on either side close in Narcissus, who, unlike
Gainsborough's Actaeon, represents not a myth of violent, antithetical merging with nature but of self-love, looking into nature and seeing himself
reflected there.[17]

When a myth or anecdote is represented by Wilson it has to do with a *fear*
of falling into the water—Narcissus or a youth climbing a tree over it; or it
has to do with controlling water by swimming or fishing in it. Wilson
begins in his early sublime landscapes with nothing but an implied chasm
between foreground and background (as in *The Murder* in the Brinsley Ford
Collection, or the *Niobe* paintings); then he fills in the gap with a known
substance, which becomes the center if not the subject of the picture—
reversing the background and relating it to the people in the foreground
without ever inviting a loss of self in it. Actaeon and Narcissus are, in effect,
the same myth, describing a human merging with nature; but Gainsborough
interprets this as being in the process of happening (fig. 24), while Wilson
stops it at the moment of division: there are a real Narcissus and a reflected
one, the water acting merely as mirror, though a dangerously seductive one.
Ultimately the water serves as a barrier, something that *prevents* humans from
reaching or completely apprehending or experiencing it as well as reaching
the source of light in the far distance. It may be a dangerous perspective back
from Turner's landscapes that makes me wonder whether Wilson's volcanic
lake is not an eye-catcher, a substitute, even a much reduced displacement
for the invisible sun, which is the other element of his landscape. The signs
of the sun are everywhere, but the sun itself almost never appears. What *is*
materialized is the hole in the middle distance, the most striking sign of the
sun because it is filled (or, as importantly, in some cases is *not* filled) with the
sun's reflections of all that is around it.

The lake marks the distinction, if not between man and nature, then
between beauty and sublimity or the ordinary and the extraordinary—a
relationship that carries us back to those early scenes in which a human
murder or passion in the foreground only feebly reflected the wild excesses of

nature. By employing the image of the lake, Wilson has found a way of mediating between these two incompatibles by way of a reflection. The lake is Wilson's statement of his position as artist. One version of *Carnarvon Castle* (fig. 15) adds to the reflection of the castle in water an artist sketching it, thus schematizing the scale of representation from the action of the surrogate artist to the watery metamorphosis to the painter's copy, which is the painting—each of which is distinct from and not to be confused with Carnarvon Castle itself.

Frequently the artist in a landscape is shown sketching the scene with a gentleman looking over his shoulder. But the natural representation of his art is the lake, which mediates between his canvas and the object he is trying to represent on the other side of the lake—perhaps in the far distance. I am suggesting that Wilson's center of gravity is not, as it would be with Turner (and in a sense was with Claude), the sun itself, but its reflection on things; and so in many pictures the sheet of water that makes up his middle distance returns the images of nature around it.[18] But the water reflects with a powerful (neoclassical?) detachment: Narcissus gazes at his reflection but does not go in—and if he did, we suspect that he, like other Wilson protagonists, would be able to swim. The lake is there for reflection, not for immersion or "drowning." The myth is perhaps best seen in Pope's version in *Windsor Forest,* where it is embodied in the nymph Lodona's pursuit by a satyr and her transformation into a still, reflecting pond, which sets up analogies between the metamorphosis of war into peace, killing into hunting, and active pursuits into the contemplative one of poetry. The calm sheet of water reflects its surroundings, making them poetic. Or, as Wilson shows, the surface can be transformed in one way or another—by a storm or by volcanic geological structures—into a surface that will not reflect—that is, for Wilson, the Avernus-type lake which is an entrance to another world whose image is withheld from us.

Gainsborough's subject is the middle distance without demarcation (or with blurred demarcation) between earth and water, between this world and the other—a sort of swamp that seems to suck in humans and animals, attracting them to its indeterminacy. As a myth to illustrate his concern, he chose the Diana-Actaeon metamorphosis, the myth of the human who sees too much (of virgin, unsullied nature) and as punishment is transformed into what he sees, nature itself (fig. 24). Wilson's version of this myth simply shows Actaeon the stag being chased away by his own hounds along the edge of Diana's lake. His *Diana and Calisto* shows Diana imperiously denouncing the pregnant Calisto before her transformation into a bear. While Wilson maintains his usual tension between story and landscape, leaving us with a sense of illustration rather than integration, Gainsborough presents a metamorphosis that is far more evocative, more essential to the landscape (into which the figures almost disappear, tonally and linearly), partly at least because it has to do with seeing. Seeing nature leads to the catastrophe of becoming part of it.

Besides the history painting *Diana and Actaeon,* there are also Gainsborough's paintings from about the same period of boys and dogs fighting (Kenwood) and of hounds coursing a fox (fig. 25). The fox is being caught and killed in a pattern of descent into a pond and a common tangle of descending serpentine lines, which has its equivalent both in the figures of Diana and Actaeon and in the entangled shapes of the boys and fighting dogs. Gainsborough in these last paintings reveals the explicit savagery underlying the metamorphosis that is his subject.

His earliest Suffolk landscapes contain a sensitivity to the social details of his surroundings soon lost when he moved to Bath and finally to London, as he gained more fashionable patronage. It could nevertheless be argued that there is a bond of a sort connecting the early landscapes that are structured on contrasting figures of farm laborers working and resting, or later drinking and wenching on the way to a harvest feast, to the late historical subject compositions of *Diana and Actaeon,* the hounds coursing the fox, and the two dogs fighting. For example, the contrast between the brightness of the upper world above the slanting horizon and the growing darkness and undifferentiation in the lower part of the composition is made to correspond in some of the paintings (for example, one at Kenwood) to the misery of the peasants, intensifying as they huddle down the dark slope and seem to merge with the vague, natural shapes.

Gainsborough's one biblical landscape, *Hagar and Ishmael* (National Gallery of Wales, Cardiff), is another Diana-Actaeon story of an expulsion from society into nature to die. In Gainsborough's painting there is no sign of the angel that will rescue Hagar and Ishmael. By contrast, in Claude's versions of the subject the most appropriate one (Munich, Alte Pinakothek) shows Abraham's house on the left and the natural landscape into which he is banishing Hagar and Ishmael on the right. This is the perfect mythic explanation for the Claude landscape, which invites its spectators, as Abraham does Hagar and Ishmael, to venture out to merge with the source of light at the horizon, a kind of benign apotheosis (presumably from Abraham's, not Hagar's, point of view). Gainsborough's version is simply a metamorphosis downward into the ground rather than up into the sky; his center of gravity is the earth's navel, Claude's is the sun.

Light, the sun, and the sky are not subjects in themselves for Gainsborough, as they are for Claude or (in different ways) for Wilson and Turner—or as sky and clouds are for Constable. But the sky and light are present, sources of illumination, silhouetting the figures on a slanting horizon line—a horizon usually close in, just beyond the middle distance. Sky serves to highlight these figures dramatically and to contrast the brightness of the upper world with the growing darkness and undifferentiation in the lower part of the picture.

In order to bring together the threads of topographical and poetic landscape, I end this chapter with a very unliterary landscape, that of Thomas Rowlandson, which is richly descriptive and yet poetic in its flowing, stylized Gainsborough-derived forms—a comic, light-hearted version of Gainsborough's profoundly reassuring (and yet disturbing) forms.

One drawing in sepia and pen (fig. 26), shows the familiar Rowlandson image of man in nature. Two men, four oxen, and a horse are dragging a fallen tree, with trees and hills in the background showing a great mass of various elaborate leafwork patterns, shadow patterns, and contour lines for the hills, played off against the small group of laboring figures. The subject is the fallen tree, which is in an intermediate state between organic growth and kindling wood. A simpler version, completely characteristic of Rowlandson, is a drawing (fig. 27, much repeated and etched) which could almost pass for a Gainsborough (whose landscapes Rowlandson copied) except for the essential difference that Gainsborough never used that strange shape of log. Neither log nor gigantic carrot, it seems a vaguely phallic shape reminiscent of the dildoes Rowlandson used in one of his pornographic drawings called *The Inspection.* [19] I think the interest of a Rowlandson landscape usually lies in the question of its middle term, the objects in the cart, the splendidly ambiguous and somewhat intriguing shapes, and the relationship between them as shapes and as representations. Whatever it may suggest as part- or whole-object, the thing carried is a large, problematic form set off against those small, animal and human figures that are drawing it.

Turning to the topographical, let us examine one of four large pen-and-ink drawings of shipyard scenes made around 1800, which gives primarily an impression of contrasting patterns of lines that delimit the different objects (fig. 28). The lines of the boards, the rigging, and the complex pattern of the sterns of the ships stand out against the large areas of white paper, the delicate lines of waves and reflections in the water, and, on the other side of the picture, against the lines of the buildings and scaffolds—and the people—on the shore. Mediating between these two interestingly different systems of lines are other people in small boats floating between ships and shore, and one large ship that is grounded, in drydock.

This drawing, insofar as it is representational (and not merely *about* the contrasting shapes and patterns), is, like the first drawing of the hauled tree (fig. 26), concerned with intermediate or borderline states of being. The significant facts of the composition are the central position of the empty space of harbor between ships and shore and the large shape of the boat which is neither in the water nor part of the structures on land. Most of this grounded ship cants to the right, making a diagonal that contrasts with the vertical line of the church steeple behind it. Indeed, the masts of the ships on both right and left are canted in opposite directions, in contrast to the upright masts in the background. Between, in the empty space, are representations of small boats and sailors either loading or unloading, plying between ships and shore. I submit that this sort of scene—or relationship—is what interested Rowlandson, as it would have (in their different ways) both the Gainsborough of ontologically insecure landscapes and the Samuel Scott of *Westminster Bridge.*

What has happened to the literary in these drawings by Rowlandson? It has become the enemy—it appears only to be ridiculed. A drawing in the Huntington Gallery shows (fig. 29) a man lounging, holding a book and reading as he sits on a man-made geometrical structure which surrounds a tree, amidst a veritable jungle of various leaf, branch, and trunk shapes, all depicted with different sorts of lines (the love of classification as principle rather than practice). The drawing is about the man with his nose buried in a book and ignoring what he ought to be experiencing. Literature is no longer privileged; indeed, it is reduced to a fragile foothold. In many drawings of gardens Rowlandson shows people turning away from books, or from statues like the Roman bust opposite the reader in this work, to suggest a redirection of verbal-visual energies toward the picturesque in nature itself.

Finally, Rowlandson marks in one sense the definitive break from the tradition of Hogarth. Enclosure was, formally as well as thematically, the subject of Hogarth's "modern moral subjects." They can be said to be an attack on physical or spiritual enclosure. Rowlandson, the extreme alternative to Hogarth, can be said to extol the breaking of enclosures, the exploding of barriers, and the collapse of man-made structures under the pressure of human (or, what was for him the same thing, natural) flesh. In his landscapes the natural shapes grow, encroach, and supersede like some monstrous cancer. Whether his model is the landscape of Fragonard, with its huge tree-shapes dwarfing human beings, or the closer model of Gainsborough, he succeeded in making natural forms overwhelm man-constructed ones and seem to be extensions of the bulging, unruly bodies of his human beings.

The subject of enclosure is also relevant to Turner and Constable, one of whom has as his subject the dissolving of the old one-point perspective box of the room through the agency of a potent sunburst, and the other the tension between barriers, hazards, and blockages and something ineffable glimpsed through and beyond those enclosing forms.

PART II
TURNER'S GRAFFITI:
THE SUN AND
ITS GLOSSES

CHAPTER 6 ❦
THE VERBAL ASPECT

On the face of it, Turner's painting is an extreme case of the incompatibility of visual and verbal structures in a single object. The dichotomy is plain in the two landmark critical studies of Turner. Lawrence Gowing's Turner makes the discovery that painting is essentially pigment on canvas, the pure form, color, and texture which are the evidences of an artist in action. John Gage's Turner is trying to reconstitute the iconography of history painting in the genre of landscape in contemporary England.[1] The paradox is that many Turner paintings substantiate both claims. In *Rain, Steam, and Speed* (R.A. 1844, fig. 30) Turner produces one of his most masterly expressions of pure paint in the forward thrust of blackness out of a hole of light—which becomes a train rushing at us along a high trestle. But then he adds (visible only upon close inspection), racing down the track ahead of the train, a tiny hare, something between emblem and pictograph, which verbalizes as "speed" and also perhaps as "transience"; and in the distance a tiny ploughman, perhaps indicating the tag "Speed the plough."[2] To this he finally adds a title "Rain, Steam and Speed: The Great Western Railway."

A less radical example to begin with is Turner's acknowledgment of the landscape tradition, *Dido Building Carthage* (R.A. 1815, fig. 31), a harbor scene with classical buildings. It hangs, according to Turner's instructions, in the National Gallery next to Claude's *Embarcation of the Queen of Sheba* (fig. 32), and it is Turner's version of a Claude, a demonstration that he could equal the old master on his own ground but also an affirmation of his roots in the great tradition. Only when you are close to the work do you recognize the Turner style in the sketchy, always slightly caricatured (or overparticularized) figures, more from the Dutch tradition than the Italian or French. Moreover, he has omitted the horizontal shoreline that closes the bottom of Claude's picture and creates the "harbor": the reflection of the sun in the water cuts the baseline of the picture in two and leads all the way up to the sun itself, which is the cynosure of the composition—to a degree quite unlike the Claude. The Claude is structured architecturally on a series of planes parallel to the picture plane at the horizon. In Turner's picture the buildings and the harbor banks curve, the encroaching foliage recoils, in the wake of the sun's rays, making the composition a vortex shaped by the sun. He has chosen the Claude body of water rather than the Gaspar—a U-shaped, harbor-shaped area which he opens at the bottom, connecting the sun of the horizon with the ordinarily (in both Claude and Gaspar) dark foreground in a single shimmering vortex.

Turner paid similar homage to other old masters, Watteau and Rembrandt, and showed Canaletto painting Venice in the manner of Turner, and Raphael displaying a landscape which looks suspiciously like a Turner. He even painted an English artist in his studio who is meant to recall Hogarth's *Distressed Poet* (or his lost *Distressed Painter*). In each case Turner fits himself into the role of a painter to whom he acknowledges a debt but transforms him into a Turner. Each reference is both homage (a connection with the tradition of great painters) and correction. The Claude *Embarcation* stands for the whole genre of classical landscape as Other, much as in Pope's Horatian imitations the Horatian text was printed on the page facing his modernization that brought out the true "genius of the place."

There is a slight story element in Turner's harbor scene: a queen, surrounded by courtiers, is pointing to some plans related to the construction that is going on around them. When the painting was shown at the Royal Academy in 1815, Turner entered a title in the catalogue: "Dido Building Carthage; or the Rise of the Carthaginian Empire—1st Book of Virgil's *Aeneid*." But even before making the catalogue entry he had added to the picture, along the wall at the far left, these same words as an inscription carved in the stone (in English). (The Claude pendant also helps by showing a queen and an implied foreign rival; just as Sheba leaves to meet King Solomon, so Dido is soon to encounter Aeneas.) The allusion to the *Aeneid* renders the word *Rise* an irony, projecting the destruction implicit in the building of Carthage and the setting of the sun implicit in its rising. In 1815 the informed viewer would also have felt a reference to France/Carthage and England/Rome. Finally, in 1817 Turner materialized the sequel, *The Decline of Carthage,* in a painting with the sun setting. His first will (1829) stipulated that the *Decline* be hung next to the *Rise,* but by 1831, in his second will, he had decided that the one painting sufficed to convey both rise and fall, and he substituted *Sun Rising through Vapour*—a landscape which demonstrated the other side of his genius, rooted in the Dutch tradition.[3]

In the foreground of *Dido Building Carthage* there is a group of children symbolically launching a toy boat (Carthaginian trade)—a touch we associate with Hogarth rather than Claude. The name of Sychaeus, Dido's husband, whose murder led to her flight to North Africa and the founding of Carthage, is inscribed on the tomb at the right. (In *The Decline of Carthage* a building at the far left is decorated with a statue of Mercury, whose caduceus is inscribed on a pediment to the right. This was the god who told Aeneas he must not tarry with Dido but proceed on his way to found Rome.)

Peripheral details like these are meant to draw our attention to an "aspect" of the work of art. Seeing aspects, or *seeing as,* is the interpretive aim of Turner's juxtaposition of his landscape with a significant detail, a title, a painting by Claude, another painting as sequel, and so forth. What we notice, consequently, is the artist's need to draw our attention to this aspect rather than another; and that the aspect to which he draws our attention is the moral one. The aspect he apparently lacked complete confidence in, but which we may now (with Gowing) see as primary, is the paint on canvas arranged in a certain graphic rhythm. This rhythm Turner wanted us to understand as a public statement about his world, but the interesting fact is the intransigence of his materials, for though he forces us to look at one aspect, we cannot help being aware of another which we may feel is more insistent.

Some of Turner's details are likely to recall Brueghel's *Fall of Icarus,* which is *about* the Flemish peasant ploughing the field, but allows a sidelong glimpse of the tiny figure of Icarus plunging unnoticed into the sea. The detail dissociates or makes peripheral the mythical from the routine of every-day life. We might see Turner's details of the ploughman and the rabbit (and the boating party far below the train), or of the boys sailing a boat, as reminders of the persistence of natural and human cycles in the presence of a sublime landscape. Certainly the figures in most Turner history paintings are details in relation to the large sweep of the composition. In some paintings the relationship can be read as a mock-heroic deflation, as when a majestic Gothic ruin is accompanied by details of contemporary debris—chickens, coops, and farm implements (as in the early watercolor, *The Transept of Ewenny Priory,* 1797, Cardiff).

In the paintings of his maturity Turner emphasizes these human details as almost pure linguistic signs. It is only a step from the speeding rabbit to the greyhound pursuing a "hare" which refers, as the picture's title, *Battle Abbey: The Spot Where Harold Fell,* indicates, to Harold Harefoot, the Battle of Hastings, and the fall of the Anglo-Saxons. The result teeters between the sublime and the ridiculous. The aspect of the hare as a tiny creature in relation to the ruins of the abbey is overlaid with the verbal pun. Engraved, the landscape appeared in *Views in Sussex* (1819) accompanied by an explan-atory note by R. R. Reinagle: "Mr. Turner has given us an episode, a hare, just on the point of being run down by a greyhound, which fills the mind with one sentiment, that of death, as no other living objects interpose to divert the mind from it." Turner has also supported the reference to death by showing the trees along the hare's path of flight changing from summer leafage to autumnal falling and winter barrenness.

Does it mar or grace Turner's great painting *Peace—Burial at Sea* (R.A. 1842, Tate), commemorating the death of the artist David Wilkie, to in-clude what is clearly a black coach on the foredeck of the ship on which Wilkie's funeral took place—a reference to the funeral that could *not* take place in London—and to include a mallard flying along the water in the lower left foreground to indicate his own (Joseph *Mallord* William Turner's) desired presence at the sea burial of his friend? The mallard itself is a beautiful shape and in no way aesthetically detracting—until one connects it by the verbal pun with the artist; and then perhaps it is only mildly annoy-ing. On the other hand, I don't think anyone would want to argue that Turner improved the painting by adding the further commentary of the pendant *War, the Exile and the Rock Limpet,* which is of limited intellectual

and no aesthetic interest.[4] These seem to me extreme cases of Turner's idiosyncratic (if not shallow) understanding of literary reference, and so of his
trivializing by literary structures his powerful graphic imagination.

In order to place Turner in the English school of landscape painting, we
must begin with Wilson's early historical landscapes, which make a great
deal of the relation between a small emblematic or historical group of people
in the foreground, and the landscape and weather conditions in the background. The Wilsonian emblem, however, becomes smaller and smaller in
Turner's landscapes. In *Aeneas and the Sibyl, Lake Avernus* (1814–15, Yale
Center for British Art) there is a rise in the foreground on which a little
drama of some kind is being played out, the round shape of a Gaspar/Wilson
lake in the middle distance, and the closure of hills in the far distance. From
these very Wilson-like scenes Turner progresses to wholly Claude compositions with no obstruction to the sunlit horizon, with tiny figures in the
foreground appearing as merely a few spots of color against the immense
receding landscape. In *The Bay of Baiae, with Apollo and the Sibyl* (R.A. 1823,
fig. 33) it is both the Apollo-Sibyl group and the more purely linguistic
rabbit and the nearby snake which explain or interpret the vast expanse of
terrain leading to the horizon.

The hare or the snake is an addition, gloss, *remarque,* or superscription,
and not an integral part of the composition like either the Brueghel Icarus or
the Hogarthian detail. Whereas in Hogarth word and image join (even
sometimes in puns as awful as Turner's), in Turner they tend to diverge. The
title and pictograph make the painting something other than its image by
itself would necessarily mean. The progression is indeed a linguistic one; a
great leap is made from the image in nature to the arbitrary structures that
develop from pictograph to hieroglyph to alphabetically constructed words
and sentences, with a result very like the evolution, and the visual effect, of
an emblem.

Spatially the linguistic structuring is literally on top of the image, and
chronologically word follows visual image. Turner himself regarded the Varnishing Days at the Royal Academy as paradigmatic: he submits a painting
that appears to be "a mere dab of several colours," as one contemporary
remarked, "and 'without form and void,' like chaos before the creation."
Then, like "a magician, performing his incantations in public," Turner
spends Varnishing Day before the inchoate, unrecognizable marks ("always
visibly and obviously made out of paint," as Gowing says) gradually adding
the representation, bringing out certain parts of the pure form and texture to
a finish, and then continuing to impose meaning in the details, title, epigraphs, and other attached documents, extending sometimes to the clauses
and codicils of his will. Contemporaries saw this phenomenon as analogous to
God's creation of the world out of chaos.[5] I rather think Turner encouraged
this notion.

The question of whether Turner regarded the studies in pure paint, the "unfinished" canvases, as his masterpieces or as merely unfinished is not easily answered. To judge by his written words, he regarded them as of secondary interest. He seldom or never exhibited them during his lifetime, and he stipulated in his will that only "finished" pictures be exhibited in the Turner Gallery; in a separate memorandum he asked that unfinished oils be shown every fifth year and unfinished watercolors and sketches every sixth.[6] While it is true that good paintings "are complete all the time so far as they go,"[7] and that this applies to Turner's paintings more than to most, I suspect that when he said that "indistinctness is my fault" (not, as it used to be read, "my forte"),[8] he was expressing his public self, the one that did finish his paintings with emblems and epigraphs.

The facts of Turner's stated intentions tend to substantiate my feeling that he was afraid to acknowledge the "unfinished" paintings, which he nevertheless kept unfinished as long as possible—on Varnishing Days exhibiting both stages and recording the process by which he moved from one to the other, and leaving the painting finally as unfinished as he dared. By the Varnishing Day procedure he may have been saying: (1) See, the design *was* there all the time; or (2) See, *I* can produce order—or creation—out of chaos; or even (3) See, this "unfinished" composition is what you *should* appreciate, but since you don't I'll give you just enough representation to understand what was there.

As Jerrold Ziff has shown, the earliest use of poetic epigraphs by Turner in the Royal Academy catalogues of 1798 and 1799 (when the academy began to accept poetic attachments to the paintings) was as a verbal equivalent to the painted landscape. This was most beautifully accomplished in *Buttermere Lake* (R.A. 1798, fig. 34) where Thomson's verses describe roughly what we see, including the rainbow:[9]

> Till in the western sky the downward sun
> Looks out effulgent—the rapid radiance instantaneous strikes
> Th'illumin'd mountains—in a yellow mist
> Bestriding earth—The grand ethereal bow
> Shoots up immense, and every hue unfolds.

It is even possible that Turner *saw* that Lake District landscape, when he first copied it on the spot, through the eyes of Thomson's lines (or Thomson's lines reproduced in Gilpin's *Lakes Tour*). More likely, he introduced Thomson/Gilpin between the first sketches and the watercolor in which he begins to place the rainbow.[10]

Then, as Ziff shows, within a couple of years Turner had developed his epigraph into a commentary on the landscape rather than merely a verbal equivalent of it. Even in *Buttermere Lake,* however, the verses do add something that is not present in the painting: "the downward sun" which "Looks out effulgent" is nowhere visible, only its effects. Turner makes it visible in the verses, which thus collaborate with the image.

Dolbadern Castle, North Wales, Turner's diploma piece for the Royal Academy (1800, fig. 35), establishes the model for his later landscapes. It shows a great wall of mountain capped by a castle tower, pictorially growing out of the mountain and silhouetted against a glowering sky, with a few tiny Salvator Rosa warriors at the foot of the mountain. But then Turner attaches to this image in the Royal Academy catalogue the lines (the first to be written by himself):

> How awful is the silence of the waste,
> Where nature lifts her mountains to the sky.
> Majestic solitude, behold the tower
> Where hopeless OWEN, long imprison'd, pin'd,
> And wrung his hands for liberty, in vain.

There is no indication in the painting of Owen, the Welsh prince imprisoned in Dolbadern Castle from 1254 to 1277, who is referred to in the verse. It is as if Wilson had attached verses to one of his Dee River landscapes, underlining the patriotic (or revolutionary) intent we have inferred from those paintings. Another early work, the watercolor *Carnarvon Castle, North Wales* (R.A. 1800, B.M.) shows a peaceful pastoral scene with a fringe of tiny figures in the foreground listening to a bard's performance, but the verses attached imply the future extermination of the Welsh bards described in Gray's poem. Turner seems to be emphasizing the disjunction, as he does more spectacularly in his later works.

As a Romantic artist Turner expressed a new epistemology, one that supposes a powerful reflexivity in the subject; he projected his imagination on a landscape, creating more literally than even Gainsborough a landscape of the mind. As Adrian Stokes has argued, Turner is the prototypical case of a landscape painter who invested his subject with part-whole relations, turning hills into breasts and tree clumps into pubic hair.[11] But at the same time Turner does not abandon the verbal dimension, indeed, is still part of the Hogarthian tradition. The figures in a Turner landscape—who always seem to be added after the fact and are often clumsily painted—are as active and readable in their actions and relationships, their expressions and gestures, as those in a Hogarth "modern moral subject." The intellectual content in Turner, though of a very different kind, is often as insistent as in Hogarth. Both artists share the problem of coming to terms with the great tradition of history painting, though in quite different ways. The work of both artists shows the split personality (perhaps an English trait given the logocentrism of their culture) of a natural and metaphysical painter, interested in purely formal problems (as Hogarth showed in his *Analysis of Beauty,* the first formalist art treatise in English) and in moral structures and messages. The difference in the oil sketches, of course, is that Turner's are really about light and its effects, while Hogarth's *Wedding Dance,* for example, is still about the dancing figures. But in both cases the vehicle is form and color. I sometimes wonder what we would think of Hogarth now if he had left in his studio, not a handful of what were clearly modelli for his "modern moral subjects," but fifty or a hundred *Shrimp Girls* and *Wedding Dances.*

Hogarth, recall, painted such oil sketches con amore, but then also produced an engraving with the objects carefully defined, inscriptions and emblems added—added, however, by way of definition not superscription. He was a painter *and* he was an engraver, and (with the significant exceptions of the finished paintings that were supposed to pass as deluxe versions of the engravings, in which he tried to combine both functions) he kept the graphic artist and the moralist separate. In his case this was a horizontal relationship between the painting and the print, the visual image and (or leading to) the verbal or literary allusions, which were in the audience's memory. In Turner's case, the relationship was a vertical one, with the visual image superscribed by literary or linguistic structures: on the image, below and around it.

Of course, the sense of "mistake" on Turner's part is exacerbated by the fact that the Turner of the large dramatic forms and shimmering color appeals directly to us in the twentieth century; the other is the backward-looking Turner who connects with Hogarth (and Wilson and Reynolds), as he does with Rembrandt and Claude. To us, I think, the great Turnerian breakthrough in history painting is the modification and reduction of all the superficies into a natural force—a storm or a raging sea, a vortex and nothing more.

At the simplest, we can say that at the end of the eighteenth century Turner, in order to elevate his landscape to the level of history painting, retained the moral-literary traces even though sometimes they were no more than a tiny emblematic rabbit or ploughman almost invisible on the periphery, or a title or epigraph that contradicts the visual. That he correctly estimated the times is proved by his election to full academician status at the age of twenty-five. But in his official Royal Academy paintings—perhaps even in his most radically innovative—he in effect superimposed a public and literary meaning on a landscape of pure form and color. What he could not understand, because he saw through the eyes of the academy and of an Englishman, was that pure form represents genuine though nonverbal thought; that the actual working out of the structure of forms was in a radical sense his real subject. Therefore he covered, disguised, or domesticated his original visual image, which he either thought he was clarifying or regarded as in some sense infra dig.

Sometimes I feel I would like to wipe out all the graffiti on Turner's paintings, judging the ideal by the unfinished canvases he left in his studio, as I would like to *read* Blake's *Songs of Innocence and Experience* on a plain blank page (i.e., without his decorations).[12] But in neither case are we offered an alternative to the combination. We may have grown up looking at Turners by themselves, certainly without the Royal Academy catalogue entries, just as we grew up reading Blake's songs alone, with large empty spaces on either side of the lines that we fill in ourselves with the associations of the words; and we may be aware of the reductive effect of some of the visual images with which he accompanied them. But Blake never published his *Songs* in any other way than with the accompanying visual images, and Turner used every method at his disposal to bring out the verbal significances of his visual images.

However much we may want aesthetically to revise, as historians we have to explain Turner as a vestige of the long controversy which pitted the body of the *visual* image against the soul as the *motto* or legend accompanying it. True, the soul requires the body (the "vesture of the soul") in order to achieve the true perfection of its nature; but the body without the soul is nothing. Sight, while ranked first among the senses, falls short of the word as the vehicle of reason, man's highest faculty. Turner is the inheritor of these arguments, which in England, with its emphasis on the word (Protestant, but powerfully supported by the presence of Shakespeare and Milton and, in his own way, Hogarth), end in the preeminence of the Turner *image* but the retention of the word to remind us of his ambivalence and sense of a pyrrhic victory.

In his own time Turner was caught in the antipictorialism of the Burke tradition,[13] reiterated in Wordsworth's "sight is . . . a sad enemy to imagination" or Coleridge's reference to the "despotism of the eye"—that the eye is subject to outward appearances, as opposed to the ear, the mind's eye. His words, "the grandest efforts of poetry are where the imagination is called forth, not to produce a distinct form, but a strong working of the mind,"[14] are at odds with the old tradition of the Sister Arts which told the artist to emblematize, particularize (the worst quality of a painting, according to Hazlitt and Coleridge), and moralize. In other words, Turner did not express a desire to combine indistinct image with indistinct words, but (paradoxically, considering contemporary criticism) used the *image* to "call forth a strong working of the mind"—indistinct but powerful—and the *words* to particularize, point, direct, and "produce a distinct form" of meaning.

It is not entirely fair to Turner, however, to conclude that he was painting no more than a landscape in the form of a vestigial emblem. The incongruity of large form and literary detail, of representation that shows one thing and inscription that says another, may serve a more interesting function for Turner than I have yet suggested. In *Palestrina—A Composition* (R.A. 1828, fig. 36) he has painted a beautifully idyllic Italian landscape, entitled it

Palestrina, the modern name for the classical Praeneste, and (in case we have forgotten this fact) attached the following quotation from *The Fallacies of Hope:*

> Or from yon rock, high-crowned Praeneste,
> Where, misdeeming of his strength, the Carthaginian stood,
> And marked, with eagle-eye, Rome as his victim.

Modern name and scene are depicted; a reference is made to the ancient site—what the scene *was* (in an excerpt from a poem which existed as little more than the series of fragments attached as epigraphs to his paintings); and a "fallacy of hope," which took place on this spot a long time before, is being enjambed with other moments in the past and present: the moment when Hannibal looked toward Rome, when he was defeated by Rome, and the present moment when Turner looks down the same channels.

The conception of a painting bringing together these different times and realities was implicit in Wilson's Welsh landscapes, but Turner nails it down, so to speak, by his titles and inscriptions, as well as by the graphic indication of such temporal intersections in the double vortex composition (see below, pp. 95–97): two vortices separated by the familiar tall feathery stone-pine (which appears in many of Turner's Italian landscapes), down one of which is the road to Rome, down the other a pastoral setting of cattle and sheep. A vortex which recedes into the horizontal distance was the basic compositional motif of the *Dido Building Carthage,* in that case created by the solid presence of the sun in the center of the canvas. There is also a third channel, the man-made one of the bridge to the left of the other two.

Andrew Wilton has argued that the Turner vortex is in origin a Poussinesque device for radial perspective that probably began with *Bonneville* (R. A. 1802, Yale Center for British Art).[15] The particular Poussin in question may be *Landscape with a Roman Road* (Dulwich Gallery). What Wilton overlooks, however, in the very Poussinesque *Bonneville* is that *this* vortical recession is crossed, blocked, and closed by repeated horizontal planes intersecting in the form of shadows and the paper-thin chateau and mountain ranges, which resemble nothing so much as the wings of a stage set. In so far as it derives from painting, the Turner vortex is an intensification of Claude's sunrise or sunset. The elements of this natural vortex, besides the presence of the sun itself, are the sense of infinitude rather than closure, and the twisting and "turning" of the horizontal planes into curves.

However, in paintings like *Palestrina—A Composition,* as well as *Calais Pier, Mortlake Terrace, Rome from the Vatican,* even *Hero and Leander,* Turner includes both channels, double or alternative perspectives down which the eye moves at different speeds. In *Calais Pier* (1803, fig. 37) there is the man-made channel, the pier on the right, and the channel of the waves that carries the boats and connects with the hole in the clouds above, creating a main downward-moving vortex. The spectator has a footing on the pier, not on the turbulent water. In *Hero and Leander* (1837, National Gallery) we see an architectural and a natural channel, the latter designated by the moon, marking out Leander's fatal swim to the distant shore of the Hellespont. One channel, usually off to the left or right side of the picture, is man-made (a bridge, pier, road, arcade, or loggia), cut across by horizontals, and closed. The other, which is usually more central, is a natural force almost always emanating from the sun.

Kenneth Clark, among others, has connected the natural vortex with Turner's pessimistic belief in the cyclic nature of history. W. J. T. Mitchell sees it as a stabilizing principle of order in Turner's world.[16] Graphically the vortex may derive from the opening in the far distance in some Wilson landscapes; but if we relate the vortex to the man-made, second channel, and both of these to the titles, epigraphs, and details that indicate "aspects" of the painting, we have to see Turner's painting as representing the intersection of different times, destinies, and alternatives. When the story depicted is classical, for example, he represents the nineteenth-century ruins, as he does around Apollo and the Cumean Sibyl in *The Bay of Baiae:* this is what will happen to the Sibyl who forgot to ask for eternal youth as well as eternal life, and also to our present civilization with its "fallacies of hope." The ancient myth and the contemporary ruins are joined as past and present, as wish and fulfillment, as the sibyl as she was and she is now (eternal, but a "ruin" wishing, in Petronius's version, for death). The same is true of "the spot where Harold fell" as it is related to past and present by the " 'are" and hound.

The intersection of different moments in time is an essential meaning of the Turner historical landscape. But it is often specified in literary rather than visual ways. Allusion, the Hogarthian strategy, operates on a purely verbal level in a painting like *Carnarvon Castle, North Wales,* in which the visual image is of a peaceful landscape with a fringe of tiny figures listening to a bard's performance, and the verses accompanying which imply the future extermination of the Welsh bards. Even when the allusion itself is graphic, the image conveys its meaning through literary rather than graphic forms. In *Venus and Adonis* (ca. 1803, Christopher Gibbs, Ltd.) Turner places the lovers in the composition of Titian's *Martyrdom of St. Peter Martyr* (fig. 68), the prototype of landscape in history painting used to express intense human emotion—the tall twisting trees and wild foliage reflecting the human "martyrdom" taking place beneath them. In the *Venus and Adonis* the composition retains its associations of both Titian (as precursor and authority) and of "martyrdom," referring ahead to the fate of Adonis that will follow in time this idyllic scene. Turner had considered using the Saint Peter Martyr composition in his *Holy Family,* where it would have served a similarly proleptic function. In the finished *Holy Family* (1803, Tate), however, he chose his more characteristic—and purely verbal—strategy of conveying the times before and after by planting a snake in the background: an emblem that indicates the cause of Christ's coming and the persistent evil in the world that will lead to his self-sacrifice.[17]

Always present, whether in the confluence of vortical forms or in the tiny emblematic detail, is a sense of the projection into a different time—a vestige of the story-telling desideratum of history painting according to Le Brun and other theoreticians (and attempted by Hogarth through similar devices).[18] But for Turner time always carries the burden of fatality. The cross on *Mont St. Gothard Pass* (1804, Abbot Hall Art Gallery, Kendal) is almost pure sign, meaning that a traveler has fallen off at this point and another will follow; and the ruins that trail off into shards scattered about the foreground of pastoral settings indicate the same message of approaching disaster intersecting with the plunge of the visual image.

The snake is a frequently used detail, often crouched in mushrooms (to Turner a sign of decay) or pursuing a hare, and occasionally expanded into a dragon.[19] Seen in relation to the vortex, it might be argued, the snake is Turner's attempt to ease the discrepancy between detail and landscape-gestalt, between verbal and visual components. As both detail and informing principle, the shape probably derives from Hogarth's serpentine line in *The Analysis of Beauty*.[20] In Turner's landscape the three-dimensional "Line of Grace," which on the title page of the *Analysis* rears upright and is connected by the epigraph from Paradise Lost with Eve's serpent and the Fall, and in the text with flames and other S-shaped forms, is turned on its side and extended into the depths of the picture space, replacing box perspective with the vortex as the defining structure of unity in time and space. In this sense the serpent relates to the reading/seeing structure of the composition, which is also its principal spatial and (when we utilize the detail itself, the title, and so on) temporal recession. But the question remains: does Turner expand the tiny snake into the principle of a vortex or does he only use the snake to explain or comment on the vortex—to denominate the vortex as fallen cycle or temporal enjambment? The coiled vortex and the tiny snake, like the image and the word, are another enjambment, and even the incongruity that sometimes appears may be taken to express the Turnerian juxtaposition of this time and that, the rise and fall of empires, and the permanence of natural form as against the "fallacies of hope."

CHAPTER 7 🐍
THE CONVENTIONAL ASPECT

As his use of linguistic structures suggests, Turner was in one sense a profoundly conservative landscape painter. This was the Turner who presented himself in his book of aquatints which he entitled *Liber Studiorum,* setting it in the tradition of Claude's *Liber Veritatis* (which had been engraved and published in 1777 by John Earlom), the record of his paradigmatic landscape designs. The *Liber Studiorum* was published in fourteen parts (71 plates) between 1809 and 1819, Turner's intention being to disseminate his designs to a wider public than could be reached by the paintings—and incidentally to demonstrate both the range and variety of his own powers and the various types into which all landscape painting ought to be divided. These compositional categories of landscape were historical, mountainous, pastoral, marine, and architectural. The *Liber* was Turner's most public utterance.

The frontispiece of 1812 (fig. 38) is an example of history painting (H., in the shorthand of the *Liber Studiorum*), and we should not be surprised to find under the design the usual Turner detritus: toppled masonry, a Roman standard and fasces, mingled with overgrown foliage, a drooping bird, and baskets holding fruit, fish, eels, and a ray. These underline the marine aspect of Turner's history as well as the rise and fall of cities that will follow upon this originary rape. The important point, however, is that Turner places a historical subject within a landscape. He has chosen Europa and the Bull: an ocean shore, gesticulating figures, and Europa being carried away on the white bull. As in the landscapes of Gainsborough, and his final mythologizing of them in *Diana and Actaeon,* Turner represents a myth concerning a human merging with nature—a metamorphosis that involves violence. But here it is the specific case of a woman abducted by a god, a male force in the form of a white bull, who is carrying her away toward what is plainly the source of light. We might regard this as Turner's attempt to mythologize in his personal way the Claude landscape subject.

The plates that follow tell us surprisingly little about what sets Turner off from other landscape painters; they tell us, rather, how he mastered the forms and models of landscape practiced by earlier artists (the reason Constable called it his *Liber Stupidorum*). They tell us, on another level, how his personal vision of landscape was evolving out of certain selected models, to be summed up in one way by his 1812 frontispiece.

For P., or pastoral, he adopts the model of Gainsborough, with the familiar pond, and cattle often in it or reflected in it.[1] Immensely expanded and elevated in the sublime landscapes, Turner's forms still correspond at some point to those free-associating lines out of which Gainsborough's landscapes were made. The typical Gainsborough landscape aspired toward the undifferentiation of texture and color toward which Turner reaches, but Gainsborough tended to draw the viewer into its depths rather than (as with Turner) force him to keep his distance, seeking out variants and details of difference such as the figures of a rabbit or a deer (or an apparent sea monster made in fact of a school of fish). Even in numbers 2 and 7 of the *Liber,* however, the closest to the Gainsborough model, Turner introduces a topographical solidity and accuracy with which Gainsborough never concerned himself.

E. P. stands for elevated (or epic) pastoral, and the model is of course Claude (no. 3). In both the P. and E. P. the sun continues to play an important role. (No. 13 is a Claude composition with the sun materialized.) In Turner's pastoral the sun, and not the Gainsborough pond, is the center of gravity, the source of the vortical form; as in elevated pastoral, the sun and not the cattle dominates. A castle sometimes becomes a surrogate for (or accompanies) the sun as an image of power as well as of antiquity.

A., or architecture, is extremely conventional: a strictly planar composition of Romanesque arches—a bridge, aqueduct, or wall of the sort used as a backdrop for the frontispiece *Europa and the Bull*. Except for the prominence—the physical presence—of the sun, the first A. plate (no. 5) could be one of Canaletto's or Scott's Westminster Bridge paintings. Number 12 combines A. and P. with a strongly planar structure and inset, a farmer—a secularized Danae—seemingly gathering sunlight in a bag, and carters carrying off the grain bags from the mill.

Turner's marine subjects adopt the Dutch model (as demonstrated by his *Sun Rising through Vapor* set against Claude's *Isaac and Rebecca* in the National Gallery). Turner maintains the flat horizontal surface of water, but there is sometimes (as in no. 10) an opening in the sky near the top—more emphatic in the final mezzotint than in the drawing—which relates to the unsettling slant of the various ships. Or rather, the ships relate to this burst of sunlight, seemingly affected or motivated by it rather than by the flat wave pattern of the calm sea. Again in number 15, *The Lake of Thun,* the horizontal emphasis of the marine subject is overpowered by the more vertical-diagonal action of the sky. Clouds, mountain intersections, and a jagged flash of lightning all point to sublime landscape scenery, with the human figures either very small or threatened, in this case on a lake. The real action is in the sky (see also *The Leader Sea Piece,* no. 20). Turner achieves this sublime effect with the sea itself, when he brings coasts and rocks to bear or merges sea and sky. But for this effect we have to turn to the painted seascapes in which the waves allow for literally mountainous declivities, as in *Shipwreck: Boats' Crew Recovering an Anchor* (1805, Tate).

M.S., or mountain scenery, is where Turner finds his forms of sublimity. The first is number 9 in the second installment of the *Liber,* where for the first time his own individual forms begin to dominate the conventional ones. And these are mountain forms, though they could have originated in cumulus clouds around the sun. The form is the vortical mountain shape focusing our eyes on the chasm or canyon, what I suppose Jay Appleton would refer to as an extreme case of the "cross-valley" syndrome.

Writers on the sublime drew attention to the intimate connection between our responses to the ocean and to mountains: we speak quite naturally of "mountain billows," Dugald Stewart notes, and conversely of "a tempestuous sea of mountains." "The idea of *literal sublimity,*" Stewart wrote, is "inseparably combined with that of the sea, from the stupendous spectacle it exhibits when agitated by a storm." "The excessive Grandeur . . . of the Ocean," according to the rhetorician Hugh Blair, arises "not from its extent alone, but from the perpetual motion and irresistible force of that mass of Waters."[2] It is not surprising that Turner brings these "immensities" of nature together, and indeed makes them virtually interchangeable, both apparently full of movement and threat—in his later paintings often introducing the sublimity of ocean as space into a solid piazza, which he manages to make appear equally unsolid (as in *Juliet and Her Nurse*). Eventually, as Hazlitt and others noticed, he turns everything into ocean (or sky or mist).

We become increasingly conscious of the sun as we turn the pages of the *Liber Studiorum. The Fall of the Clyde* (E.P., no 18, fig. 39) equates sunlight and the burst of the waterfall. The scattering of nymphs bathing along the bottom gives the picture mythological resonance, but it is the sun slanting down from the upper left corresponding to the falls that makes the picture Turner's. The equation of the sun and uncontrollable energy sets the Turner E.P. off from the model of Claude, showing that for Turner the sun is a force in itself. Not merely a magnet, a force of attraction, or a focus as in Claude, it is an active center of energy pouring into the foreground, coming out to meet the spectator. In *The Little Devil's Bridge* (no. 19, labeled M.S.) Turner uses the bridge-span as the circular-vortical opening through which the sun pours, and this motif is summed up in *The Via Mala* (no. 78).

In other words, by this time Turner's generic categories are beginning to break down. Whether he intends it or not, the M.S., M., E.P., and H. subjects are resolving into the simple categories of sublime, beautiful, and picturesque. The P., in fact, by this time could stand for picturesque. In number 17 the Gainsborough structure has become a foreground filled with the familiar Turner debris. The same happens to an architectural subject, as in number 21. E.P. usually designates the beautiful. The rest of the generic categories—mostly M. and S.P.—are drawn upon for sublime scenes, which are essentially the vortically oriented ones. By number 36 Turner has brought the sublime into H., which takes its text from Spenser's *Faerie Queene*, making use of a mountain landscape and the intersection of blasted tree trunks behind the figures. As early as number 19 the small foreground detail—here the animal skeleton—has begun to characterize the threat of danger within the landscape.

We are now in a position to talk about the figures in Turner's landscapes. Andrew Wilton is the scholar who places the greatest emphasis on these figures.[3] The "awful silence," the "majestic solitude," and other aspects of sublimity in the natural scene of *Dolbadern Castle* (fig. 35), are given additional force, Wilton argues, by being related to the experiences of a specific human being—the "hopeless Owen" of the verses, who, though unseen, is the protagonist of the natural drama. The human figures of the soldiers at the bottom right of the composition also give us a human reference, one that is within the painting rather than its accompanying verses. I think they are somewhat at odds, but the reinforcement probably intended by Turner points to the principle which John Gilbert Cooper enunciated in 1755: "even the ruins of an old Castle properly dispos'd, or the Simplicity of a rough-hewn Hermitage in a Rock, enliven a Prospect, by recalling the Moral Images of Valor and Wisdom . . . amiable Images, belonging to the Divine Family of Truth."[4] In *Dolbadern Castle* the "moral image" of the figures on the canvas is one thing, in the verses, another (presumably "liberty").

For purposes of comparison, we can look at Philippe de Loutherbourg's *Avalanche* of 1804 (fig. 40), in which the natural disaster is seen entirely in human terms. There are four figures, beginning at the farthest remove with a wayfarer carrying a walking stick, showing astonishment but safely out of the path of the disaster. He stands for us. Then there is his utterly terrified dog; and, closer to the disaster, a woman and man showing their individual signs of mortal terror—she fleeing, he praying for deliverance. Finally, there are two figures who are engulfed by the avalanche: one a man falling from a collapsing bridge, the other only a face and arm disappearing in the snow.

This is technically Burke's sublime, for it leaves the viewer outside the picture as secure as the observer within, a mere meditator on the human effects of a natural catastrophe. Burke's "delight" refers not to the terrified victim but to the safe spectator who can identify with the terrifying source of the danger, sublimating terror into delight.[5] Loutherbourg, however, injects a very great deal of story-telling between us and the landscape: the natural scene exists only for the humans, as a moral exemplum for their meditation.

Turner, at his most sublime (fig. 41), makes part of the terror the unimportance in every sense of the human survivors; and at his least sublime, he allows the humans to become comic clutter. It is at this point that the Turnerian sublime intersects with the Turnerian P., or picturesque. I am arguing that the sublime shifts toward the picturesque in proportion to the size of—the extent to which Turner brings close—those roly-poly bag-of-potatoes people (as Ruskin called them) he uses for staffage. The sublime, concerned with death and self-preservation, shifts toward the beautiful as it becomes concerned with love and social relationships. Turner paints, on the one hand, avalanches and shipwrecks, and on the other, parties, festivals, and love stories. But these may intersect, and even the beautiful usually carries with it implications of the sublimity of what is going to follow. Thus he tells the story of Romeo and Juliet or Hero and Leander, for beauty is a "fallacy of hope," and the love of Dido and Aeneas and the others is only a delusion that will end in the destruction of the Carthaginians by the Romans.

Turner also takes Burke's emphasis on the ocean as "an object of no small terror," and thus depicts vastness, vagueness, and obscurity of all sorts. For when people become a small fringe along the shore or beneath the mountains, then the sea and/or mountain or sky becomes the real subject of the picture, and this is the Burkean area of vagueness and obscurity—of undifferentiation, in which dark, confused, uncertain images, as Burke said, "have a greater power on the fancy to form the grander passions than those have which are more clear and determinate."[6]

Turner takes his leave of Loutherbourg, however, who still painted in the social idiom of Boucher. One way he does this is to remove the secure place Loutherbourg always allows for the viewer.[7] Turner puts his viewer in the position of the endangered person himself, leaving him no ground to stand on. Thus we can regard Turner's sublime as the shrinkage of the human in relation to the natural phenomenon: man's insignificance in the face of nature. Or we can see Turner as either reducing the humans (the historical) to a mere vestige of a landscape, or adding them to the landscape as a hold upon history.

In paintings that are E.P. or picturesque, he adds people who function as Loutherbourg's do. In the painting usually known as *Pope's Villa* (fig. 42), we meditate on the group in the left foreground as they meditate on the relics of the great poet's villa. The result is closer to a small version of Wright of Derby's *Air Pump* (Tate) than to any Wilson I can think of, where the figures simply add an emphasis to the foreground of the country house or park.

Pope's Villa is a typical Turner elegy. The house is the new one of Lady Howe that is being built on the ruins of Pope's demolished villa. On the nearer side of the Thames we see men (and a couple, man and woman, like the pair in Wright's *Air Pump*) meditating on the ruins of some such structure as Pope's villa. We see a broken Corinthian capital (which cannot have come specifically from Pope's villa) and the frame of a picture—perhaps a portrait, perhaps a view of the old villa before its destruction. There are also verses by Turner in one of his notebooks, but not (presumably) published to accompany the painting when it was exhibited, titleless, in Turner's gallery.

But as these human figures become larger and more particularized, they reveal Turner's seeming equation of the human and the picturesque (what contemporaries felt to be "Shakespearean," to judge by the comic grotesques who also populated Scott's novels);[8] and as they grow to fill up the space, the picture itself becomes picturesque. It is appropriate to compare this crowded landscape with the unfinished ones, the empty ones, or the late ones (including cityscapes), in which the people are tiny, indistinguishable, calligraphic touches. It is, I believe, in the latter that we feel the distinctively Turner sublime, which is felt through disorientation—and not disorientation of the figures within the landscape but of the spectator outside. A landscape of mountains and bare plains, equally of swirling clouds and smoke or snow, waves or mist, is one into which the viewer projects himself in vain, only to find no foothold, and so to find something else—the sublime incommensurability of his reach and his grasp, of himself confronting an unformulable nature.

We know that the human is central to the sublime, but what Wilton has not acknowledged is the fact that the human is implicit in the perception of the scene itself: such a picture as Turner paints forces the viewer to become the spectator-participant in the scene (even in some sense the artist). Turner's little people, as they are particularized and enlarged, stand between us and the scene with which we are asked to come to grips. The small figures are so small, so distant—creating a kind of middle distance (rather than foreground)—that they cannot serve in the usual way as surrogates or as mediators between us and the picture. They tend to become *part* of the dangerously unstable area that challenges us. I think these facts draw our attention to the significance of Turner's reducing the people—often indistinguishable from the billows of fire or smoke or the mountains, or reduced, as in *Avalanche in the Grisons* (fig. 41) to a tiny house being crushed by gigantic forces—to part of a sublime phenomenon itself.

And yet we do sometimes make the leap when, as in *Staffa—Fingal's Cave* (fig. 48), a single touch of red can be made out against the black of the ship, itself tiny in a vast seascape. The touch of red, which at first looks like another of Turner's gauche intrusions, in fact gives the sense of minute human life and activity deep inside that distant ship—something within which we, the viewers from afar, do associate ourselves.

Perhaps it is useful to remember the old landscape structure of the "Times of the Day," where gods or allegorical figures appeared in the sky and humans below in the landscape, which was the real subject of the picture. Turner's figures appear all along the bottom of the landscape; they are sometimes gods and sometimes humans. I would agree with Wilton that the second is the more successful solution when the figures are kept small. Turner uses the gods as legitimation for his highest flights of history; but the use of humans relates the individual victim to the illimitable space with which he contends. He is not only our surrogate but that of the other contender within the picture, the artist. As the well-known case of *Snowstorm* (R.A. 1842, Tate) shows, Turner the artist is invisible at the heart of the storm, lashed to the boat's mast, and he is also on this side of the canvas rendering the conflict between the artist and nature.[9] We are, he shows us, in various ways witness not just to our own situation, but also to the artist's attempts to encompass the unencompassable by showing it unencompassable yet constructed on formal principles that connect one painted landscape to the next and can be generalized as, say, a Turnerian vortex.

For one conclusion we must draw from the evidence of this chapter is that the vortex cannot be explained either as "pure form" or as truth to nature. Turner continues to insist on the accuracy of all of his representations, and he probably believed this; but the fact is that in the large compositions, and even to some extent in the sketches, nature is shaped to an a priori pattern. I believe it is for this reason that he habitually depicts the most fluid of subjects, sea and sky, or rock formations seen through mist, and so frees himself to produce his swirling vortices—the one stable element of which is the center of light which is (or is represented by) the sun.

CHAPTER 8 ⚚
THE REVOLUTIONARY
ASPECT: THE SUN

Both Turner and Constable painted the Chain Pier at Brighton. Constable's painting (fig. 61) is about the pier and the foreground objects rendered palpable, picturesque (in the sense of those Turner people that sometimes crowd his foreground). Turner's subject (fig. 62) is the light itself and how it makes pier, sails, and water appear. In Constable the sun is where the spectator stands, and so objects appear to be emerging from darkness, picked out by the light on their surfaces. Turner makes the spectator look at the sun, showing a gradual materialization of light with intervening substances, a gradual supplementing of an initially light area with darker tones. His sun at the center, between two supports of the pier, dissolves the pier (as it dissolves a stretch of the railing in *Mortlake Terrace,* for example). He paints the profound ambiguity of a sun that is not (as it is usually painted) overhead or behind us but near the horizon line, either rising or setting—sometimes it is impossible to tell which.

The sun is a presence in almost every Turner landscape. It may make itself felt only through a medium of mist or clouds, but often Turner's storms seem to evoke the whirlwind of Ezekiel with "a fire infolding itself, and a brightness . . . about it, and out of the midst thereof as the color of amber, out of the midst of the fire" (Ezek. 1:4). Sometimes the sun is palpable. To quote one contemporary viewer writing of the *Regulus* (B.I., 1837, fig. 43), "Standing sideway of the canvas, I saw that the sun was a lump of white standing out like the boss on a shield."[1] It is safe to say that the sun is most prominent when the scene is most symbolic and least descriptive.

Turner chose as pendant to his *Dido Building Carthage* one of the few Claude landscapes in which the sun itself appears as an object, not diffused by haze or off to the side casting oblique rays; and yet it looks dim compared to his own (figs. 31–32). We look directly into his sun: not to the right or left of it but straight into it, which means at the source of light and energy. The sun splits the picture down the middle, dissolves the stable Claudian harbor into a vortex, opens it at the bottom, and leaves us as viewers no place to stand. It literally curves the verticals and diagonals of Claude's architecture into a vortical recession which makes even the trees seem to twist in recoil from the sun.

This characteristic structure intensifies over the years, but it emerges from the beginning with surprising rapidity. At first we saw Turner experimenting with all modes and styles, and these he laid before us—his wares, his virtuosity demonstrated—in the *Liber Studiorum.* But already the sublime was the important mode, and it was sun-oriented. Then and later, the distinction between his sketches of particular effects, colors, or details and the paintings he worked up into compositions for sale or exhibition obtained. Contrast, for example, the on-the-spot sketches of the burning of the Houses of Parliament in 1734 with the finished views in Cleveland and Philadelphia. The sketches are only concerned with the effect of fire related to the buildings and the river. But the finished canvases reflect considerations of the sublime, the Fallacies of Hope, and the decline of nations—concepts for which Turner has sought visual equivalents. He is not satisfied with simply reproducing the effect of a phenomenon, which was sufficient for the sketch.

The shape behind the finished painting is the Claude landscape's central sun materialized, and more particularly the Claude seaport, which Turner uses to show the effects of the sun—not only its light reflected on surfaces but seemingly its force on objects. In one sense, he is a powerfully reductionist painter of the Claude landscape, a primitivist who eliminates every extraneous element except the source of light on the horizon. As he grows older he becomes more mannered, less various, more intense and narrow—or focused—and this means that as his forms become less topographical-descriptive and more literary, they are reduced to the single one I am describing. In a characteristic late oil, presumably unfinished, *Yacht Approaching Coast* (fig. 44), the sunburst cuts the picture in half, both upward and downward. This gives an idea of the original form of a Turner "color beginning" before it becomes an exhibitable history painting—say, *The Bay of Baiae*—the landscape, the human figures, their projected story, the emblems, and the title that assume its shape.

It is possible to argue that the idea of the sun preceded the form which Turner worked out to express it, that he was working toward a congruence between the content and the graphic image. *Europa and the Bull,* which he uses as the frontispiece to his *Liber,* is followed by *Apollo and Python* (1811, Tate), in which the god of light is pitted, in a Salvator Rosa landscape, against the serpent emerging from or withdrawing into this utterly dark cave (see below, p. 92). The myth is one in which the god of light is shown in conflict with the powers of darkness, including the equation of dark with evil, light with good.

In *Regulus* (fig. 43) the myth and the form coincide: sight and blindness, light and darkness, power, defiance, and heroism. The sun Turner painted in *Dido Building Carthage* moves toward extremity in this story of the Carthaginians' revenge on the Roman general, which was to cut off his eyelids. Most versions of the story say this was done to prevent him from sleeping. Turner takes him into the sunlight, which suggests the idea of blinding by excessive light. The Carthaginians are in the lower lefthand corner with a barrel of spikes prepared for another stage (or version) of Regulus's punishment. But they themselves are literally being swept away by the strength of the sun. The sun, like the fall implicit in rise and the darkness in light, is also—in Turner's conjunction of present and future—destroying Carthage, rolling away all the Carthaginians who are torturing Regulus, as they simultaneously disappear into his approaching blindness.

There is a tiny, pale figure on the steps to the far right, who becomes Regulus in the print that followed the painting.[2] This is one of those cases where Turner associates the viewer of the painting with the tiny figure deep within who is involved in the action itself. It is essentially the situation he recorded in *Snowstorm,* where viewer and artist (whom he equates) are both participants inside the storm that whirls about them as they look at the painting and actors at the center of the landscape, tied to the mast of the ship that is rocked by the storm. They are both the direct participant blinded by the sunlight in *Regulus* and the tiny figure being led into the sunlight deep within the painting. In *Juliet and Her Nurse* (R.A. 1836) they are both the doomed Juliet, source of dawning light ("Juliet is the sun," as Romeo says), and the artist who is himself the creator of the light that illuminates Juliet and therefore the Piazza San Marco, coming from the west instead of the east where the *natural* sun rises.[3] As these paintings show, Turner brings together a natural and a created (poetic, painterly) sun, the one a sun of destrúction that blinds Regulus and separates Romeo and Juliet, the other a sun of human creation that sets before us a world of both realities.

To see where the natural sun of *Dido Building Carthage* leads, we can add to *Regulus* three other paintings. *Ulysses Mocking Polyphemus* (1829, National Gallery, London) shows that the blaze of the sun is both the rising of Odysseus's sun and the setting of Polyphemus's. The sun was originally superscribed (the lines are now almost lost) with Apollo's chariot of the sun—an indication, perhaps, of a typical unwillingness to let the sun do its own work. Turner still needed the horses of Apollo (specifically, the horses of the sun on the Parthenon frieze) as well as the actual sun.[4] He also needed the touch of fire from the Cyclops' forge, both to set off the true sun of Odysseus's victory and to suggest a displacement of the bloody socket of Polyphemus's eye. The most graphic element in his literary source, *Odyssey,* Book 9, focuses in a horrible way on the gouging out of the cyclop's eye. In both the *Regulus* and the *Ulysses,* Turner has taken peripheral aspects of the story and dwelt on them, and in each case this involved the putting out of eyesight with fire—the fire being the sun.

In the various paintings of *The Burning of the Houses of Parliament* (1835, Cleveland and Philadelphia) the sun has become a literal fire destroying the seat of English government in the same kind of gesture Guy Fawkes had once planned. And in *Slavers Throwing Overboard the Dead and Dying—Typhoon*

Coming On (R.A. 1840, Boston Museum) the setting sun smears the sky with blood symbolizing the fate of the slaves cast overboard and devoured by sharks; at the same time it creates a long, slender funnel which presages the avenging typhoon of the title.

From *Regulus* to the "color beginning" *Yacht Approaching Coast,* the sun's shape and the shape of its emanations come to determine the shape of the composition and then the shape of the canvas itself, replacing the normal rectangle of a landscape with a circle. Everything in the picture, from the waves to the clouds and the people, is determined—both created and destroyed—by this source of energy. Over a large number of paintings the sun becomes associated with, on the one hand, fruition, warmth, and energy, but, on the other, with plagues and apocalyptic conflagrations and blood-baths. It rises and sets; it burns and lights; it is the source of color, life, and energy, the ultimate fulcrum of the vortex, the colorless white in front of which opaque substances produce warm colors—the yellows and reds and oranges that define the vortex.

Of the many proverbial senses of the word *sun* available to Turner, I single out four: *sun* as a metonymy for life, as in "I 'gin to be weary of the sun," Macbeth's words when he hears the news that Lady Macbeth is dead and Birnam Wood is coming to Dunsinane; and closely related to this meaning is the sun as source of all power, as god. (Turner is supposed to have said shortly before he died: "The sun is God.")[5] Then there is Lucretius's warning, "The sun will blind you if you persist in gazing at it" (Sol etiam caecat, contra si tendere pergas). These senses are connected by the Jewish God whose countenance is like the sun: "Thou canst not see my face: for there shall no man see me, and live."[6] They are also connected by the sun of Plato's myth: man is forced to leave the darkness of the cave, where he sees reality only as shadows cast by a bonfire, and look straight into the sun. First, Socrates tells us, he will be blinded, but eventually he will be able to make out objects with far greater clarity than before, as he will be able to see and understand the sun itself. In Ripa's *Iconologia* the sun is Truth that has to be veiled like the blinding Truth of the poet, which to be bearable must be obscured with allegory. There is a sense, not too purely metaphorical, in which the haze, Turner's "medium" as Hazlitt called it,[7] is the veil of allegory covering and concealing Truth, which, like Turner's sun, is blind-ing to ordinary eyes. There is another sense in which the figures and the story Turner adds represent the veil of allegory which protects us from the sun. This sun is nourishing, but when it does occasionally break through the veil, the result is apocalyptic destruction.

The locus for the congruence of blindness and insight for Turner's genera-tion was the pair of suns in Milton's apostrophe to his blindness in the invocation to Book 3 of *Paradise Lost.* Like the bonfire and the true sun in Plato's myth, Milton's external sun, to which he is blind, is contrasted with "thou Celestial light / Shine inward . . . that I may see and tell / Of things invisible to mortal sight." The confrontation of man and sun is also clear in Satan's apostrophe to the sun (Book 4): he is regarding and being regarded by the sun (God), as both conscience and sign of all he has lost, and the exchange brings him closer than at any other time to self-realization.

The sense of duality is apparent in the fourth sense of the word *sun,* as rising/setting (in common parlance, phrases applied to declining politicians—"more worship the rising than the setting sun," etc.). Dugald Stewart, writing of sublimity, discusses a circumstance

> which conspires, in no inconsiderable degree, in imparting an allegorical or typical character to literal *sublimity.* I allude to the Rising, Culminating, and Setting of the heavenly bodies; more particularly to the Rising, Culminating, and Setting of the Sun; accompanied with a corresponding increase and decrease in the heat and splendour of its rays. It is impossible to enumerate all the various analogies which these familiar appearances suggest to the fancy. I shall mention their obvious analogy to the Morning, Noon, and Evening of Life; and to the short interval of Meridian Glory, which, after a gradual advance to the summit, has so often presaged the approaching decline of human greatness.[8]

In Turner this is the sense, fully developed by the early 1800s, that the rising sun *implies* its setting; indeed, that the apparently rising sun is in reality setting, as in the *Dido Building Carthage.*

So far we have placed Turner's sun in relation to the verbal structures of the proverb. We need to examine a number of other contexts beginning with political imagery. Turner grew up during the upheavals of the 1790s in France and (dimly reflected) in England. The conservative reaction of 1815–20 and the subsequent crises of the 1830s and 1840s, which seem to have upset him, found their expression in imagery first set out by the French Revolution.

The traditional meaning of the sun as God and therefore as his vicegerent, the king, followed from its being the source of light and warmth and power. At the outset of the eighteenth century Louis XIV surrounded himself with the imagery of Apollo and called himself the Sun King. Around the middle of the century, by a kind of polemic reversal, the sense of light was shifted by the *philosophes* to "enlightenment," the individual human reason, and the king and church became the darkness (and so ignorance) which the light attempts to penetrate and dispel. (Or perhaps we should say that the *philosophes* grafted onto the sun as God the iconographical tradition of the sun as Truth chasing away the shadows of the mind.)[9]

The French Revolution was widely described, in its first phase, as a sunrise, and the most commonplace set of associations revolved around the contrasts of light-enlightenment-freedom. At the first celebration of Bastille Day, 14 July 1790, a vast chorus (in the driving rain) commended the new French nation to the sun: "pure fire, eternal eye, soul and source of all the world." In England, Sir Samuel Romilly wrote: "a kingdom, which the darkest superstition had long overspread" now greeted "the bright prospect of universal freedom and universal peace [which was] just bursting on their sight." In James Mackintosh's words, "we cannot suppose that England is the only spot that has not been reached by this flood of light that has burst in on the human race." And when the revolution inevitably disappointed these sanguine expectations, we hear William Hazlitt referring to the hopes for kind feelings and generous actions which "rose and set with the French Revolution. The light seems to have been extinguished for ever in this respect."[10]

Hazlitt's passages on his experience of the French Revolution as a new dawn, a bursting of sunlight on a dark world, are summed up in "On the Feeling of Immortality in Youth":

> For my part I started life with the French Revolution, and I lived, alas! to see the end of it. But I did not foresee the result. My sun arose with the first dawn of liberty, and I did not think how soon both must set. The new impulse to ardour given to men's minds imparted a congenial warmth and glow to mine; we were strong to run a race together, and I little dreamed that long before mine was set, the sun of liberty would turn to blood, or set once more in the night of despotism. Since then, I confess, I have no longer felt myself young, for with that my hopes fell.[11]

This passage runs the full gamut of light associations from birth and youth ("ardour") to age, from "dawn of liberty" to setting "once more in the night of despotism," and from "warmth and glow" to "blood."

Edmund Burke, who saw the revolution from the other side, made his first references to this imagery in his *Philosophical Enquiry* of 1757, where darkness is sublime and light is not: "But such a light as that of the sun, immediately exerted on the eye, as it overpowers the sense, is a very great idea. . . . Extreme light, by overcoming the organs of sight, obliterates all objects, so as in its effects exactly to resemble darkness."[12] And so again, as in *Regulus,* sun and total darkness are one. This same fierce glare, this power or uncontrolled energy seen as sublime in his *Philosophical Enquiry,* becomes thirty years later, in his *Reflections on the Revolution in France* (1790), the enlightenment rays that have been intensified by the revolutionaries into "this new conquering empire of light and reason" which dissolves all "the sentiments which beautify and soften private society," and indeed (as the metaphor shifts for him) rudely tears off "all the decent drapery of life," first from the queen and then from society. The true sun, as he sees it, enters

> into common life, like rays of light which pierce into a dense medium, [and] are, by the laws of nature, refracted from their straight line. Indeed in the gross and complicated mass of human passions and concerns, the primitive rights of men undergo such a variety of refractions and reflections, that it becomes

absurd to talk of them as if they continued in the simplicity of their original direction.[13]

His image of man's intricate and complex nature as the reality it is essential to preserve in society is precisely the opposite of the revolutionary's view of man as an obstruction to the beneficent glare of human liberty.[14]

By implication, Burke posits two suns: the royal or natural sun which is, in England at least, refracted through the prism of human nature or human possibility; and the false, usurping sun of the human reason, which he sees is "not the light of heaven, but the light of rotten wood and stinking fish—the gloomy sparkling of collected filth, corruption, and putrefaction."[15] This is the false light cast by Swift's enthusiasts and Pope's dunces, the light of the "new philosophy" which its adherents perceive as a "glorious blaze."

For Burke is reacting against the metaphor for revolution formulated by the Reverend Richard Price shortly after the fall of the Bastille:

> I see the ardor for Liberty catching and spreading. . . . Behold, the light you have struck out, after setting America free, reflected to France, and there kindled into a blaze that lays despotism in ashes, and warms and illuminates all Europe! Tremble all ye oppressors of the world! . . . You cannot now hold the world in darkness. Struggle no longer against increasing light and liberality.[16]

Price raised the imagery of enlightenment into one of conflagration, which Thomas Paine developed in the opening of his notorious chapter 5 of *Rights of Man,* part 2 (1792): "From a small spark, kindled in America, a flame has arisen, not to be extinguished." But, he added, "Without consuming, like the *Ultima Ratio Regum,* it winds its progress from nation to nation, and conquers by a silent operation," and the fire ends by being sublimated into the sun's warmth, the natural burgeoning of plants, and the universal spring of revolution.[17]

For some indication of the power of the image of the sun-become-fire, we need only compare the words of Turner's fellow Royal Academician, the Irvingite James Ward, which combine religious enthusiasm and millenarian fervor with Lord Byron's lines relating revolution abroad to revolution at home. Ward, in *New Trial of the Spirits* (1835, the year after the burning of the Houses of Parliament), puts it this way:

> God is not to be mocked! The vivid lightnings are gone forth! Farm house conflagration. York Minster conflagration, Senate House of Kings, Lords and Commons burnt—'I will overturn! overturn! overturn!' Ezek. XXI.27. King, Church, Government, and people beware!

Byron's lines in his *Curse of Minerva* (1812) may in fact have been still in Turner's mind when he painted his two versions of *The Burning of the Houses of Parliament:*

Say with what eye along the distant down
Would flying burghers mark the blazing town?
How view the column of ascending flames
Shake his red shadow o'er the startled Thames?
Nay, frown not Albion! for the torch was thine
That lit such pyres from Tagus to the Rhine:
Now should they burst on thy devoted coast,
Go, ask thy bosom who deserves them most.
The law of heaven and earth is life for life,
And she who raised, in vain regrets the strife.

[ll. 303–13][18]

We can sense in Turner's sun something of Burke's sublime, but also the revolutionary stripping away of veils and mists from the face of the naked sun, which becomes a source of heat as well as light. The artist joins the patriot, trying to make men see what *he* has seen by looking directly into the sun (while other artists look into the cave and see only shadows cast by marionettes in the light of a bonfire). One way to explain Turner's landscape structure is to say that he has returned to the world of the cave to tell us what he has seen out there and to force us to look at it ourselves.

Turner's poetic alter ego was William Blake, whose etching *Albion Rose* (back dated 1780 to correspond with the Gordon Riots) shows England rising out of slavery as a youth bursting Scamozzi's textbook diagram of the proportions of the human figure: he breaks the circle in an expansive sunburst, his hair twisted into flamelike points, much as Turner's sunburst destroys the perspective box of the Claudian landscape. In his poem *The French Revolution* (1791) the king is still the sun, but obscured by clouds, and a new dawn is rising to replace him. The imagery is of the sun of democracy versus the night of the old order, whose false "light walks round the dark towers of the Bastille." Lafayette, the new revolutionary light, is "like a flame of fire," and when he lifts his hand, "Gleams of fire streak the heavens, and of sulphur the earth."

The two suns of Plato and Milton are thus either the natural sun versus the philosopher's deluding light, or the aged setting sun of monarchy versus the young rising sun of democracy. As these alternative interpretations might lead us to suspect, with the disillusionment following the French Revolution the sun became a radically ambiguous symbol. In *America* (1793) Blake already shows "fiery Orc" (the spirit of revolution) amidst flames, either (depending on the coloring of different copies of the book) standing out from the flames like Albion or being engulfed by them—emergent or consumed. In Shelley's *Triumph of Life* (1822) "the [natural] Sun sprang forth" in a world of spring and sunlight, and all things responding "Rise as the Sun their Father rose." But the world of the poet's dream is sunless, plantless, and dead, with only "a cold glare, intenser than the noon, / But icy cold [which] obscured with blinding light / The sun." This is the chariot leading the triumph of life, its light inadequate to direct its way; and this wandering chariot drags behind it the enlightenment heroes—in particular Rousseau, their spokesman—who have outlived their ideals.[19]

Burke's true sun has become, in Coleridge's *Rime of the Ancient Mariner* (1798), the sun-of-reason which "now rose upon the right" when the Mariner has killed the albatross, and which the sailors take to be a sign that the Mariner was right to kill the bird "that brought the fog and mist." It is the sun of reason or practical convenience which carries the mariners to the sea of death, wherein, as Robert Penn Warren expressed it, "the sun itself, which had risen so promisingly and so gloriously like 'God's own head,' is suddenly 'the bloody Sun,' the sun of death—as though we had implied here a fable of the Enlightenment and the Age of Reason, whose fair promises had wound up in the blood-bath of the end of the century."[20] On the other hand, Burke's false light, "the gloomy sparkling of collected filth, corruption, and putrefaction," becomes precisely the slimy snakes in the moonlight—the light of the imagination—the acceptance of which leads to the Mariner's rehabilitation.

Turner makes use of similar lighting effects (which include gleaming serpents) but his sun is all-sufficient and requires no moon as complement. If he thought about Coleridge's sun, I am sure it meant to him God's wrath and the Mariner's conscience, bloodying the sky in *Slavers* or exploding it in *Regulus,* aimed at the Mariner, as the "glittering eye" of the "bright-eyed Mariner" himself is leveled at the wedding guest. The sun's significance depends on whether the viewer is sinner or penitent, and consequently on whether the sun itself is external or internal. The literary sun which influenced Turner, if any did, was the sun that beats down upon the monk Ambrosio in M. G. Lewis's *The Monk* (1795). Following scene after scene of immurement within dark churches, monasteries, and dungeons, the sun finally bursts forth: Ambrosio is plucked from his Inquisition dungeon and cast down to the ground under the glaring, burning, punishing sun, which assumes the attributes of a stern and angry God to whom Satan has relinquished his victim—"The Sun now rose [not as in the *Ancient Mariner* 'upon the right' but] above the horizon; its scorching beams darted full upon the head of the expiring sinner"—and with it come myriad insects and eagles from the sky. And to complete the apocalyptic end of Ambrosio, we are told it took him "six miserable days" to die, and on the seventh a violent storm arose and he expired in the midst of a deluge: the order of Genesis is here reversed, and the general structure of a great many Turner canvases adumbrated.

I refer not only to Turner's paintings of the Deluge itself but to the way in which his paintings repeat the order of Creation. Hazlitt's hostile criticism is pertinent: "The artist delights to go back to the first chaos of the world," he said of Turner, "or to that state of things when the waters were separated from the dry land, and light from darkness, but as yet no living thing nor tree bearing fruit was seen upon the face of the earth. All is without form and void." Contemporary accounts of how Turner built up a painting on Varnishing Day show the same pattern.[21] Starting with an emphatic *fiat lux,* Turner separates land from sea, painting dark over (or up from) light in precisely the reverse of the conventional procedure followed by painters in oil, who start with dark glazes and work up to the high points of light.[22] But he stops short of finished creation, or at least suggests a precarious point of time at which chaos is about to reassert itself. Carthage is both abuilding and declining, destroying Regulus and itself.

I have postponed until now discussion of the actual practice of the landscape painter, expressed in his need to control and arrange his natural materials. Jay Appleton, in *The Experience of Landscape,* notes that the sun can either illuminate a landscape or participate as a component of it: but the latter is difficult because "the eye cannot contemplate it except at the risk of great discomfort and even physical damage" and it "obliterates everything else," is "so blindingly bright that we can see nothing. Some limitation must be placed on its brilliance so that it approaches the same scale of light intensity as the landscape it illuminates."[23] To make the sun manageable, the artist reflects it on surfaces of other objects (clouds, trees, buildings) or interrupts the passage of its light, partially or totally, by placing objects between sun and observer. Both possibilities, however, depending on the size of the object or the degree of its opaqueness, can deprive the viewer of the unimpeded prospect to the horizon which determines the Claude landscape, and which Appleton sees as one of the psychological norms of landscape. The sun is, in Appleton's terms, the "supreme prospect symbol," as "not only by far the most powerful source of light but . . . also symbol of distance on a supra-terrestrial scale." Prospect allows a way of escape; the observer himself tends to be in a shaded foreground (the Claudian coulisse), seeing but not seen, so that "prospect and refuge can be at least partially achieved simultaneously."[24]

This whole process is reversed by Turner, who confronts his viewer with the sun, giving him total prospect but depriving him of any refuge whatever in the foreground or middle distance. The sun penetrates to his innermost refuge, leaving him naked and without a place to stand, let alone conceal himself. He is face to face with the ultimate, whether we call it God or Truth or Self.

The sun in a landscape can be regarded—certainly was so regarded by earlier painters—as the divinity that suffuses the "Book of Nature." Its influence is comparable to the Christian doctrine of the Incarnation, as God descends into man and man receives "a measure of divinity which brings him within reach of God."[25] It is important to remember that behind Burke's sublime lies John Dennis's, which was powerfully sun-oriented. The most sublimely terrible idea, says Dennis, is that of an angry god, and involved in the idea of the sublime is a desire for engulfment. The sublime, he says "gives a noble Vigour to a Discourse, an invincible Force, which commits a pleasing Rape upon the very Soul of the Reader; that whenever it breaks out where it ought to do, like the Artillery of Jove, it thunders, blazes, and strikes at once."[26] Here the sun and the sublime are connected with God the Father, a specifically "angry" God. Dennis, and later Burke, leave little doubt that the sun (like other sublime objects) is a symbol of the threatening father. As Freud pointed out, in most languages the sun is male as opposed to "Mother Earth."[27] In terms of this verbal contrast, the basic Turner composition is a penetration of earth by sun, an overpowering ("a pleasing rape") of the earth, which opens up before it. If a vortex is the central informing principle, the general composition takes the form (and often the representation) of a harbor, illuminated and indeed defined, if not scooped out, by the sun. If a paint rhythm can project a metaphor, we might say that existence is a harbor, a fringe of awed, recoiling spectators. The verses from Revelation that Turner attached to the Royal Academy entry of *Angel Standing in the Sun* (fig. 45) speak of the Angel (the sun) as devouring the whole world: a "supper of the great God . . . [at which the sun will] eat the flesh of kings and the flesh of captains and the flesh of mighty men," and so on (Rev. 19 : 17, 18).

What does it mean, then, for Turner to compel his viewers (and himself) to look straight into the sun? Addison distinguishes beautiful from sublime as a passive response to experience from an active one. Whereas it is "but to open the eye" to experience beauty, sublimity satisfies our desire "to be filled with an object, or grasp at anything that is too big for its capacity" (the "thing too great" is defined as the "Supreme Being"). The end recommended is submission, but the process begins with an active gesture, and to Addison the sublime is liberating, aggrandizing, and exhilarating. If Burke finds it alienating and diminishing, it is because he is afraid of it at the same time that he is drawn to it. But both agree that the sublime refers us forward to ultimates, to confrontation with and exercise of power, while the beautiful refers us nowhere beyond the self and a regression into the repose of infantile rest.[28] Turner, in these terms, is pitting the viewer against the landscape and its Creator, and finding himself sharing the roles of both viewer and creator.

In discussing the sun as father symbol, Freud recalls the myth of the eagle who, because of his close relation to the sun, tests his offspring by making them look into the sun "and requires of them that they shall not be dazzled by its light." He is thus behaving, Freud tells us, "as though he were himself a descendant of the sun and were submitting his children to a test of their ancestry"—that is, a "mythological method of expressing his [own] filial relation to the sun."[29] One way to "grasp at" or be "filled with" the father-god-king is metaphorically to take his place, calling yourself the individual human reason and him the darkness; or to identify with him, taking the quality of pure power and altering it to something comprehensible like the creative energy of the revolutionary or the artist. In the same way, Turner's homage to Claude (or to Rembrandt, or Canaletto) transformed each artist into a Turner, or insinuated a Turner *between* that artist and the spectator. And so with the sun he takes on the greatest of all natural authority symbols, removes its veil, makes it his own artistic subject/signature, and sees himself accordingly as creator/destroyer, parallel to its positive and negative aspects.[30] There is in the sun as the "eye of God" the sense that when the artist paints the sun he is painting himself, and Turner's sun-centered landscapes may be, as Lindsay has suggested, self-portraits.[31]

Thus far we have seen what the Turner sun as an image could have meant to a contemporary who looked at Turner's pictures, and—to judge by a number of these pictures—to Turner himself. We also know that Turner *wanted* his contemporaries to understand these things but despaired of communicating them.[32]

In the late painting, *The Angel Standing in the Sun* (1846, fig. 45), Turner superscribes the sun with the figure of a seraphic angel, highest of the nine orders (burning with ardent desire for God).[33] But, though the picture plainly represents the Angel of the Sun, and this is supported by the title, the epigraphs appended in the Royal Academy catalogue tell us it is the avenging Angel of Revelation and the Angel of Darkness in Samuel Rogers's poem *The Voyage of Columbus*. Like those earlier Turner suns, this is a sun and no sun, light as darkness (or blindness), an occlusion between us and the natural sun. But the angel is also, quite literally, Turner himself, superimposed on the sun as a near congruence of both mythologizing and gloss. His arms are raised and the right one brandishes a sword which makes a semicircular arch like a rainbow in the air, with birds flying in the track of the arch. Ruskin had described Turner three years before, in *Modern Painters* (1843), as "standing like the great angel of the Apocalypse, clothed with a cloud, and with a rainbow upon his head, and with the sun and stars given into his hand." The passage was picked up a year later by the Reverend John Eagles and savagely parodied in an attack on Turner in *Blackwood's Edinburgh Magazine*.[34] Turner has represented this angel, and below him has inscribed smaller pictographic figures related to the Reverend Eagles and other detractors, whom we can make out to be Cain fleeing from the body of Abel over which Adam and Eve mourn, Delilah bending with her scissors over a sleeping Samson, Judith contemplating the head of Holofernes, and the chained serpent of Revelation 20 : 1–2.

All the revolutionary overtones of the sun are subsumed under this personal, artistic significance. Blake, for the same reason, chose to depict the revolutionary figure of Albion as a sunburst breaking not political but aesthetic rules, the doctrine of the Vitruvian circle. But Blake's Albion is still Albion (England); Turner's angel brandishing the sword on the Day of Judgment is only an emblematized version of the Turner who smears the sky with appropriately bloody sunsets and who predicts vengeance on the slavers or sets the Houses of Parliament afire.

CHAPTER 9 ❧
THE OTHER
SUN

We are now, perhaps, in a position to speculate on the power of the train image in *Rain, Steam, and Speed* (fig. 30). Until one of my students showed concern for the safety of the hare I had not thought of it as being endangered by the train. Granted, they are on the same trestle, but the rabbit is over to one side, and if there is a Turnerian joke involved it would seem to be the fact that the rabbit is outrunning the train. This, however, was only an uninformed impression. When I put the hare in the context of other Turner hares (he insisted on calling them hares), I realized that almost all are being threatened by a serpent, or at best a greyhound. In the verses attached to *Apollo and Daphne* (R.A. 1837) Turner writes:

> As when th' impatient greyhound, slipt from far,
> Bounds o'er the glebe to course the fearful hare,
> She, in her speed, does all her safety lay;
> And he, with double speed, pursues his prey.

Under the word *hare* in books of proverbs we find ideas of impending calamity.[1]

The hare is usually, however, threatened by a serpent. The fire burning at the front of the locomotive (where it would not normally be seen) helps to suggest a fire-breathing dragon—as in George Cruikshank's drawing of a train-engine opening its fiery mouth to devour a passenger (1840).[2] The train, seen as a reflection of the iconographical tradition and a reversal of the usual vortex emanating from the sun, is a gigantic black serpent coming at the hare and us, black as Python in the confrontation of sun and darkness in *Apollo and Python*.

We should recall *Apollo and the Sibyl: The Bay of Baiae* (1823, fig. 33), where the snake is stalking the rabbit in the context of the Cumean Sibyl who, granted eternal life without eternal youth, suffers the same sort of defeat at the hands of time that is suggested by the serpent vis à vis the hare. And so, returning to *Rain, Steam, and Speed,* we might argue that the train and the hare fulfill the same relationship. We can now modify the interpretation of the hare as emblem or, in conjunction with the ploughman, a verbal tag, and see it as one of various forms of locomotion emanating radially from a single vanishing point: rabbit, ploughman, rowboat, and train. The train is simply another example of the human attempt to defeat time. The train is, above all, a man-made substitute which, no more than the hare, can succeed. The larger contrast, of which the hare would seem to be Turner's gloss, is between the Great Western Railway of his title and the lovely pastoral crossing of the Thames at Maidenhead seen below—a *locus amoenus* swept across by the new railway bridge and train.[3]

In this sense we can see the great black phallic serpent heading straight at us as the negative of Turner's sun which often equates total light and total darkness. The dark train and the sun in a painting like *Regulus* are both forces of energy that are bearing down on us, as palpable in their effect on us as on such intervening objects as the hare. But *Rain, Steam, and Speed* shows how Turner distinguishes total light from total darkness: they have the same effect but are obviously different, as natural is to human, as real to imitation, as life to art. The train is a substitute, an alternative, a black sun. It is painted in what Turner called material or earth colors, as opposed to the aerial colors of the sun. In the same way, as the analogy with *Apollo and Python* suggests, the snake or dragon was related to the powers of darkness and earth (the qualities Blake, too, understood the snake to represent).[4]

We thus have a chain of associations: train, serpent, darkness, material colors, and the attempt to defeat time. All of these are in opposition to the sun, to natural time against which men strive in vain, and therefore to the sun as god. Behind the black train-engine that contends with the yellow sun (only ironically, as a side issue, with the hare) we detect Turner's admission that the sun cannot be painted by any human artist with material pigments no matter how overweening his egotistical sublime.

There are also landscapes in which Turner paints an object—usually a ship's sail—between us and the sun, or off to one side of it, or even opposite the real sun. I believe this object serves not just as a surrogate sun but as an admission by the artist of the impossibility of actually representing the sun's light without an intermediary of some sort. Even in *Yacht Approaching Coast* (fig. 44) the yacht's sail is needed to augment in some way the blazing sunlight which *is* the picture.

This structure appears at its most emblematic, its most literary, in *The Sun of Venice Going to Sea* (R.A. 1843, fig. 46). The sun is itself invisible, its presence problematic. To judge by the facades of the Venetian buildings on the horizon, and by the verses accompanying the Royal Academy entry, the sun is behind the spectator, who faces the boat. This boat carries the sign of the sun painted on its sail, as well as the words "Sol de Veneza Mi Ragi . . . [i.e., *raggia*—shine on me]." But not only is the sun replicated on the opaque, material sail of the ship, but the city of Venice behind it (Doge's

Palace, Campanile, and San Marco) is also represented on the sail intervening between the viewer and the real Venice.[5] There is a whole series of interventions between spectator and sun, as of signs for reality. Then, of course, Turner also adds the verses from his *Fallacies of Hope:*

> Fair Shines the morn, and oft the zephyrs blow,
> Venezia's fisher spreads his painted sail so gay,
> Nor heeds the demon that in grim repose
> Expects his evening prey.

The verses themselves are an adaptation of Gray's lines in *The Bard* (ll. 71–76). These palimpsestic lines, with their echoes of sublimity and doomed bards, turn the image of sunrise into one of sunset and darken the image into death and the decline of the Venetian state (fallen in 1797)—a theme as persistent as the allusions to transience in *Rain, Steam, and Speed* and *Battle Abbey.*[6]

We might recall the floating fire pump in the foreground of the Cleveland version of *The Burning of the Houses of Parliament* (1835), on whose side are the words SUN and FIRE, separated by the sign of the sun that refers to the Sun Fire Office insurance company. The ironies focus around the sign, the man-made artifact, the utterly impotent fire engine in the face of the real, consuming natural force, the fire.

The structure in which the sun is accompanied by an opaque sail can also be seen in a straight seascape, *Chichester Canal* (Tate), or, in a more negative and symbolic way, in *Peace—Burial at Sea,* and above all in *Angel Standing in the Sun* (fig. 45), where the surrogate sun is at once a negative sun and the painter-creator's sign of a sun. If it does not intervene between us and the sun, it substitutes for the sun—or is a displacement of it, a manageable allegory that relieves the intensity of its centrality, in the same way, perhaps, as the title, verses, and literary allusions do.

Some corollaries are called for. Turner tends to show the sun in the sky at a point where it is either rising or setting—that is, at a moment when light and dark or light and shade, or air and earth (aerial and material or earth colors), or the sky and the profound dark depths of water are in proximity and conflict. This meteorological situation calls for the figure (or anti-sun) between spectator and sun who obstructs the light as it rises or sets. By intensifying the sun, Turner intensifies the gloom of the foreground—the detritus, the shadowed, shaded objects and figures that intervene. What this amounts to is the agon of light against dark which is the essential Turnerian drama and for which he seeks myths in the story of Apollo and Python. His art is, in a sense, about this agon, this particular version of chiaroscuro (so different from Constable's, which is a way of highlighting, drawing out significance, illuminating the dark—usually the past—and freshening the moldy, decaying relics of the past). It was for this reason that Turner was drawn to Goethe's conclusions about color, in which darkness as well as light is required to produce color sensations (as opposed to the Newtonian position that light alone is necessary). He needed both.

A second corollary is the fact that this drama of chiaroscuro, related as it is to the juxtaposition of sun and a sail or some other opaque object, is also a dramatization of Turner's realization (as an artist) that however much he wants to paint sunlight, by which he means the aerial colors, he knows he is trapped by the medium of his art itself to do so in muddy pigments. As James Heffernan has observed in his excellent essay on Turner's color, "Turner's problem was a way of representing these pure combinations of aerial color with material pigments"—themselves an obstruction between us and the sun and/or the object.[7] This is any artist's realization that the two forms of light, aerial color and material color, are in fact the same, subject to the same fate. It is the insoluble paradox of light versus the representation of light in the only possible way, by pigment, which is restated in the larger issue of the illusionary recession behind the surface of the canvas versus the integrity of the surface of the canvas as paint. Though (as I have said) Turner begins with a white ground and builds up his shades, representations, emblems, hieroglyphics, and alphabetic constructions on top of it, he does not leave the white sun alone either. While the color may not change from the white of the ground, the texture does—he piles up impasto until the sun is as palpable as the dark superimpositions.

What is the solution for a painter who wants to paint the sun and its sunlight in a world of material objects that only absorb its light in muddy excrescences, and with his own material oil paint? One solution is to paint the prismatic media that lie between sun and object—mist, atmosphere, or even surfaces of water. When Hazlitt writes that Turner paints "representations not properly of the objects of nature as of the medium through which they were seen," this "medium" is the "air" of Wilson's bon mot ("Claude for air"), and amounts to the second element of the Turner landscape.[8] First is the sun, the source of illumination and color, and then the air between that refracts the sun—or all the refracting elements, which in effect trope the sun in a graphic way, and so make it publicly acceptable. But then, third, the medium is represented, materialized also (inevitably) in the paint or the "hand" of the artist.

What, then, is the meaning of the opaque object which Turner interjects between sun and medium? I take this to be his allegorizing of the natural force, and I take the allegorizing to mean that he acknowledges the paradox, or the contradiction or the impossibility—the temerity—of painting directly with human pigments the aerial substance. A second way to face this problem, then, is to paint an allegory on top of the admittedly inadequate, false image of a sun—at its most positive, a mythological Apollo and his chariot of the sun, or an Angel standing in the sun; at its most negative a black, mourning symbol of death that obliterates the sun.

I should add that the same procedure is used by Turner with the vortex generated by the sun. The painting *Peace—Burial at Sea* (itself a circle or octagon) has at its center the black ship with its circular paddle wheel. *Snowstorm* works in the same way. Though its lines of force complicate a simple vortical shape, the same circle of the paddle wheel is at the center, generating the sense of the round picture, circular motion, vortex, and endless repetition.

How does the sun, duplicated in an opaque object—perhaps a train which materializes one aspect of it, its energy, harnessed by man—relate to the other sort of sun-duplication Turner uses so frequently: the adding of a second, man-made, human sun? This is the motif Turner may have learned from Wright of Derby, who often sets a natural source of light—usually the moon—against a man-made source: a lamp, a forge, or a candle. The forge of Polyphemus, for example, we have seen to symbolize a secondary, vanquished sun (versus Odysseus's rising sun), and a bloody, burnt-out eye. Juliet glowing with love in *Juliet and Her Nurse* serves the same function. In *The Fighting Temeraire,* being tugged to her last berth to be broken up, the second source of light and energy is in the red fire on the ship's deck. The train in *Rain, Steam, and Speed,* with its fiery engine, must also be seen as another version of the man-made and secondary sun.

I suppose we should recall the true and false suns of the French revolutionaries. In his *Song of Los,* Blake opens with a false sun covered with hieroglyphics and worshipped by a kneeling figure, and ends with a true (revolutionary) sun purged by Los of its Urizenic runes and now blood red—hammered out by Los (both sun and song, equated as the work of poetry). Besides the opposition of false and true, Blake adds idol-worship versus creative labor (which he also relates to age versus youth, darkness versus light, clothed versus naked).[9]

This secondary sun, which emanates from a man-made enclosure, is analogous to the material sun Turner produces with his paint. With it Turner as artist acknowledges himself to be in a way analogous to the blacksmiths, stokers, and other producers of this secondary light source. He is Promethean in so far as his act represents the artist's defiant challenge to the true sun, making of his second sun a Promethean stealing of fire. In this sense, the myth of the Cyclopean light in *Ulysses Deriding Polyphemus* becomes central to Turner, tying into *The Fallacies of Hope* and all his statements about rising and setting, decline and fall. It says that those who imitate the creative energy, the power of the sun, will fail. But it also says that failure is built into the object of imitation as well as into the act of imitation. For he who imitates the sun must also imitate its setting and disappearance. Like the sun, he too will sink and vanish.[10]

But perhaps there is yet another explanation, suggested by a writer in *The Spectator,* 11 February 1837: "the only way to be reconciled to the picture [by Turner] is to look at it from as great a distance as the width of the gallery will allow of, and then you see nothing but a burst of sunlight."[11] A spectator seeks his distance from a late Turner painting in order to see the picture as representation (as Reynolds recommended one do with Gainsborough's portraits), but also to avoid being blinded. Is it for this reason that Turner adds something that intervenes or that diverts? Is it to keep from blinding the spectator or merely to absorb the power of the sun?

A painting which sums up much of what we are saying is the remarkable *Staffa—Fingal's Cave* (R.A. 1832, fig. 47), Turner's first canvas showing steam power pitted against the forces of nature. The secondary sun has been reduced to a spot of red on the side of the black steamboat—hardly visible from more than a few feet away from the canvas (indeed, related to stray splatters of red paint). This is the second, the human source of light, set against the hot, glowing sun that is almost at horizon level a little to the right. It is also indication that inside the boat is human activity.

The question about this painting is whether, as John Gage has suggested, this is a case of Turner's adding a poetic reference in the title after the fact, which is unsubstantiated in the painting.[12] This interpretation depends on the fact that Fingal's Cave lies out of sight on the other side of the promontory represented. In fact, the shape of Fingal's Cave is visible just behind the smoke emitted by the steamboat's funnel, and moreover this cave-shape is repeated in the larger arch of clouds through which the sky breaks above the island. The arch of the cave, as Gage notes, "since its discovery in the 1770s . . . had been regarded as the natural 'original' of both the Gothic and the Classic styles in architecture."[13] The verses added in the Royal Academy catalogue (from Scott's *Lord of the Isles,* canto 4), referring to the "surge that ebbs and swells" and "From the high vault an answer draws," connect the words *high vault* with the graphic vaults above and below, those of the sky and the cave. The arch of the clouds and of the cave-mouth (and the smoke from the steamboat, which also arches), and even "the irregular, columnar structure of the island against the incisive, upright rhythms of the steamer's funnels," as Gage acknowledges, produce the message: "Art, as usual with Turner, puts up a brave show in the face of nature."[14] If this perception of the painting is accurate, then the contemporary critic who said "all is in unison in this fine picture" was correct.[15] *Staffa—Fingal's Cave* is an example of a Turner painting that integrates landscape and literary reference, as well as landscape and human reference—in that one tiny spot of light, barely distinguishable, with which the viewer can connect with a poignancy that is more usually obliterated by a heavy-handed picturesqueness. This painting would be my answer to the many clumsy additions of which Turner is guilty in other paintings, as well as a supreme instance of the characteristic Turner interplay of the two suns—the human artist and the God of nature.

CHAPTER 10 🦢
THE VORTEX:
REPRESSION
OR REINFORCEMENT

From an investigation of Turner's sun it is apparent that the graphic image itself has beneath it, waiting to be exhumed, puns, proverbs, and other verbal structures: some merely inherited and not understood by Turner, unconsciously carried along, but many serving as a conscious part of his meaning. There is a sense in which a verbal structure may be at the nucleus of a Turner painting as well as on its periphery.

The Turnerian vortex clarifies this issue while also propelling us into pure speculation. Art historians would tell us that Turner discovered this form in Thornhill's Greenwich ceiling or Rubens's Banqueting House ceiling—in short, in the experience of baroque art. There is, however, no vortex of this kind in either ceiling, or in any other English ceiling he could have seen. If Lindsay's thesis about the origin of the vortex[1]—that it might be traced back to the doodles in the sketchbooks which become representations of entangled, copulating bodies—carries any validity (and I think, even without reference to the sketches, it does), the first impulse might have been either a form that engendered, suggested, or took the shape of a primal scene; or a representation that engendered the form; or even the word itself—to copulate, to join, to unite, or the simplest copula, *to be*—that lies behind both of these, initiating the characteristic Turnerian enjambment of different times, places, and fates.

Charles Stuckey has argued that the vortex may find its confirmation in Turner's own name—that there is a graphic movement corresponding to the verbal one from "Turner" to "turn" to "wheel," "circle," and of course "cycle," and even to "ring" (as in *Undine Giving the Ring to Masaniello* [Tomasso Aniello, *anello*-"ring"] of 1846).[2] This would not, however, be merely a significance Turner read into the vortex late in his life, but rather the origin of the form itself in the child's concern with its own name. Indeed, it would join the primal scene and the pun of the copula *to be* with the earliest self-identification.

We are already aware of Turner's adult penchant for punning—not only using "hare" for Harold Harefoot but signing his own name with a sketch of a mallard (for his second given name, Mallord).[3] We recall the story told by Thornbury of Turner's love of play—entertaining children and himself being "playful as a child"—from which he received the nickname, after once capsizing a vehicle he was driving recklessly, of "Over-Turner."[4] But the primal pun would have established itself before Turner ever took up a brush. We know that Farington heard him remark that the father of his rival, Girtin, was a turner. His own father was *not*—he was a barber, but with the vortical pattern of the barber pole as his sign.[5] The point is that there is a verbal source for the vortex in the name Turner (Latin *vertere,* to turn), and a visual source in the father's barber pole, and they come to the same thing.[6]

At this point the word and the image are almost indistinguishable. Obviously somewhere in the dim past there had been an ancestral turner, prior to the name, whose sign would have been a coffee-grinder or a Saint Catherine's Wheel or some turning device—which Turner could have seen as readily as a barber's pole.[7] The heraldic sign or the shopsign originated as a name on which a visual pun was made, and the name itself—Turner, Baker, Smith, or Miller—harked back to a metaphor, a trope of some kind related to the visual practice of the occupation.

We can only emphasize the importance to Turner of his name, especially toward the end of his life when he provided in his wills, not only for a Turner Gallery of his paintings, but for a biennial award to be called Turner's Medal, a charitable institution for male artists called Turner's Gift, an annual dinner for the Royal Academicians on his birthday (presumably to be called Turner's Day), and £1000 for a monument carrying his name in St. Paul's Cathedral.[8]

Alain Grosrichard has remarked on "the transference of the need to name the world to the prior need of naming oneself. To name the world is to make the representation of the world coincide with the world itself; to name myself is to make the representation that I have of the world coincide with the representation that I convey to others."[9] We have seen the importance to Turner of *naming,* in the sense of adding words to visual images. In practice this becomes the naming of the Other—the sun or the vortex made by (or which creates) the sun, which can be named in terms of the surrogate sun (or son) who is the creator (painter) named Turner. Thus, as Rousseau realized, "man's first language had to be figurative," and there is "some degree of conceptuality (or metaphor) from the start, within the very act of naming."[10] The real point of origin for any kind of communication is not the image in nature (as representation) but the subject expressing himself in relation to the Other: "that is a giant to me; like me the sun is also a Turner," and so on.

Thus a Turner is "one who turns or fashions objects of wood, metal, bone, etc., on a lathe" (*OED*)—a maker or craftsman, but one who operates through, or shapes by means of, rotation of the object. With the noun go all the senses of the verb: rotation, a spinning around something, a twist (perhaps also the turning implicit in the coupling of lovers); a convoluted form corresponding to one whole revolution; and so a change of direction or course ("the wind has turned"), a deflection or deviation from a course, and change or transformation in general. What we see is a number of senses which allow for the connotation of a turner as a revolutionary, in the sense both of an artist transforming his art and a man his society, reversing the order or arrangement of the object—upsetting, deranging, or unsettling, and hence rebelling ("the worm will turn"). The "Overturn, overturn, overturn" of Ezekiel 21 : 27 has its various echoes in English radical literature: "a *metathesis*, translation, overturning, and total amotion . . . that the Beast's government may never have a being more in England."[11]

If the vortex form originates in a pun, its meaning—layer upon layer— would go something like this: Turner, my name; a maker or an artist; a constructor of vortices in particular; a revolutionary; He who revolves the earth ("as the world turns"). We have already examined the conjunction of artist and God; with revolutionary *and* God we are at the heart of the vortex itself: a tension of conflicting forces, an ambivalence toward the sun, and a need both to change the order and to maintain it.

I do not mean to argue that the word and concept were necessarily prior to the image for Turner, but only that it is not safe to assume that they were not. We have established a verbal impetus before as well as after the graphic image has been made—and this second verbalization is then an attempt (on the part of the artist, in Turner's case) to recapture an original meaning, obscured by the graphic image which has become what Gombrich calls an "open sign"[12] possessing almost unlimited significances or interpretations.

The sort of juxtaposition we have seen in Turner's "emblematic" paintings can be regarded in a number of ways. The relationship of the visual image to the commentary might be seen as a sop to authority or as self-delusion. Perhaps Turner is getting this obligatory literary aspect out of the way in the verses and title of the Royal Academy catalogue, and then dropping it, so that he (and we) can enjoy the sublimity of his image. For, once the picture was hung in a house—or in Turner's studio—there were no words or verses attached to the frame (as in Hogarth's engravings or in many Pre-Raphaelite paintings) and the collaboration of word and image was broken. I find this explanation less than satisfactory, however, because it does not explain the basic relationship between form and representation, let alone the words or visual puns included inside many paintings.

To this Turnerian process we might compare Coleridge's addition of a prose context, a preface, to his fragmentary poem "Kubla Khan."[13] He seeks to express, or in fact to change, the meaning of the poem by the contiguity of another "text" rather than by active revision of the object itself. Coleridge, however, does this to free or open up the fragment to meanings beyond itself, while Turner tries to define and close off the limits of meaning. With his marginal glosses to *The Rime of the Ancient Mariner*, Coleridge projects the idea of a symbol, locating and acknowledging the source of meaning in the object. Turner consciously turns his symbol into an allegory, suggesting that he feels an object has meaning only within the context supplied by the superimposed interpretation.

For what Turner demonstrates is an attempt to absorb the natural object in the subject, or make it a symbol for his own state of mind; but at the same time he acknowledges the existence of the gap within a failed language. Perhaps for Turner, as for Coleridge, the essential problem expressed in all his work is to reconcile "I am" and "it is," the inner and the outer life. Turner as painter demonstrates the problem even more sharply and poignantly than Coleridge. One has to suppose that for him the painting was an incomplete object symbolizing a self that he recognized as his own yet felt alienated from. His own very shaky sense of selfhood had to be materialized constantly in paintings along with their explanations, and all of them hung in a gallery where his self was thus aspiring to a state of completeness which extended to his instructions that only finished paintings be shown. One must suppose that the great "unfinished" pictures made him uneasy about a self not yet grasped, and of course his studio was stacked with these, which we now consider his masterpieces. Even the finished ones—*Dido Building Carthage* and the rest—were ignored; visitors report that Turner could not bear to look at them, and we know they rotted and mildewed and flaked. And yet he continued to prepare them for their role in the Turner Gallery that was to be attached to the National Gallery.

Thus Turner in his visual phase produces a number of marks on a canvas, transforming what is present into a symbol of something much greater but fundamentally inaccessible. This is the act of painting in which the "it is" becomes the "I am." But the self that engendered the graphic image seems as distant from "I am" as Descartes's subject from its object, and now the "I am" has to be further reconceptualized by words into an "it is." The gap is between the experience of the conception in the mind and the result as it exists as an object; and this entails a further attempt to recapture the origin of the image in either experience or concept: by recreating its inner personal significance at the moment of its creation, or perhaps sometimes finding one for it after the fact. To do this Turner is willing to sacrifice the freshness of the experience (recorded in the sketchbooks, even painted on the canvas) to what is more respectable, the reconstruction of the concept, the emotion, the "I am" which pretended to be "it is."

We cannot leave unsaid the possibility that Turner is not trying to express the truth at all but only to repress the original meaning and substitute one he feels is more public and respectable, one he may have discovered during the painting of his picture or after the fact. Perhaps a better analogy is not with Coleridge's "Kubla Khan" but with Richardson's multiple revisions of *Clarissa,* which patently demonstrate his conviction that something had surfaced in the first edition that needed covering up. We can see Turner seeking to impose an acceptable meaning—one that includes even the very personal allusions he seeks to communicate in the late paintings—as a way of concealing a true, perhaps discreditable, meaning which he senses is expressed in the object, while, like Richardson, unconsciously exposing himself.

Turner seems to interpret the incomplete, even fragmentary, quality of the painting (what is not present, not shown, not carefully or completely defined) as an indication either that the actual vision or its experiential quality has been lost, and that what remains—or has been transmitted—is at best a shadow of that vision; or that something made him stop before he had completed the representation and now makes him disguise it. To complete it, to recreate it as it ought to have been, he believes that verbal forms are required, perhaps to show that it began (or should have begun) as words in the sense of concepts or poetry, rather than as perceptions or personal trauma.

Is this repression? It is true that the words attached to the painting may often clarify the more profound and disturbing implications of the painting.[14] The glosses or superimpositions are themselves often subversive. But perhaps there is something more disturbing to Turner than "Fallacies of Hope." They are doubt-ridden, these glosses and Fallacies of Hope, but they are overt. Perhaps the ostensibly disturbing content is only an act of penance, a self-retaliation on Turner's part, which displaces his problem to safe materials. The glosses may serve to repress something Turner cannot publicly acknowledge, the personal ego-energy he fears to own, the personal name of Turner that is his real subject, or, perhaps, his failure—his knowledge that his aspiration to paint the air is in fact impossible of fulfillment.

My argument has been that if we take the sun as Turner's symbol for self-transcendence at the same time that it is linked by the artist with self, then we can see how the rest of the act of painting can be regarded as repression of this unwelcome knowledge. Turner superimposes a series of revisions that humble, chasten, curb, suppress the exuberance of his actual gesture—his hubris of believing he can paint the sun, and above all of making the sun a self-portrait—by devising a plot of failure and doom in the cosmos. Put most simply, he displaces this visual, painterly sun to a literary one on the viewer's side, between sun and spectator.

The alternative explanation is to say that Turner's Apollo in his chariot in *Ulysses Deriding Polyphemus* and the Angel standing before the sun are not glosses but Turner's awareness of the inadequacy of signs to represent things—the limitations of even the highest-aspiring artist.[15] Knowing that he cannot represent the sun itself, he consciously adapts an allegorical mode in which he offers a double representation—an acknowledgment of personification as a part of any perception of nature even of the source of light itself, the sun. Even the sun can only be seen as covered (like the Man in the Moon) by an Apollo or an Angel.

In this reading, Turner's paintings themselves express the act that is mythologized in the stories he illustrates. This is the punning self-portrait I have alluded to, Turner as a Promethean or Apollonian painter with the heliotropic power of his own name. Turner is the painter who looks straight at and paints the sun: it is in the middle of his canvas, his subject, his god, and the object of his representation, both this other and his self. This reading also explains something of the viewer's awkward feeling of finding himself in the position of challenging and yet being put down by the source of all light and energy and power.

Turner's pessimism about communication is perhaps primary. The glosses on *The Angel* and other pictures reflect his despair at a public that has turned away from what he considers his most important work. Thus, when he shows *The Morning after the Deluge,* painted in the positive (plus) colors that follow from sunrise, he nevertheless replaces the symbol of communication, God's covenant of the rainbow, with prismatic bubbles, signs of fallacious hope. The other covenant symbol, the bronze serpent beneath the figure of a recording Moses, is equally dubious. It is both a covenant between God and Moses and a prefiguration of Christ, the ultimate covenant between God and man;[16] it also carries Turner's usual associations of serpents with the Fall and aggression against rabbits and small creatures, and suggests the cosmic pessimism of the circular structure of the painting. It will all happen again; disobedience, night, and flood will follow sunrise and forgiveness.

The covenant, however, takes us all the way back to an early painting, *Buttermere Lake* (fig. 34), in which the rainbow is no literary "covenant" but does connect, in a more profound because more symbolic way, the distant scary mountains with the sunlit community beneath the mountains and on the edge of the equally remote, blank lake. Here Turner is saying a great deal about covenants, about man and nature, sublime and beautiful nature in peaceful coexistence, but he does so without turning to allegory—without admitting the failure of communication in the sign that leads him at last to such allegorical works as the Deluge paintings. In this early work he has shown the other way of painting landscape, which Constable was to explore in a more tendentious way—but was also to abandon in despair.

PART III
CONSTABLE AND
THE SUPPRESSION OF
LITERARY LANDSCAPE

CHAPTER 11 ❧
THE STOUR VALLEY

Coleridge tells of his conversation with John Thelwall, in "a beautiful recess in the Quantocks": "I said to him, 'Citizen John, this is a fine place to talk treason in!' 'Nay! Citizen Samuel,' replied he, 'it is rather a place to make a man forget that there is any necessity for treason.' "[1]

The period through which Turner and Constable lived was in many ways dominated by the French Revolution (1789–1815). The revolutionary art that accompanied the French Revolution was an art that either represented the experience or idea of revolution or stimulated people to a revolutionary consciousness. The art of the French themselves (in particular of Jacques Louis David) sought to stimulate not rebellion but the consciousness of an official idea of the revolution (e.g., as a reclaiming of Roman republican virtues). Because the revolution received an official representation, immediately institutionalized, France did not produce what we might call a revolutionary art—an art that overthrows academic assumptions of what art should be. The neoclassical style in which the revolution was represented had itself been a reaction against certain aspects of the rococo style in the 1780s: this was its revolutionary credential. Otherwise, it drew attention to the antiquity and stability of the new order. Constable, no lover of the French Revolution, wrote of the painting of David and his school, "which sprung out of the Revolution," that they "exhibited their stern and heartless petrifactions of men and women—with trees, rocks, tables, and chairs, all equally bound to the ground by a relentless outline, and destitute of chiaroscuro, the soul and medium of art."[2]

The distinction I wish to make is between an art that *represents* revolution—as, say, some of Turner's sunbursts and natural cataclysms may be said to do—and an art that is itself, in terms of artistic tradition (just as a conventional revolution is of political tradition), revolutionary.

Simultaneously with the political revolution in France a literary/artistic revolution took place in England, which is best seen in the landscape painting of Turner and Constable and the nature poetry of Wordsworth and Coleridge. Blake wrote poetry and made graphic designs that represent the phenomenon of revolution. Turner not only employed revolutionary metaphors in his paintings but was a "revolutionary" painter in his replacement of objects in nature by his painterly medium, itself a metaphor for the artist's sensibility. Much more strikingly out of step, however, was Constable. Like Wordsworth, he was "revolutionary" in seeking a basic change in the artist's subject and source of inspiration. He was far more militant and programmatic than the trimmer Turner, who still thought of landscape as being book-oriented—indeed, continued to think of the Royal Academy as his mother—and tried to conceal his revolutionary art beneath public iconography.

For if we transfer the word *revolution* from politics to art, we have to mean simply the overthrow or scrapping of the established artistic hierarchy. Only the most advanced artists of the time, Gericault and (in a different way) Delacroix, realized at once the awesome turn Constable was giving to the tradition of post-Renaissance European painting. We can read of his intention in his letters, as we read the same sort of sentiments in Wordsworth's preface to *Lyrical Ballads.* By comparison, the eighteenth-century attempts at artistic change—for example, Hogarth's *Four Times of the Day* in landscape, or his *Harlot's Progress* or even Blake's illuminated books in history painting—were merely subversions of hierarchical assumptions, parodic rebukes that at best developed in some artists a "revolutionary" consciousness.

To understand what Turner and Constable accomplish, we should recall Hazlitt's description of Wordsworth, who "like Rembrandt, has a faculty of making something out of nothing, that is, out of himself, by the medium through which he sees and with which he clothes the barrenest subject." His "mind magnifies the littleness of his subject, and raises its meanness; lends it his strength, and clothes it with borrowed grandeur."[3] Landscape was a way for a poet or painter to render self-portraits even more private and personal than those of Rembrandt. Wordsworth summed up the principle when he wrote that the poet's "materials are to be found in every subject which can interest the human mind," which should include "low and rustic life."[4]

Hazlitt's description of Shelley followed the same line: "Poetry, we grant, creates a world of its own; but it creates out of existing materials. Mr. Shelly is the maker of his own poetry—out of nothing."[5] Hazlitt's well-known comment on Turner was that he paints "pictures of nothing and very like." In other words, his paintings represent not so much objects themselves as "the medium through which they were seen."[6] And although Hazlitt did not comment on Constable, it is significant that Constable himself in 1824—perhaps having read Hazlitt—believed that his business as a landscape painter was "to make something out of nothing, in attempting which, he must almost of necessity become poetical."[7]

Constable's ideological revolution in painting lies in the elevation of independent landscape, free of both literary texts and the human-centered assumptions of Claude and Turner. He is reacting against the painter's potential for being (in Martin Price's words) "victimized by the claims of verbal meaning." The term *literary* in my title for this part of the book refers to the complementary aspects of conventional landscape painting which Constable wished to suppress: one was the imitation of landscapes painted by earlier artists, and the other was the telling of a story, the allegorizing or otherwise tarting up of the landscape.

At the very outset of his career in 1802, Constable wrote to John Dunthorne, the local handyman in East Bergholt with whom he had sketched in the fields as a youth, that there are two ways of painting landscape: one is by

"running after pictures and seeking the truth at second hand," and the other
by endeavoring "to get a pure and unaffected representation" of the scene.
This is the well-known passage in which he says: "There is room enough for a
natural painture. The great vice of the present day is bravura, an attempt at
something beyond the truth. In endeavouring to do something better than
well they do what in reality is good for nothing."[8] In 1824 he wrote the
passage about making "something out of nothing" to his closest friend, John
Fisher. Roman ruins, he says, are

> the most grand & affecting natural landscape in the world—and consequently
> a scene the most unfit for a picture. It is the business of a painter not to contend
> with nature & put this scene . . . on a canvas of a few inches, but to make
> something out of nothing, in attempting which he must almost of necessity
> become poetical.[9]

Constable is opposing this doctrine to the academic one "that subject makes
the picture." What rendered suspect the great six-foot canvases of the Stour
Valley that he exhibited at the Royal Academy in the 1820s, and kept him
from being elected a Royal Academician until some twenty-five years after
Turner, was the unredeemed lowness of his subjects. While omitting the
literary elements, he painted local English countryside on the scale and with
the bravura (regarded by contemporaries as brash color and technique) of the
history painter.

   The rule of Constable's theory is probably best demonstrated, however, by
an exception, *The Cornfield* of 1826 (fig. 48), which, unlike his more common horizontal compositions, is an upright shape opening on a central axis
constructed on an unbroken progression from foreground to distance, bottom
to top. This spatial progression becomes metaphorical as marked by the
signposts of a youth drinking out of a stream, a middle-aged farmer in the
middle distance with a plow and a wheat field ready to harvest, and a church
tower on the horizon—all of which corresponds to some such topos as the
"Ages of Man," the church tower being an emblem of faith or hope in the
afterlife.[10] The tower was not visible from that point on the ground, and
indeed the finished version of the painting should be contrasted with the
depopulated landscape of the oil sketch (Birmingham, fig. 49), which shows
how the ground originally looked to Constable on a certain day in 1825.

   To "do something better than well," one is apparently allowed to add a
church tower and other staffage, or one can paint a symbolic structure (a
monument, a ruin) that is extant and then perhaps comment upon it using
dramatic perspective, lighting, and brushwork. *The Cornfield,* in its gentle
way, ushers in a series of symbolic landscapes of Constable's final decade:
Hadleigh Castle, Stonehenge, Old Sarum, and *The Cenotaph to Sir Joshua Reynolds
at Coleorton.* In the watercolor *Stonehenge* (1836, fig. 50), with its overtly
symbolic subject and its prominent rainbow and agitated sky, he even in-

cludes a tiny emblematic rabbit juxtaposed to the ancient Druid ruin, painted on a separate piece of paper and pasted onto the painting. It was literally "something beyond the truth," something added. (This rabbit, in fact, preceded Turner's hare in *Rain, Steam, and Speed* by seven years.) One question we shall want to answer is whether that superimposed rabbit is emblematic of the way these later excursions into symbolization relate to the refusal during the earlier years to paint "literary" landscape. We shall be relating three periods: that of the oil sketches and small paintings of the Stour Valley executed between the time of the letter to Dunthorne and 1819; that of the six-foot canvases of the Stour Valley which Constable exhibited at the Royal Academy from 1819 to 1825; and the last decade of his life, from 1825 to his death in 1837, when the paintings (beginning as a continuation of the six-footers) departed from the Stour Valley setting, turned to symbolic subjects, and were augmented by the mezzotint prints of the *English Land-scape* series (1830–33) and by Constable's "official" pronouncements in the letterpress for that series and in his lectures delivered at the Royal Institution and elsewhere (1836).

In his "Bible of Hell" Blake worked out a model for the functioning of revolution based on what he saw across the Channel after 1793, from Robespierre to Napoleon, which showed an act of revolt followed by an internalizing of the overthrown tyrant in a worse tyranny. The landscapes of Turner and Constable, in their different ways, also represent a revolt against literary, political, and other appropriations of nature followed by an act of appropriation of their own. Their practice leaves us with the question: What does Constable's "nothing" prove to be? Of what, in fact, does his "revolution" consist, since nothing can be created ex nihilo?

In one of the lectures of 1836 Constable summed up his doctrine of "natural painture" in his analysis of a winter landscape by Jacob Ruisdael:[11]

> This picture represents an approaching thaw. The ground is covered with snow, and the trees are still white; but there are two windmills near the centre; the one has the sails furled, and is turned in the position from which the wind blew when the mill left off work; the other has the canvas on the poles, and is turned another way, which indicates a change in the wind. The clouds are opening in that direction, which appears by the glow in the sky to be the south (the sun's winter habitation in our hemisphere), and this change will produce a thaw before the morning.

Ruisdael, Constable says, "has here told a story" of the weather, and he contrasts this successful landscape painting with another Ruisdael landscape in which "he attempted to tell that which is out of the reach of the art." In this painting, called "An Allegory of the Life of Man," which reminds one of Constable's own *Cornfield,* "there are ruins to indicate old age, a stream to signify the course of life, and rocks and precipices to shadow forth its dangers. . . ."[12]

This is a remarkable passage: I know of no writer on art before Constable who offered such a radical interpretation of landscape. It was evidently part of his own practice. As though he could not convey all the information he wished in the painting itself, he labeled a late topographical view *Englefield House, Berkshire, the Seat of Benyon de Beovoir, Esq.—Morning* (1833, private collection). Further information was sometimes recorded on the backs of canvases; on an early cloud study he wrote: "5th September 1822, 10 o'clock, Morning looking South-East very brisk wind at West, very bright and fresh grey clouds running very fast over a yellow bed about half-way in the sky" (London, National Gallery).[13]

The fact that Constable was painting ruins and precipices as he spoke the words about Ruisdael only underlines the contradiction we are seeking to understand. Even in those words he cannot restrain the metaphorical activity of his mind. Notice that "glow in the sky" becomes first, geographically, "the south" and then, metaphorically, "the sun's winter habitation." In his remark on Ruisdael's "telling a story" of the weather there is an implicit metaphor of narrative. Though the difference is striking, the model for his remarks is nevertheless Charles Le Brun's analysis of Poussin's history paintings as poetic narratives with beginning, middle, and end.[14]

This is a landscape that depicts meteorological change. Constable's words about a beginning, middle, and end of the weather should be contrasted with the Reverend John Eagles's recommendation that landscape depict a point of ideal time when day and night or two seasons meet.[15] Constable is not concerned with an ideal, timeless time—nor is Turner. Both are concerned with a pivotal moment in time: Turner with a point of choice or of transition in man's fortunes between rise and fall, victory and defeat, and other metaphorical equivalents of facts of nature—day and night, sunrise and sunset, summer and winter—whether of time or weather. Constable often shows the weather before and after in a single canvas because his sky is a broad expanse and the weather is in motion. This moment of change in weather from sun to rain or calm to storm is the moment in which the viewer is situated. Whether Constable can paint this meteorological story without loosing metaphors of the sort Turner consciously exposes is the question we are considering.

Meteorology is, however, distinct from topography, at least as it was practiced by painters from Siberechts to Wilson. Wilson's or Turner's atmosphere raised or poeticized the country house—"destroyed" it, according to John Harris, because it replaced exact description with more painterly concerns. Constable wrote in 1822 about his not having seen William Beckford's spectacular pseudocastle, Fonthill: "I never had a desire to see sights—and a gentleman's park—is my aversion. It is not beauty because it is not nature."[16] A straightforward representation, like that of Englefield House, he labeled "Morning," and in the final painting further stipulated atmospherics by adding lowering storm clouds. Harris agrees that Constable, too, indicated "his disdain for the house as a subject," but "atmosphere" meant something very different to him than it did to Turner.[17] Turner's subject was the atmosphere itself, a layer in space that refracted the sunlight; Constable's subject was the objects transformed by atmosphere, how it changes them or brings out in them certain hidden qualities. In a curious way, however, he allows it to intervene, to become a layer in space, as Turner did. I refer to those specks of white from his palette knife which came to be called his "whitewash" (Turner's word for it) or, in Edward FitzGerald's words, "that white sky-mud which (according to Constable's theory) the Earth scatters up with her wheels in travelling so briskly round the sun."[18]

Constable explained this whitewash as his way of suggesting the "dewy freshness" of a scene, and there are many anecdotes of his defense of his "whitewash" as the very essence of a landscape that is "beautifully silvery, windy & delicious—. . . all health—& the absence of everything stagnant."[19] But these statements pose questions. What does the added layer of texture *represent?*—"whitewash" or "dew"; atmosphere or augmentation; a palpable screen between us (or the painter) and the scene, separating us from it, or a property of the object itself, light reflected off it, an augmentation of its tactility?

Constable is famous for two statements: one in which he describes the atmosphere of his painting as "lights—dews—breezes—blooms and freshness," and the other in which he refers to the tactility of objects: "old rotten Banks, slimy posts, & brick work," to which he adds: "I love such things."[20] How does he reconcile freshness and rottenness?

These words appear in a letter of 1821 to Fisher, devoted to the six-foot canvases he was painting, and in particular to *The Hay Wain* (fig. 54), which Fisher had bought from him. Having described the old, rotten, slimy objects he loves, Constable goes on to say (contrasting himself to Shakespeare, who "could make anything poetical," i.e., "something out of nothing"):

> But I should paint my own places best—Painting is but another word for feeling. I associate my 'careless boyhood' [the phrase will reappear ten years later in the letterpress to *English Landscape*] to all that lies on the banks of the Stour. They made me a painter (& I am grateful!). . . .[21]

And he adds that *The Hay Wain* "is one of the strongest instances I can recollect" of such Stour scenes. He is intensifying in the six-foot canvases the intention he developed in the years of experiment and observation that preceded them. But in those studies and paintings, too, he is concerned with a personal past, and therefore with aging wood, moss, damp, and physical decay, associated in particular with the mills, locks, and canals through which his father had carried out his business in the valley. This concern runs through all of the Stour Valley paintings, becoming the distinguishing feature or rationale of the showpieces he exhibited at the Royal Academy.

But how does this pastness of the objects he represents relate to the "freshness," the "health," and "absence of everything stagnant" in the atmosphere? The whitewash as "dewy freshness" was one more form of intensification introduced in the 1820s to augment the highlights and the deliberately unfinished technique that distinguished the Stour Valley landscapes of the earlier period. In strictly topographical terms, these highlights created the stereopticon effect in Constable's most three-dimensional paintings, denoting spatial relations in an almost maplike way, and at the same time pulling the object and the viewer closer together. But in terms of his aim to regain his "careless boyhood," the highlights, the later flecks of white, presumably represent either the blurred nostalgia of the observer/recreator,[22] or perhaps more schematically, a light growing out of darkness, in which he sees objects, substances, people, relationships, all coming alive (or returning to life) as they are activated by light. We are tempted again to detect a metaphor in natural equivalents. As distance tends to suggest memory or hope, so perhaps dark equals the past and light equals the dewy freshness of the present, or a brief caught moment which merges past and present.

At one point, in one of his more bumptious letters to Fisher, Constable contrasts his own "fresh" landscape with another in the same exhibition which he says is "like a large cow-turd—at least so far as color & shape."[23] In his own painting he presumably tries to join in one object and one moment the immediate, "fresh," and "dewy" present and the old, rotting, mossy past.

An important difference between Constable and Turner is that the latter painted looking into the sun, while Constable painted with the sun behind him or (as in *The Hay Wain,* originally called "Landscape: Noon") directly above him.[24] Turner paints dark shapes emerging from light (a light or white ground); his paintings are about light, and the foreground figures are merely impingements upon that point of origin, that creative source, that self-portrait of the painter as creator of a world. Constable, however, has an apparently (only apparently perhaps) far humbler aim—to depict objects, substances, people, relationships, topography, by showing them emerging into the light out of darkness. The highlights, later the flecks of white, are movement and texture to take hold of. The sense of depth, distance, precisely demarcated space, and relationship is quite remarkable in his paintings, due partly to his emphasizing highlights as texture.

Looking back from 1830 on these early paintings, as he prepared to present his mezzotints of "*English* Landscape" that would rival the general term *landscape* (or classical, Italian, or Alpine landscape), he chose the elements that must have seemed to him "English." He passed over the six-footers of the 1820s to return to the smaller, more intimate and intense visualizations that preceded them (and on which they were based). He used these small sketches or recreated them in an even more intense version of that early style to represent (as he put it in the letterpress to *English Landscape*) "one brief moment caught from fleeting time." These sketches tell us that Constable did not want to paint "landscape" in the general sense that Turner did—in the principle forms and genres laid out in the *Liber Studiorum*, or in the categories of "sublime" or "beautiful" into which these genres resolved themselves. He was interested primarily, as his meteorological notations attest, in the representation of a particular time and place, very close to what Wordsworth called a "spot of time." And if at one level of generality the place was East Bergholt and the Stour Valley, at another it was England.

What, then, are the basic qualities of an "English" landscape according to Constable? These elements, whatever they are, have molded most Englishmen's idea of their landscape ever since—from the time of the man who, riding in the same coach with Constable as it entered the Stour Valley, remarked to the painter, with no idea of his identity, "Yes Sir—this is *Constable*'s country!"[25] In Constable's own terms, we have seen, the qualities are dewy freshness and rottenness.

In more general terms, what he does is join the information of topographical landscape with the sensuous experience of the landscape as seen, or perhaps better—to explain the extreme intensity of the chiaroscuro (another favorite Constable term)—as remembered. He intensifies the sunlit areas and the shade, producing the brightest and most intense greens. (Which goes some way toward explaining the public concern when the Tate Gallery's *Stoke-by-Nayland* was attributed to Lionel Constable. It had seemed to sum up the Constable landscape with its intense green tree and sunlit grass *because* Lionel was drawing on his father's most obvious characteristics.) He also conveys a sense of limited scale, limited spaces; a concern for establishing exactly where a property, hill, or field ends and another begins, the point of jointure or transition. Spatial relations are of primary importance—the precise relation, not the sense of infinite extension which was essential to the Turner landscape. This also included a concern with the relationship of earth and sky, of cloud formations in the sky and their shadows on the earth, and so in a more general way of smooth and rough, of enclosure and openings into the distance or in the midst of things. There is a greater emphasis than in most landscape paintings on trees, which fill up much of the space; the effect is, once again, to intensify the area that is *not* trees. One element, we shall see, that all the six-foot canvases of the Stour Valley have in common is that they are river scenes—often relating pond and river, mixing stagnant and running water.

Strong contrast and great concern for spatial relations and demarcations, and in the most general way a desire to communicate information—a certain information, extensive and emphatic: in fact, Constable attempts to convey *all* of the sensory experience of a place. Thus the objects on the ground and in the sky, *as* objects, is what he represents, and only secondarily Turner's subject, the sun and the atmosphere that surrounds these hard objects and transforms them as the poet transforms his experience.

As early as 1797, in *Remarks on Rural Scenery* by his London friend J. T. Smith, Constable had a policy statement in relation to which he could place himself. This slender book, "with twenty Etchings of Cottages, from Nature; and some observations and precepts relative to the picturesque," argued that landscape painting "does not necessarily exist in grandeur, *exclusively* or *alone,*" but also "in the most *humble*" as well as "the most *stately* structures, or scenery" (p. 6). The artist, Smith says, must turn from the neat, well-kept cottage to

> a far more profitable subject—the neglected fast-ruinating cottage—the patched plaster, the various tints and discolorations, which, like the garments of Otway's witch, shall
>
> 'Seem to speak variety of wretchedness'
>
> —the weather-beaten thatch, bunchy and varied with moss—the mutilated chimney top—the fissures and crevices of the inclining wall—the roof of various angles and inclinations—the tiles of different hues—the fence of bungling workmanship—the wild unrestrained vine.... [p. 9]

Smith is, of course, relaying the picturesque ideas of Gilpin, Knight, and Price. But we can see how differently Constable and, say, Gainsborough would have illustrated this passage (Gainsborough with, to continue the passage, his "ragged children—the intrusion of pigs—and the unrepaired accidents of wind and rain"). Smith starts off with Gainsborough (p. 7), who is evidently the artist he has in mind, and emphasizes his stylized, unnaturalistic aim. But Constable would have compared the freedom of poetic license that Smith allows the picturesque artist with the duty of the topographical artist, for whom "every absurdity, as well as beauty, must be faithfully depicted, or his drawings will not hand down to posterity that *local* and particular truth, which it is expressly his business and purpose to transmit" (p. 14). The Gainsborough-type artist takes Smith's advice to "retire into the inmost recesses of forests, and most obscure and unfrequented villages" (p. 12). Constable is intrigued by the picturesque elements Smith enumerates, and some of these are his own, especially in so far as they denote age and the past. But in his early work he is clearly more concerned with where he *was,* not with where he might go to search out picturesque conventions or invent them, and with faithfully depicting "that local and particular truth."

Nevertheless, if we look at the pre-1819 landscapes (and indeed, at Constable's landscapes in general), we also notice the tension between the desire to represent the landscape exactly as it was—to recapture a memory of the past—and the need to express the painter's feeling (response) and control over this landscape. There is no such tension in the landscapes of Gainsborough, who can be relied on to ignore almost entirely the topography and the informational content of the scene for formulae, for purely poetic or formal relations. Constable thrives on the tension between the most powerful sense of illusionistic depth and the need to hold the spectator's eye on the surface of the canvas—on the fact that this landscape is painted, recreated by a particular sensibility.

Perhaps we can say that precise demarcation or distinction between spatial areas is Constable's obsession and that his concern with paint expresses it. We might say that he suppresses the human-centered assumptions of the Claudian landscape with such fervor only in order to allow the human to return in another way, in the person of the painter—in his wish to paint "one brief moment caught from fleeting time" in a representation of vines and flowers overrunning man's artistic structures and therefore memory. The tension is between man and his works and nature as a challenge to his supremacy: between cultivated and uncultivated, canal locks or boat-building and natural forms or growths. Two of his greatest paintings of the earlier period are *Boat-building near Flatford Mill* and *Dedham Lock and Mill* (1815 and 1820, respectively; fig. 51)): both show the most marvelous articulation of space as form, information, and emotional charge and release. In another pair, *Golding Constable's Kitchen Garden* and *Flower Garden* (ca. 1815, fig. 65), the accurate spatial representation has as its foil the formal relations between the vertical and horizontal lines of the man-made structures and the unfixed, overflowing shapes of the trees and fields. The result is a close-up, greatly intensified version of the interest in a Koninck landscape of flat fields or a Hobbema of trees and clearings with the occasional house or mill.

Beginning in about 1825, demarcation takes the form of a tension between canal locks and leaping horses and birds taking flight. The fact of the canal system and the enclosures—the hedgerows that divided the fields—had an important and determining effect on Constable's landscape painting. William Marshall described his impressions of the east Norfolk landscape in 1787, in *Rural Economy of Norfolk:*

> The enclosures are, in general, small, and the hedgerows high, and full of trees. This has a singular effect in travelling through the country: the eye seems ever on the verge of a forest, which is, as it were by enchantment, continually changing into inclosures and hedgerows. . . .[26]

The edge-of-the-woods phenomenon was one Constable presumably grew up with, but the larger impression is of the segmentation we have seen to be a characteristic of his Stour Valley paintings. The process from Tudor times onward, as W. G. Hoskins has shown, was one of the division of fields, through inheritance-divisions and through enclosures, into ever smaller units. "By far the most conspicuous element in the new landscape," Hoskins writes, "were the small, hedged fields—small, that is, by comparison with the vast open fields that had preceded them, which usually ran to several hundred acres unbroken by a single hedge."[27] We do not need to suppose that enclosures hit East Bergholt in particular (they did not until too late to have had much effect on Constable) to see a general pattern of experience involving the division of large open fields into ever smaller demarcations: "The result was a fantastically small set of fields—many of them only an acre or so in size, some as little as half an acre." With enclosure came "a complete transformation" of the English landscape, "from the immemorial landscape of the open fields" to "the modern chequer-board pattern of small, squarish fields, enclosed by hedgerows of hawthorn."[28] I am suggesting that Constable's visual image of a landscape may have contained a nostalgia for the open field, a desire to escape from demarcation and subdivision into the open field.

Closely related in contemporary theory to the contrast of cultivated to uncultivated is the near equation we sense between utility and beauty as opposed to untouched nature and disorder, perhaps danger or hazard. As John Barrell has shown, the emphasis on cultivation and enclosure led poets and writers on agriculture—and probably Constable too—to think in terms of divisions and segmentation, demarcation and closely observed spatial relationships. As Thomas Batchelor wrote in *The Progress of Agriculture:*

> But, Industry, thy unremitting hand
> Has chang'd the *formless* aspect of the land . . .
> And hawthorn *fences,* stretched from side to side,
> Contiguous pastures, meadows, fields divide.[29]

A painting like *Dedham Lock and Mill,* with its almost maplike emphasis on the spatial relationships between locks and open areas beyond, is only a very complicated version of a basic Constable landscape structure, which can be seen at its simplest in *Cottage in a Cornfield* (1833, but probably based on a version of 1818; fig. 52).[30] This structure consists of demarcations, barriers, fences, gates, and so on, beyond which stands a cottage, farmhouse, or vicarage, around which (usually to the right) one glimpses an uninterrupted distant stretch of sunlit meadow, closed in by trees on the horizon. There may be donkeys or even people present, but, comparatively, they are only accents.

In *The Hay Wain*'s celebration of pastness Constable has chosen the particular moment at which the grass is being cut to make hay, which will serve as fodder for the animals during the winter. One feature that distinguishes his landscapes, even the earliest of them, and that worried contemporaries with their established ideas of landscape painting, was the fact that they depict not "landscape" but farming, milling, canal-transport, and various kinds of labor—of the sort one would have expected generically to find in realistic subject pictures. Perhaps this is why he called *The Hay Wain* "Landscape: Noon." Leslie, in his biography of Constable, writes: "I have heard him say the solitude of the mountains oppressed his spirits. His nature was peculiarly social and could not feel satisfied with scenery, however grand in itself, that did not abound in human associations. He required villages, churches, farm-houses, and cottages. . . ."[31] Even Turner paints either a genre scene (a blacksmith's shop) or reduces his figures in relation to a picturesque cityscape, market-day, or landscape. Constable's figures are placed precisely in relation to their own landscape, in which they live and work and function. They are an integral part of it, and when they are barely visible, the landscape nevertheless shows the effects of their work. (This is what worries John Barrell, who sees the landscape as relatively empty because the signs of people's labors are there and, he believes, Constable suppresses the laborers themselves as disjunctive elements.)[32]

Constable disturbs by painting, often on a large scale, the farming activity and, even more, the economic elements of the local countryside: though this is precisely what later made Constable's landscape England's. It is almost as if he had transplanted Canaletto's or Bellotto's busy cityscapes to an English country setting, full of workers as well as near-idle strollers and boys fishing. The subjects of his major paintings are now ploughing, harvesting, dung-spreading, or canal transport.

In one sense Constable picked up the English conversation picture, the scene depicting a family sitting in its own park with its own house in the background, its own animals, domestic and sporting, in appropriate and precise spatial relationships to one another. But—most important—he omits the family, or the member of the family who is in fact viewing the scene and so is unnecessary *in* it. The point of view is, in Barrell's sense, proprietorial. He is painting for himself the perspectival series of country-house views we associate with Lambert and Wilson. Whether or not he knew Bellotto's Dresden and Warsaw scenes, the aim of painting an area recreated street after street, viewed from various directions, was his own. In Constable's painting the "property" is the countryside, his own, which is only a stretch of about two miles wide and six across, part of the Stour Valley, on either side of which are ridges which rise to some 150 feet in height. He worked, as Leslie said, "within the narrowest bounds in which, perhaps, the studies of an artist ever were confined," but his aim could "be best attained by a constant study of the same objects under every change of the seasons, and of the times of day"—to which he added, "he was fond of introducing the tower of Dedham Church, which is seen from many points near Flatford" (p. 286). In the context of history painting, the seasonal aspect refers back to the "Times of the Day" and to Lambert's seasonal contrasts; the different perspectives on a common area refer to the series in which a country house or a city is depicted from all directions and with the precision of the cityscape painter rather than the ordinary landscape painter of the time.[33]

The sketches Constable made in the Stour Valley in the 1800s were systematically painted around the valley, looking down into it or across it and recording different views connected by certain controls or stable landmarks—such as Dedham Church tower and Stratford St. Mary's, one regular and the other irregular. Constable is following the principle of the pictorial circuit (the principle on which many English gardens of the mid-eighteenth century were constructed) on the one hand, and the complete topographical record on the other. He literally walked around, looking into the valley, and never looked *out* of the valley, away from it.[34]

When he did go down inside the valley, he painted a single object from all directions, circling it. He looked at Flatford Mill from different angles and then looked out from the mill to Willy Lott's cottage, the canal, the distant meadows glimpsed through a row of trees. Whether a lock, a mill, or a canal, these were all personal places, usually owned or worked by his father. He seldom (perhaps never) painted the house of a stranger, anyone without strong personal connections to the Constables. From his own house where he was born, he looked out at the other houses and fields roundabout, and drew and painted them. His originality—what distinguished him from a topo-graphical painter like Bellotto or Paul Sandby—consists in the emphasis on the "impression" of a particular viewer, perhaps what Constable liked to call the "dewy freshness" he wished to convey, and not the objectivity of a camera obscura.

Constable was trying to recapture and represent an experience, and his method of painting was not unlike Wordsworth's description of the opera-tion of the poetic imagination: he talked of recreating the scene he knew as a child; he went to the scene and made careful sketches (Wordsworth says you should go and then later register what you saw, when the unimportant will have faded from memory), but then he waited for years, and in his London studio put those sketches together to "recollect in tranquillity" the scene as it impressed itself on him in childhood. The sketches produced the data, the Stour Valley locations, events, and seasons, the transmission of life experi-ence out of which (or through which) Constable much later, in the six-foot canvases, attempted to recover something from the past, to define himself in terms of his childhood surroundings, and reconcile genre and decorum in landscape painting, with its English subject, presenting these year after year in the Royal Academy exhibitions as his major works.

Of course I am oversimplifying: the degree of remove from direct study of nature varied greatly during Constable's working career. The Tate *Flatford Mill* was probably painted largely on the spot; the first six-foot canvases were reflections on immediately preceding studies from nature; while the late six-footers were distant memories. But the result was in general a combination of particularity of time and place, reflected in season, cloud formations, light and shadow, and the desire to recapture the past: "a scene is revisited," as M. H. Abrams has written of Romantic nature poetry, "and the remembered landscape ('the picture of the mind') is superimposed on the picture before the eye . . . a persisting double awareness of things as they are and as they were. . . ."[35] This may take the form of the fresh dew and the rotting boards, or of the sketches and paintings that lead up to the full-scale childhood recollection in broken paint and passionate brushstrokes, and then to the final "finished" reconstruction which balances the primary and secondary recollections, the object and the subjective transformation of it into what it *was.* This last, six-foot Royal Academy painting constitutes the process of reconstruction or of harmonizing the two or more points in time, the studies not only of solutions to compositional problems but their varying degrees of particularity or stages of memory and recreation. Even the "finished" painting remains relatively, or partly, unfinished, expressing the tension at the center of Constable's conception of landscape between past and present, memory and description, connotation and denotation, subjective and objective, evocation and representation, and the closed-eye image of the past and what it is before the eyes now in clear focus.

CHAPTER 12
THE SIX-FOOTERS

What distinguishes the major compositions Constable exhibited at the Royal Academy from 1819 onward is, first, the fact that they are immensely spacious in comparison with the sketches from nature which preceded them; and second, that part of this spaciousness entails a focusing in a monumentally simple shape on a single aspect of the landscape experience. At least until *The Hay Wain,* almost all of Constable's paintings can be explained as attempts to get everything in the natural landscape on canvas (sometimes on a series of canvases). Considering the fact that he regarded the six-foot canvases as topographical and quintessentially English and local—even personal— landscapes, I shall begin with their deviations from the descriptive: that is to say, from the smaller paintings which preceded them, from the "natural painture" he described in the letter to Dunthorne, and from the strict transcription which he argues is part of the scientific "truth."

The views of Willy Lott's cottage in the sketches and smaller paintings, for example, show the canal dividing the composition down the middle, trees on both sides, pretty much as the scene still looks today (fig. 53). Constable was standing on the edge of his father's property at Flatford Mill, painting a cottage away from which (legend had it) Willy Lott spent no more than one or two nights in his whole lifetime. In the six-foot *Hay Wain* (R.A. 1821, fig. 54), however, Constable has moved the vantage point to the left and cut down the trees and underbrush on the right side of the canal to create an opening off the main axis into the meadow.[1] Everything now points in that rightward direction, toward the haymaking that is going on in the distant meadow (presumably the empty cart's destination), with no closure on the right.

My assumption is that Constable modified the topography for the heroic version because he needed it to fit his own idea (since he rejected those of other painters) of "necessity" in a "poetical" composition. In the oil sketches of Willy Lott's cottage (including the exhibited piece of 1814 in Ipswich, fig. 53) there is an obvious and easy escape route for the eye, straight down the middle of the composition. In the six-footer, Constable makes it by no means so easy, shifting it to the right and, indeed, forcibly opening a place where in the landscape itself there was no access. The obvious, true escape route was suppressed so that a different, and perhaps nonexistent, one could be created. The difference is that the route to the right leads to the meadows and harvesting.

Stratford Mill (R.A. 1820, private collection) had already had its right side opened up by Constable's moving the vantage point to the left and emphasizing the treeless tow-track along the right bank of the river. With these two compositions of 1820–21 can be contrasted *The White Horse* (R.A. 1819, Frick) which immediately preceded them, in which Constable had not yet found the composition he was working toward, but (a matter we shall return to) in which bodies of water play a much larger part. The *Examiner* critic had contrasted *The White Horse* with Turner's landscapes at the same academy exhibition and concluded that, unlike Turner, Constable "does not give a sentiment, a soul to the exterior of Nature," but "gives her outward look, her complexion and physical countenance" only. It may well be as a response to this sort of criticism, as Alastair Smart has speculated, "that the second of the six-foot canvases, the *Stratford Mill* of 1820, is more concerned with the expression of the artist's response to Nature's moods."[2]

Following *The Hay Wain*, Constable painted *View on the Stour* (R.A. 1822, fig. 55), in which he complicated the canal in the foreground by adding barges and bargemen, in effect taking the place of Willy Lott's cottage on the left but moving it toward the center. We may see the barges as Constable did (as he wrote to Fisher), as the "rich center" of the picture, but they also mark a break, a discontinuity in the planes which prevents the eye from easily connecting foreground and distance.[3] They are obstacles (powerfully tactile, like the mossy, slimy foreground) that hinder us from reaching the other part of the painting, the open sunlit fields in the distance. The

broken paths the eye is forced to follow in these landscapes should recall the
*un*broken progress from foreground to distance, along a central axis, used for
allegorical purposes, in *The Cornfield.*

   The next large painting, *A Boat Passing a Lock* (R.A. 1824, fig. 56), is an
upright form (though repainted in the horizontal shape two years later) to
emphasize the height of the rough foreground structure of the lock, which
filled the space of the barges and extended along the whole front. This
painting caps all the earlier ones dealing with the relationship between locks
and open areas beyond. *Dedham Lock and Mill* was such a painting; even the
boat in *Boat-Building near Flatford Mill* served the blocking purpose. *The
Cottage in a Cornfield,* as I mentioned earlier, was the simplest example of
such a composition, and *Parham Mill, Gillingham* (R.A. 1826, Yale Center
for British Art), the most extreme: the mill structure and pond are in the
foreground, with a waterwheel in action, and visible over this is a thin slice
of bright meadow with the meandering stream (from which the mill operates) connecting meadow and foreground. *Boat Passing the Lock* only makes
the most impressive use of this man-made structure placed in the center,
with the sunlit meadow visible over its top (and crowned on the horizon with
a conventional symbol, a church tower).

   What is taking shape in these paintings reaches fulfillment in *The Leaping
Horse* (R.A. 1825, fig. 57), the first of the six-footers to abandon a specific
locality, to generalize the Stour Valley, and to move landmarks around. Here
Constable repeats the composition established in *The Hay Wain,* replacing
(as in *View of the Stour*) Willy Lott's cottage with barges; and by further
lowering the spectator's viewpoint, he makes the heap in the foreground
more emphatic, more palpable, and of an even more immediate tactility.
And in this case his verbal description shows us what *he* saw as he painted.
He wrote to Fisher: "It is a canal and full of the bustle incident to such a
scene where four or five boats are passing with dogs, horses, boys & men &
women & children, and the best of all old timber-props, water plants, willow
stumps, sedges, old nets, &c &c &c."[4]—I think our visual impression of the
foreground is accurately caught by this verbal piling up ("bustle") of objects,
many more than we actually see, and these augmented by three ampersands.

   In a later letter to Fisher, Constable described the feeling of the whole
picture as once again "lively—& soothing—calm and exhilarating, fresh—&
blowing."[5] Finally, he described the overall composition in a letter to a
prospective buyer: "Scene in Suffolk, banks of a navigable river, barge horse
leaping on an old bridge, under which is a floodgate and an elibray [eelery or
eel trap], river plants and weeds, a moorhen frightened from her nest—near
by in the meadows is the fine Gothic tower of Dedham."[6] Constable's crucial
punctuation is that dash, followed by the added clause pointing to the light,
meadows, and church tower—an eternal sunlit moment beyond the decaying
confusion of the foreground, the lock and eel trap and weeds down "under"

the bridge. Significantly, it is precisely here on the foreground confusion that we find the dewy "whitewash" which connects the foreground and the gleaming, broken paint that designates the distant "meadows"—an emphasizing of the relationship between foreground and distant sunlit meadow in *The Hay Wain*.

Constable's careful approximation of verbal syntax to graphic structure should be contrasted with C. R. Leslie's description, which (as one might expect from the painter of *Uncle Toby and the Widow Wadman*, V & A) focuses on the story incident of the boy and the horse:

> The chief object in its foreground is a horse mounted by a boy, leaping one of the barriers which cross the towing paths along the Stour (for it is that river, and not a canal), to prevent the cattle from quitting their bounds. As these bars are without gates, the horses, which are of a much finer race and kept in better condition than the wretched animals that tow the barges near London, are all taught to leap; their harness ornamented over the collar with crimson fringe adds to their picturesque appearance, and Constable, by availing himself of these advantages, and relieving the horse, which is of a dark colour, upon a bright sky, made him a very imposing object.[7]

In the figure of the leaping horse, Leslie is pointing to a detail of Stour Valley routine. He is also right in detecting something of his own kind in the rearing horse that leaps up away from the bridge. The freshness, represented by the dewy "whitewash," is perhaps *symbolized* by the leaping horse, which is moving away from the several locking, trapping, closing elements and toward the sunlit "meadows"—a word with associations of haymaking and cattle-grazing.

Alongside Constable's written statements we also have the commentary of his revisions, which can be seen by comparing the full-sized sketch (fig. 58) and the finished Royal Academy painting. In the sketch the right is closed by a "willow-stump," which in the final version is moved into a position supporting the central obstructions, strengthening the lock, between us and the peaceful meadow in the distance. This shift also leaves the horse's path open, or almost—for Constable nevertheless feels he must add a tiny church tower, as he had done in *A View on the Stour,* at the far right edge of the canvas, a kind of closure cum religious symbol—and mention it to his prospective buyer.

These steeples, we may conclude, are added not just for reasons of formal closure but to reinforce the sunlit meadow by a symbol (of faith, hope, etc.); and this is to be distinguished from the steeple used as part of a semantic structure (steeple, cornfield, farmer, boy), as in *The Cornfield.* Then we notice that the moorhen, the tiny bird at the bottom right of the painting, is in fact as marginal (and seemingly added) as the rabbit in *Stonehenge.* But it is posed to parallel the leap of the horse, out and away from the milieu, and

Constable draws verbal attention to it (we might otherwise have missed it). It is, therefore, yet another symbol in this painting.

The river, too, takes on a status somewhere between a horse-related symbol and part of a study in demarcations. It is a rushing torrent until its fury is sluiced off through the lock. Then it runs on smoothly to the meadow (where harvestlike activity is going on). The lock controls or regulates the flow of the river to keep it from becoming either too rapid or too stagnant—too dewy-fresh or too slimy. Actually, there are three areas of water to be distinguished: the rushing torrent coming in from the left; the runoff in the foreground, through the sluice (from which the moorhen is taking off); and the peaceful sheet of water which is coeval with the distant meadow, creating a single sheet of sunlight.

The unobtrusive symbols in *The Leaping Horse* hardly prepare us for the enlarged vertical barrier of the ruined tower in *Hadleigh Castle* (R.A. 1829, fig. 59), a more conventional version of the rotting foreground shapes, but now no longer indigenous to the Stour Valley scene. Constable has moved out of his native valley and made a Gothic convention the subject of his painting. And yet the structure I have described still remains dominant: beyond all this foreground symbolism is the brilliant expanse of light-filled water (and the spot of sunlight on a distant peninsula, hardly more than a touch of paint) now picked out in a cloudy prospect under dark and threatening sky. And as if to draw attention away from it (as he closed *The Leaping Horse* at the right with a tiny church spire), Constable directs the sun's rays to the far right edge of the picture. This is also a painting to which he appended lines of verse à la Turner, lines from Thomson's *Seasons* which conclude a passage on light as the source of earthly life: "Far to the dim horizon's utmost verge / Restless, reflects a floating gleam."[8]

With all of this Turnerian trimming, Constable then, in 1831, produced *Salisbury Cathedral from the Meadows* (fig. 60), which is the ultimate development and emphasis of the structure he began with *The Hay Wain*. Here we see the same unsteady foreground of *The Leaping Horse,* with the same upright piles, and the most intense sunlit meadow he ever painted, now under an unsettled sky and literally at the end of a rainbow.[9] The forest is in the same position on the left, and the rectory fulfills the role of Willy Lott's cottage on the edge of the trees, but added as massive reinforcement is the body of the cathedral itself.

The same general structure we have described appears even in *The Chain Pier, Brighton,* the six-footer of 1827 (fig. 61): the length of the pier traversing the middle distance is broken just before it reaches the right edge of the canvas, opening a vista to the sea beyond. Though the break appears at the right, once again Constable adds a closure—a boat to match the church towers, but in this case much closer to the viewer and more prominent in the sketch.

Now let us see what sort of composition this is that Constable has developed and compromised (or emphasized) with such symbols as the tower, the cathedral, and the rainbow. In the opening of the composition to the right (only perfunctorily closed by a church tower or a beam of sunlight) and the emphasis on the obstructing foreground and middleground planes, Constable is deviating from the conventional Claude structure, the model for all literary landscape. A Claude is a pure prospect; and as John Barrell has shown, for both landscape poets and painters this landscape served as an excuse to ignore "the immediate disorganized foreground" in favor of "the malleable area beyond"—or at least to manifest an uneasy tension between what Thomson called "little scenes of art" and the "awful solitude" in which "great nature dwells." This organization, as Barrell notes, is a landscape that holds nature at arm's length, making it safe. In this sense the foreground is ordered by having a few figures who moralize or mythologize the prospect. Using Barrell's terms, "the immediate, disorganized foreground" versus "the malleable area beyond," we can distinguish Turner's need for the "malleable" elements from Constable's concern with the physical reality or density of objects. In Turner's landscapes all we see is prospect; the fringe of foreground incident, which is moral or emblematic, merely allows him to produce a landscape which, though no longer resembling a Claude, retains the general structure and principle or spirit of a Claude.[10]

Constable defines himself in relation to Claude, whom he loved, by painting a relationship between the foreground, where the viewer or painter "stands," and the prospect to the horizon. But he has dropped the coulisse on the right, and he extends the one on the left, turning it into a dense and palpable object in its own right. Both foreground and middle ground are, in Claudian terms, impediments between viewer and horizon: the foreground is an uncertain terrain (water and edge-of-water phenomena), heavily painted, and the middle distance is a rectangle of dense, nearly impenetrable wood reaching from the left about halfway to the right, beyond which opens, in place of Claude's horizon light, a sunlit field extending into the distance, closed by a line of trees on the horizon. Even past the blockages of the foreground and middle distance, there are only one or two interrupted patches of light, which you find your way to perhaps more intensely as a result of the obstacles over which you first have to struggle.[11]

These characteristics are, of course, present to varying extents in the six-foot canvases. But they tend to become more emphatic with each landscape. The picture comes to represent, in Jay Appleton's prospect-refuge terms, the "edge-of-the-wood" phenomenon, "in which the open view on one side is balanced by the woodland on the other";[12] except that Constable does not balance them: he reverses the prospect-refuge symbolism, making the foreground and the woods turbulent and threatening, and the distant clearing a peaceful refuge. These woods in Constable's landscapes never serve as a refuge, seldom beckon one in, in fact must be regarded as a hazard, because the viewer's sense is one of relief and release as his eye finds the opening into sunlit meadows. It is the feeling less of prospect than of reach, and the knowledge that one will be safe and peaceful way out there, not in here close among the turbulence of trees, foliage, and rough, close-up objects, which have to be felt, grasped, and lovingly associated with by the viewer/painter, but in a situation where the general effect is of hazard and uncontrol.

Let me now propose some hypotheses to explain the various elements of this composition which Constable imposes upon his topographical views of the Stour Valley. Beyond mere reaction against the Claudian stereotype, he was certainly influenced by northern European landscape—for example, by Rubens's *Landscape with a View of the Chateau de Steen* (then in the collection of Constable's friend Sir George Beaumont; now in the National Gallery, London, fig. 63), an edge-of-the-woods composition which opens onto a distant sunlit meadow at the same time that it stops the viewer and makes him linger over its sensuous, tactile details. But as the effect intensifies in *The Leaping Horse* and the paintings that followed, we see the more personal influence of those Ruisdael landscapes (two are in the National Gallery, e.g., fig. 64) in which the foreground is dark, obstructed, the whole sky overcast, and the viewer feels the desire to project himself over all the foreground, past the church or castle to one small spot of brilliant sunlit meadow in the distance, where he feels at rest.[13] Constable's description of a Ruisdael, which I have quoted, is immediately preceded in that lecture by his admiration for Ruisdael's painting of English weather—"those solemn days, peculiar to his country and ours, when without storm, large rolling clouds scarcely permit a ray of sunlight to break the shades of the forest."[14] If we can interpret "scarcely" to mean a single ray of sunlight, we come close to a description in words of the composition we have seen, even when Constable avoids the overcast sky.[15]

From the graphic prototypes I turn to a personal configuration. The horizon behind Constable's house in East Bergholt has been picked out by Charles Rhyne from the many topographical views taken from the windows of the house in 1810–15 (figs. 65, 65a).[16] Constable begins to construct in these descriptive views a personal iconography—or at the very least a control system, something on which to anchor his landscapes—from the places associated with his earliest childhood and centering on the house in which he was born (the nexus of all associations, according to Archibald Allison). This house, which Constable used much later as the frontispiece of his mezzotint series reproducing his paintings, *English Landscape* ("though to others it may be void of interest or any associations," he wrote, "to him [i.e., Constable] it is fraught with every endearing recollection"),[17] was a point from which he painted views in all directions.

From one window (sometimes from a higher floor and sometimes a lower) he painted the house's flower and kitchen gardens, beyond them East Berg-holt Common, and across the horizon (from left to right) the windmill where he worked as a youth and first learned to observe the formations of clouds, and then the long, dark rectangle of wood at the right edge of which was the rectory where he first met Maria Bicknell, the sunlit meadow open-ing to the horizon in which they used to rendezvous and walk together, and then another (closing) copse of poplars. Maria's uncle, the rector (Dr. Rhudde, referred to by Constable in the letters as simply "the Doctor") had put a stop to their courtship, because he thought Constable the struggling painter was an unsuitable match. From this window Constable wrote to Maria on 22 June 1812: "I see all those sweet feilds [*sic*] where we have passed so many happy hours together—it is with a melancholy pleasure that I revisit those scenes that once saw us so happy—yet it is gratifying to me to think that the scenes of my boyish days should have witnessed by far the most affecting event of my life." The "scenes of my boyish days" (another version of the "careless boyhood" he spoke of to Fisher) are here mentioned in a passage that is clearly about his present relations with Maria. Two years later, still separated, Constable wrote from the same place:

> I believe we can do nothing worse than indulge in useless sensibility—but I can hardly tell you what I feel at the sight from the window where I am now writing of the feilds in which we have so often walked. A beautifull calm autumnal setting sun is glowing upon the gardens of the Rectory and on adjacent feilds where some of the happiest hours of my life were passed.[18]

From other windows he painted the views of East Bergholt Church and the out-buildings toward the High Street. But it is the configuration looking toward the rectory that is most obsessively repeated and obviously most cathected with the associations of his frustrated love for Maria, his memories of furtive meetings with her (against the wishes of her family), and his separation from her, during which he painted the scene repeatedly, some-times telling her in letters of his feelings as he did so.

The fact that Constable painted from within the house looking out through windows is probably significant for two reasons. For one, he could move up and down. If we compare the finished oil in Ipswich with the pencil sketch made from a lower window (V & A), we see that in the latter there is almost no meadow visible between the vicarage and the nearby tree in the kitchen garden. The blockage consists not only of the tree immediately below him, which from a higher floor can be seen over but from this lower window blocks out the meadow, but also of the intervening walls, fences, houses, trees, and gardens.[19] In the garden, with his back turned to us (and Constable), is a laborer digging in the soil.

Though the window itself is never shown,[20] it has to be, with the knowl-edge of time and place (sometimes written on the painting) and the letters to

Maria, part of the picture's emotional context, the refuge from which Constable can see without being seen. What we derive, among other things, is a sense of his house as a triangulation station, a refuge from which different readings can be taken of certain hostile aspects of the outside world. We receive the experience of someone who is looking out of a refuge/prison to contrasting areas of sun and shade, freshness and staleness—which for him take on the significance of present and past. From these windows Constable made the sketches that were (as he wrote to Fisher) "nothing but one state of mind—that which you were in at the time."[21] Several years later, in a London studio far from the familiar scene, distant views of Flatford or Stratford Mill were transformed into landscapes comprising "more than one state of mind," which nevertheless held to the composition of that one segment of the horizon line seen from the upper floor of the house. The place of the rectory, for example, may be taken by Willy Lott's cottage with its associations of home, marriage, and so on—or, superimposed, with associations of the rectory—but in any case, with ambivalent feelings of both refuge and hazard, peace and threat. It can also be replaced by a canal barge or by a cathedral. But some form of it remains in the same relationship to the rectangle of woods on the edge of the meadow, imbued with the same ambivalent feelings.

In the letters to Maria, Constable is consistently equating temporal and spatial relationships: "let us look forward to the time," he writes, ". . . when we shall have the inexpressible happiness of seeing each other again." Using space to represent a plunge back into the past, he "revisits" those "sweet feilds" in which they passed "so many happy hours together," and the letters are punctuated with references to "so far as we are apart"; "it is really an age since I saw you"; "we are two hundred miles apart and . . . it is a month since I had the happiness of a letter from you—one line to say that you are well would be some alleviation of this wretched absence."[22]

The landscape serves the purpose of elegy, filling up the absence Constable felt so keenly. Landscape and Maria are so closely linked in the letters as to be almost indistinguishable. "How much real delight I have had with the study of landscape this summer," he starts out. "Either I am myself improved in 'the art of seeing Nature' . . . or Nature has unveiled her beauties to me with a less fastidious hand." The "delight" he has in landscape painting is here related to the unveiling of a female Nature's charms (who is "less fastidious" than in the past). The act of painting he connects with other "delights" associated with female beauties unveiled (intermingled with the emblem of Nature or Truth unveiled by the artist). But, he then adds, returning to Maria, "I am writing this nonsense to you with a really sad heart, when I think what would be my happiness could I have this enjoyment with you. Then indeed," he concludes, "would my mind be calm to contemplate the endless beauties of this happy country."[23] Then, in different mood, painting becomes the obstacle that stands between them—the profession that is distrusted by the Doctor and Maria's parents: "In several letters I have omitted to say any thing about painting or of what I have been doing in that way—but it is a subject on which I cannot write to you with any pleasure. It seems to be our greatest enemy but nevertheless I love it more and more dayly."[24]

We can now add to the meadow's associations of haymaking and cattle-grazing, bucolic love trysts. Although Constable has displaced the breasts and buttocks that Adrian Stokes sees in Turner's landscapes to a topography of meeting-places, he is nevertheless describing and painting a landscape of desire. The femininity of landscape was a convention he would have breathed in with the air (see above, p. 10) but he reduces the conventional symbols to the quiet, sunlit, beautiful meadow and the active, male shapes of the woodland in the foreground.

Thus Constable, when he monumentalizes, takes a particular place that is highly cathected for him and imposes its forms on other places to make them equally important or—as it must have seemed to him—universal. But he also adds to the exact representation he sought certain general principles of landscape, which he evidently hoped would not lessen the sense of "English Landscape" or of a particular Constable landscape. Though he claimed not to be interested in general principles—the ideas of the "beautiful" and the "picturesque"—but only in a particular place and time, in fact the six-footers show him moving for reinforcement and emphasis from one of these categories to the other. They served as equivalents to his own emotional state of remembrance.

We have discussed the middle and far distances, which we may regard as the beautiful meadow held at arm's length and blocked by shapes in the foreground that are, in a small way, sublime. But the aesthetic, generic category that should correspond to his emergent composition is "picturesque," a type that is "more concerned with the individual features than with creating a general structure to contain them."[25] The picturesque had at first merely introduced (through William Gilpin and others) rules of roughness and irregularity, intricacy and surprising juxtapositions of detail, into the conventional Claude structure. But in Constable's paintings the "picturesque" theory contributes to a situation in which the gnarled and twisted tree, the "picturesque" object, dominates the picture. The Claudian coulisse, no longer framing the prospect, has been moved in toward the center and foreground itself to become the subject. Constable's *Dell in Helmingham Park* (1830?, Tate) is nothing but a huge tree branch emphasized by the remarkable tactility of the paint; many of his oil sketches are, in this sense, "picturesque."[26] Constable is a genuinely picturesque artist in his concern with objects—rough and irregular, mossy and slimy—which are felt, grasped, and associated with by the viewer. But the viewer is always permitted a fragmentary prospect, a small escape route to the horizon. We might say that Constable, replacing the Claudian structure with picturesque blockage, nevertheless projects us over the boats, laboring bargemen, weedy river-banks, and mossy locks to relief in a limited prospect revealed beyond.

It will be useful to examine by contrast one of the most accurate of Constable's topographical paintings, *The Stour Valley and Dedham Church* (R.A. 1815?, fig. 66). The novel feature is in the left foreground. As the equivalent of the kitchen garden in the view that included the skyline of woods and vicarage (fig. 65), here we see a large pile which, in the terminology of Stour Valley farmers, is a muck heap, and in Constable's own words, a "large cow-turd." There are sketches for the scene which include the muck heap, and so it is quite likely that it was actually there when Constable drew the scene. It also serves a technical repoussoir effect, thrusting yet farther away the details of the valley itself. But it is not merely a formal element. It is being dug into, used by farm laborers who are putting the muck in a cart to take it down and manure the fields in the valley we see spread out before us.[27] The picture was painted for a friend, Miss Philadelphia Godfrey, daughter of the local lord of the manor, who was marrying Thomas Fitz-hugh.

In so far as this pile is manure, it has now been transformed into rich fertilizer, overgrown with creeping green vines and little clumps of plants. Though slightly unusual as a symbol for a wedding picture, its relationship is obvious to the ordered, distant fields which thrive on the disposition of dung and refuse, and temporally will follow from it. This obstruction in the foreground will lead, with seasonal change, to all that beauty and utility; and the relationship is essentially the same as in the way cut through to the fields and the haymaking in *The Hay Wain;* or the way to the distant meadow beyond the garden being tilled by the laborer in *Golding Constable's Kitchen Garden.*

In literary terms, the structure is georgic, that most characteristic of eighteenth-century English poetic forms, whose potential extended from the complex *paysage moralisé* of *Windsor Forest* and *Grongar Hill* down to the sheer farming manual of *Sugar-Cane, The Hop Garden,* and *The Fleece.*[28] In georgic terms, the foreground of this picture consists of clumps of decomposition and decay like the bovine corpse of Virgil's fourth *Georgic* out of which bees and nations regenerate. Constable's high viewpoint makes the valley beyond appear ordered, causally related to the foreground muck heap, and he crowns—or seals—the relationship with a church tower. This relationship is an adumbration of his general arrangement of the picturesque object, of extreme tactility, of broken paint, a representation of lush disorder, *and* (on the other end of Constable's verbal dash—) the distant countryside— panoramic, organized, painted in smooth, continuous strokes.

The georgic is, of course, only a literary reflection of the age-old reliance of the farmer on the rhythm of the seasons that has replaced the eternal spring of the pastoral (in graphic terms, the Claudian) Golden Age, by ploughing, sowing, and reaping—most dramatically by regeneration out of a maggoty corpse. It is well though, with Constable (especially in light of his later paintings) to remember the political dimension of the georgic poem: the symbol of regeneration becomes the rusted sword or the soldier's rotting corpse turned up by the plough, and civil war always casts a shadow over harvest, as winter does over spring (Constable wrote in *English Landscape,* "the uncertainty of spring is proverbial").

In a letter to Maria, as it happens, Constable expressed his acerbic view of the marriage of Philadelphia Godfrey to Mr. Fitzhugh, who is (Constable tells Maria, from whom he is still at this time sadly separated) "extremely rich . . . and a college friend of Mr. Godfrey's. I believe he is near thirty years older than Miss G. but in the plenitude of his wealth that was not *thought* of. He is a most gentlemanly and agreeable man," Constable adds with how much irony it is hard to tell, "and I am told there is very great attachment between them."[29] He is recognizing the parallel between Maria's situation and Philadelphia's, and the familiar terms of loss and distance in time and space creep into his description of the painting commission. It is to be "a picture of 'the Valley' for Mr. Fitzhugh (a *present* for Miss G. *to contemplate in London*), which I think *you* would like could *you* see it" (emphasis my supposition). He turns immediately to the parallel subject of himself and Maria: "fate is still savage . . . I lament every moment of my life the absence of your society and feel the loss of it in my mind and heart—but it is for you that my heart is rent," he concludes, returning to the equation of her and Philadelphia.[30] I suggest that Constable is finding his georgic structure confirmed in experience—and if we had an equivalent letter to John Fisher, we might find a ribald connection between the muck heap and the money of the elderly husband, if not the husband himself. It is the "muck heap" that makes the order of marriage, harvested fields, and even the commission of the painting possible.

If the Philadelphia Godfrey story confirms in words something of the sense of relationship we feel between Constable's occluded foreground and distant prospect, we can see the situation even more clearly four years later, in May 1819, by which time Maria and John have finally been reunited and married. Constable had just completed his first six-footer, *The White Horse,* his most ambitious painting to date, and though it had been well received, he was being urged (as we have seen) to give his landscape more "soul" or "senti- ment." At this point he made one of his infrequent visits to East Bergholt to settle some family affairs. In particular, "the Doctor" (as he referred to Dr. Rhudde, Maria's uncle who had delayed their marriage) was dying. Consta- ble arrived in the village "just as the bell was tolling for the Doctor"—and he noted the coincidence that he died on his (Constable's) mother's birthday (which he got confused—it was in fact her *wedding* day). He wrote to Maria: "But I will endeavour to forget those unhappy divisions & violent agitations which were real afflictions to both of them [for which read "us," as in his own marriage] in this world, trusting they are now in [a] scene where nothing but peace & love & joy can reign."[31] Note well the escape from the "unhappy divisions & violent agitations" to the "scene where nothing but peace & love & joy can reign," the verbal equivalent of that distant sunlit meadow.

To the subject of Dr. Rhudde's death Constable juxtaposes the landscape of East Bergholt: "Every tree seems full of blossom of some kind & the surface of the ground seems quite lovely—every step I take & on whatever object I turn my eye that sublime expression in the Scripture 'I am the resurrection & the life' &c, seems verified about me." In short, now that he is happily married, he returns to East Bergholt and reads into the death of his old enemy, Dr. Rhudde, the experiential structure he is about to impose on his paintings of the Stour Valley: a complex relationship between death, decay, fertilization, spring, and resurrection.

First, there was the vicarage at the edge-of-the-wood in the middle distance, beyond which stretched the open meadow. Then there was the foreground compost heap, which connects causally, metaphorically, and generically (as georgic) with the valley. In the Boston *Stour Valley and Dedham Church,* with muck heap, cultivated valley, and church tower, the fructifying aspect was primary, and renewal was the subject. The situation becomes more complex in the canal-lock pictures of the 1820s. Here the foreground, a raised towpath or canal bank, which is made to look like the same ridge overlooking the Stour Valley, is both a water-channel (as rich in plant-life as the compost heap) and a barrier, consisting of upright posts and crossbeams.

The meadow becomes the object of perception on the other end of an ever more tenuous and difficult route. From *The Hay Wain* and *Stratford Mill* to *The Leaping Horse* and the paintings that followed, the painter moves from a fairly high (a georgic or topographical) vantage point down to a lower one, at or below ground level, which enlarges the occlusion and emphasizes the viewer's entrapment and need to get out over the occluded area to the distant meadow. The meadow itself is broken up by rivers and other divisions, or becomes a sheet of water. The lower vantage point is now intensified, perhaps melodramatized, by the obstacles added in the foreground. The picturesque muck heap has become not only the slimy, rotting riverbank but a canal lock in close-up, literally a locked passageway guarded by a gate and an army of fence posts. These posts, and the transposed willow stump (especially the strange long stick in the foreground), are assertively phallic barriers.[32]

As the 1820s proceeded, the barrier aspect was emphasized by its exaggerated size, the spectator's lower viewpoint, and the heavy impasto of paint that seems to draw it closer to the viewer and keep him farther away from the sunlit meadow. *The Leaping Horse* prepares us for the enlarged vertical barrier of the ruined tower in *Hadleigh Castle,* a more conventional version (perhaps the historical counterpart) of the rotting foreground shapes, but also a more threatening one, lacking the potential for georgic renewal in organic decomposition. With the Gothic trimming, the picturesque becomes overtly sublime, a towering obstruction to a beautiful spot of rest in the far distance, prevented by a sublime power symbol, the ruined tower.[33] The low vantage point and the frantic brushwork of *The Leaping Horse,* the horse itself, of course, a Burkean symbol of the sublime, has become a view from a height only to accentuate the jagged terrain that offers no place to stand, the scattered human figures, the tower broken but still blocking, and the precipitous chasm. The whole distant prospect, sea and all, remains chaotic and unformulable, with only that one tiny spot remaining an idyllic place of limited, isolated sunlit space.

Finally, we come to *The Cenotaph to Sir Joshua Reynolds at Coleorton* (R. A. 1836, fig. 67), in which there is nothing but foreground—a very shallow space with one tiny clearing and the usual spot of sunlight, but now completely closed in, a cul-de-sac in an otherwise impenetrable wall of trees. At the center of this closed space is the monument to the dead genius of English painting, here conflating Constable's homage to Sir Joshua Reynolds and Sir George Beaumont.[34] The only opening is the small patch of sky directly overhead. The paint surface is now even more tactile and dense, but depthless, a wall rather than an indicator of spatial relations and demarcations.

CHAPTER 13 🦯
ADDITION AND
SUBTRACTION:
LANDSCAPE AS DIVESTED
HISTORY PAINTING

These are the paintings Constable was to sum up in the lectures on landscape he delivered in 1836. The Ruisdael winter scene is not the only model he offers there. As his example of how "landscape is the child of history"[1]— that is, of history painting—he singles out Titian's *Martyrdom of St. Peter Martyr* (fig. 68), which I suspect was in his mind when he painted *Dedham Vale* (R.A. 1828, fig. 69), and his few other upright compositions (including, though reversed, *The Cornfield*).[2] The heavy, dramatic weight on one side of the composition offered an alternative to the placid Claude composition. Titian's painting was the great exemplar of landscape expressing the violent emotions of the human actors in a history painting (we have seen Turner's reverent use of it).

Constable draws attention in Titian's painting to the "union of history and landscape" in a scene which takes place, he tells us, "on the skirts of a forest,

and the time verging towards the close of the day. . . . The choice of a low
horizon greatly aids the grandeur of the composition." He comments on how
in the foreground "we are startled by the rush of an assassin on two helpless
travellers, monks, one of whom is struck down, and the other wounded and
flying in the utmost terror"—violence, most immediately terrified flight,
seen from a low vantage and reflected in the swirling movement of the trees.
"We see a deed of horror perpetrated with the utmost energy of action," he
tells us, "in a scene hitherto one of stillness and repose." And, he concludes
(once again implying that verbal dash), "At the top of the picture, through
the loftiest branches of the trees, a bright and supernatural light strikes down
on the dying man, who sees in the glory a vision of angels bearing the
emblems of martyrdom; and illuminating in its descent the stems and
foliage, contrasts with the shadowy gloom of the wood."[3] The edge-of-the-
wood phenomenon, the low horizon, the energetic and chaotic foreground,
even the top of the picture with the area of "bright supernatural light" (the
meadow effect reinforced by sun rays and rainbows)—all are here. Constable
is describing the Ruisdael scene (to which he also refers in the lectures), and
his own, in terms of one of the best known history paintings.

Deaths and martyrdoms are the subjects Constable chose to illustrate his
thesis about the origin of landscape painting.[4] Notice that his examples are
not mythological; they are from the Christian tradition, but they are not the
Nativity or even Christ Healing the Sick. The most generic examples he
adduces are the Passion, the Crucifixion, and the Entombment:

> The cross must be fixed in the ground, there must be a sky, the shades of night
> must envelop the garden (the scene of the agony), and a more awful darkness
> the Crucifixion; while rocks and trees naturally made a part of the accompani-
> ments of the sepulchre. Here, then, however rude and imperfect, we are to look
> for the origin of landscape. It was first used as an assistant in conveying
> sentiment, and being found completely successful, was cultivated by succeed-
> ing painters, until at length it became a distinct branch of art.[5]

Constable has simply *removed* the history from a history painting—leaving
the landscape which was the background of the Passion, Crucifixion, or
Entombment. "Landscape" is history painting with the history (or the literary myth, the human protagonists) removed. The history is not, as Turner
would have it, added in a corner to legitimate the landscape. The landscape is
arranged and activated *as if* there were heroic figures contesting within it,
violently and passionately, and natural shapes replace the foreground human
ones, while the same escape route points to a distant spot of peace which
Constable described in his favorite historical landscape as "a vision of
angels."[6]

However, as he said in one of those 1814 letters to Maria, "I love the trees,
the feilds, better than I do the people."[7] Who *are* those people and what is

the action he is omitting or displacing onto nature? He explains in the lecture how Saint Peter's zeal in carrying out his religious duties as a Dominican inquisitor "had given great offence to a powerful family, who employed an assassin to waylay and murder him." His reason for Saint Peter's martyrdom (unnecessary to specify in the circumstances) sounds rather like a version of his own situation vis à vis "the Doctor" on the one hand, and the Royal Academicians on the other, intensified by the fact that Maria was by this time dead.[8] The painter too is the martyr: even Titian, he remarks, "was by no means high in reputation when he produced this great [landscape] work, and so inadequate was the remuneration he received for it . . . ," and so forth, describing a plight he also attributes to Domenichino, another of his examples of historical landscape painter.[9] Constable's point that great landscape painting was never understood is another case of the linking of his landscape painting and the enforced separation of lovers that runs through the letters to Maria and shapes his view of the external world.

I suspect that the tension in these final paintings is between what is absent and what is present: between the crucifixion and the disturbing landscape. It is the same sort of tension we have felt in the relationship between what Constable says and what he shows. When he *talks* in public about his landscape painting, he talks in terms of origins—he wants to trace landscape back to its beginnings—and does so by still finding a place for his unliterary landscape in the tradition of history, as if there were no other way, as in praising Ruisdael's *Winter Landscape* he could not avoid maintaining the history/story/literature metaphor of narrative ("telling a story"). He cannot get out of his head the idea that pictures and poems are the same thing. He is not willing to talk about his landscape in formal terms because these are not really *his* terms (as they are, say, Gainsborough's), and he is not *able* to talk in his own terms, which are perhaps of desire and could only be put into words in his letters to Maria. Thus he leaves us feeling a disturbing tension between his need to express a personal image, a landscape of his affections, and his need to align his work with an artistic tradition (make it history painting) and with conventional modes of symbolization.

Just at the time of the lectures, Constable was also exhibiting at the Royal Academy his painting of *The Cenotaph to Sir Joshua Reynolds at Coleorton* (fig. 67). This is in one sense another tarted-up landscape, for Constable has added the busts of Michelangelo and Raphael, inventing them ("to add a further dimension to his tribute to past art, perhaps even to suggest a pedigree for British art," as one critic has put it).[10] One need only compare the Royal Academy painting with the pencil sketch of 1823, which like the oil sketch of *The Cornfield* is empty, unpopulated: there is no clearing in the forest, no pair of busts, no stag.

The stag is present, in relation to the three artifacts, as a natural element, but the more striking feature is the absence—for in fact it is one of those divested symbols to which Constable refers in the lecture on the origin of landscape painting. The stag is the remains of a *Legend of St. Eustace,* from which the crucifixion that appears between its antlers (literally a crucifixion, not a crucifix or cross) has been removed. The stag is very close to the one in Dürer's celebrated engraving (fig. 70), but its hind legs are in slightly more extended motion and its head turns toward the viewer. Dürer's stag also stands, as Constable's does, between two bunches of tree trunks, but as only one part of an extremely complex composition: he is high in the upper right of the picture space. The echo of Dürer applies only if we place ourselves in the position of the other missing element of the legend, Placidas (the Roman general who has been persecuting Christians, is out hunting, and is about to shoot the stag). If we regard the protagonist as displaced to the position of the viewer, toward whom the stag is turning his head, then we have to recall that in the legend he spoke: "Placidas, why pursuest thou me?" At which point Placidas fell from his horse like Saul/Paul and was converted, becoming Eustace.[11]

I must, however, mention two facts: that besides Dürer's well-known engraving there were not many representations of Saint Eustace (or Saint Hubert) available to Constable, and those were largely drawings. The legend of Saint Eustace was not a major referent for nineteenth-century Englishmen.[12] Second, there *is* a representation of a story concerning a stag in Constable's own oeuvre—in fact, the one history subject in his *English Landscape* is an illustration of Jaques and the stag from *As You Like It,* II.i. (fig. 71). What Constable would have had in mind was the print after Hodges's illustration of the scene in the *Boydell Shakespeare* (vol. 1, 1805, pl. 25), which is essentially an enlivened or populated landscape. In Shakespeare's text, the First Lord is describing to Duke Senior a scene involving Jaques in the Forest of Arden. Jaques, the melancholy conservationist, sees a wounded stag with (he says) "Big round tears / Cours[ing] one another down his innocent nose / In piteous chase"—"augmenting" an adjacent brook with its tears. This stag must be Shakespeare's (or Jaques's) memory of the stag who speaks to Saint Eustace, but whose words apparently were not heeded in this case. Jaques, the First Lord explains, "moralizes" the spectacle "into a thousand similes." More specifically, he interprets it as a man abandoned in his adversity: "being there alone / Left and abandoned of his velvet friends," he is allegorized by Jaques as "misery doth part / The flux of company. . . . Sweep on, you fat and greasy citizens," says Jaques; " 'Tis just the fashion. Wherefore do you look / Upon that poor and broken bankrupt there?"[13]

When Constable introduces the stag into *The Cenotaph,* we may say that he turns back to the Dürer representation of the saint's legend itself but continues to show the secularized, un-"moralized" version—yet retaining the memory of Jaques's particular application of the moralization to himself, including a pond which may carry over from the brook "augmented" by the tears of Jaques's stag.

But another intermediary in the graphic tradition must have occurred to the contemporary spectator: Claude's *Ascanius Killing the Stag* (Oxford, Ashmolean), which was in London by the end of the eighteenth century. It was this killing of a stag that started the war between the Trojans and Latins: a scene of ominous portent, as opposed to the cheerful scenes Turner painted which, like the rainbow bubbles of *The Deluge,* were nevertheless "fallacies of hope." Claude's stag, reversed, is in approximately the pose of Constable's, but the resemblance to Dürer's stag remains stronger and, I think, primary.

There is yet another intermediary, however; this one literary. There can be little doubt that Constable knew the passage in Thomson's "Autumn" which brings to a close his meditation (Jaques-like) on English hunting (ll. 426 ff.):

> The stag, too, singled from the herd, where long
> He rang'd the branching monarch of the shades,
> Before the tempest drives.

He is expelled from the "shady depth," "and sobbing sees / The glades, mild opening to the golden day" (i.e., the clearing). He is, in short, Jaques's stag:

> he stands at bay;
> And puts his last weak refuge in despair.
> The big round tears run down his dappled face;
> He groans in anguish; while the growling pack,
> Blood-happy, hang at his fair-jutting chest,
> And mark his beauteous checkuer'd sides with gore.

If Constable's *Jaques and the Stag* directly illustrates *As You Like It,* then his *Cenotaph* can be thought of as subtracting Jaques; or as illustrating Thomson's poem, which has eliminated Jaques by transforming him into the presiding poet.

Have we lost Saint Eustace along the way? Perhaps, but we have seen a layering process in which the legend of Saint Eustace, Shakespeare's *As You Like It,* Claude's *Ascanius Killing the Stag,* and Thomson's *Seasons* have built up a tradition which Constable finally brings to a vivid fulfillment.[14]

The Cenotaph was painted for the 1836 Royal Acacemy exhibition, the last year it was held in the old Somerset House quarters, and so it was an appropriate homage to Sir Joshua Reynolds, whose palette Constable had donated to the Royal Academy. Thus the painting is primarily an elegy to Reynolds and to the end of an era—perhaps (like Hogarth's last print, *Tailpiece*) to the end of things in general. In this context the stag is a symbol of majesty trapped—dying because of man's hounding him to death. He is not the "monarch of the shades" but the stag "at bay"; he is not Reynolds but Constable himself, standing in the ambience of Reynolds, Raphael, and

Michelangelo. The message to Placidas as well as Jaques, I suppose, is addressed to the Royal Academicians and other spectators at the exhibition of 1836, those people who have disdained Constable's landscape painting.[15]

But rather than the paranoid undertones, we should stress the genuine sense of suppression here—not repression, because Constable is quite conscious of what is being withheld. The story is implicit, framed by the busts of Michelangelo and Raphael, charged with all of its emotion, but without the literary or symbolic elements, which have been removed, leaving the landscape to speak for itself. The tension in these final paintings of the 1830s is between what is absent and what is present; between the crucifixion and conversion that are withheld and the symbolic busts (garden sculpture of undeniable probability in a park like Beaumont's) of Michelangelo and Raphael that are added. And these are joined in a setting which did already contain a symbolic cenotaph in a park full of personal memories for Constable of friendship and patronage.

Looking all the way back to 1819, we can conclude that instead of telling a story, Constable either goes to the memories of his childhood, constructs a story of the weather (which corresponds to the childhood associations but becomes increasingly dramatic and anxious), or paints actual ruins which carry their own implicit story, evoking a past, an absent story. Or he takes a legendary scene and subtracts the legendary elements, leaving the charged setting. This practice does not really contradict his opinion that the artist should begin "by study equally legitimately founded in art" but then match it against nature. He takes fragments of a Dürer or a Titian but transforms them, by divestiture, into what he calls a natural landscape.

In *The Cenotaph* Constable places Raphael opposite Michelangelo. In 1795 he had made a series of large pen drawings after Nicolas Dorigny's engravings of the Raphael Cartoons in Hampton Court Palace. We know he also made trips to Hampton Court to see the originals.[16] I wish to suggest that from these paradigmatic history paintings, these central works of High Renaissance art, fixed in his memory by his own copies of them, Constable (consciously or unconsciously) chose the long rectangular shape and the simple planar arrangement of masses in his six-foot landscapes of the Stour Valley. The familiar shapes of the Cartoons offer yet another explanation for his composition of the six-foot canvases and are, in the sense he proposed in his lectures of 1836, history painting transformed into landscape.

Raphael's designs in the Cartoons, as Sidney Freedberg has written, are "distinguished by a concentration, a deliberation, and a monumental force of statement that are different from any prior mode of Raphael's expression,"[17] and indeed of any other Renaissance artist. The scenes Constable uses are not the axially balanced ones (*The Death of Ananias* and *Paul and the Proconsul*) but the more directional designs, primarily "*Feed My Sheep*" (fig. 72), *The*

Sacrifice at Lystra, and *Paul Preaching at Athens,* and to a lesser degree, *The Miraculous Draught of Fishes.* In these Cartoons there is a large, roughly rectangular crowd of people assembled densely on one side. The space that separates this crowd of unbelievers (in *Paul Preaching* and *The Sacrifice*) from Christ or an apostle on the other side gives great emphasis to the interval, which opens up the closed scene. The masses of the people and the single numinous figure are set out in strata parallel to the picture plane, and they tend to crowd the picture space except for the interval—which opens a prospect to the horizon. There is, as Freedberg notes, a resemblance to classical relief style, "a rectangular density of figures in one clear plane, or subdivided into planar strata."

The significant fact to remember is that Constable copied Dorigny's engravings, not the Cartoons themselves. Dorigny reversed the Cartoons, recreating the left-to-right reading structure of the tapestries for which the Cartoons were made. Constable follows Dorigny, placing his large rectangular mass of foliage on the left (reinforced by a barge or building, ultimately by a cathedral) and the interval on the right. He omits the apostle, the agent of conversion or miracle, or rather translates him into, not just the empty numinous space, but sometimes a tiny religious symbol, a steeple (or only a tree). The important impression is of the massing on the left and the opening from this claustrophobic, blocking area into the distant fields—extensive in *"Feed My Sheep"* and *The Hay Wain,* more difficult of access in *Paul Preaching* and *The Leaping Horse.* The composition explains something of the monumental effect of these landscapes, and it can be glossed by Constable's words about landscape being history painting with the story removed, leaving only the charged setting. The effect is very different from Turner's landscapes, on the one hand, and from Claude's, on the other—though it is possible to see how Constable used the Claude forms as the basis for a rationalization of the Raphaelesque ones.

CHAPTER 14 🌾
ENGLISH LANDSCAPE

Addition is the mode of the mezzotint prints of his paintings Constable published in 1830–33 under the title *Various Subjects of Landscape, Characteristic of English Scenery.*[1] Added are verbal commentary and poetic analogies. We have to begin, however, by noticing that in at least some cases subtraction was also involved. Most of the paintings reproduced in the series are the small oil sketches. From the expansive, monumental versions of these sketches in the six-footers Constable moves to compressed chiaroscuro versions in the *English Landscape,* which simplify them into dramatic contrasts of light and shade. Thus, instead of *The Hay Wain,* Constable reproduces *The Mill Stream*, and many of the most striking works are the direct topo-graphical sketches which are in fact—as he may have realized—his most radical conceptions. When he does include a six-footer, the result (as with *Hadleigh Castle* or *View on the Stour*) is a rather contracted version of the original, probably taken from the oil sketches rather than the final product, but in any case looking out of place alongside the vignettelike sketches.

The six-footers built in their own "poetry," but the small on-the-spot views—which in *English Landscape* he presents as the very essence of his landscape vision—did not speak for themselves. They had to be poeticized for general consumption.

It is not difficult to imagine Constable's response to the review of the first installment in *The Spectator* of 25 February 1831, which complained of the "extreme blackness and coarseness" of execution in the mezzotints, neverthe-less conceding that "their rough execution we do not so much object to, as it appears to imitate the style of painting in the originals . . . these hasty mez-zotint scrapings display great feeling . . . and contain some strikingly natural and simple compositions. We fear however, that their manner of execution will prevent their due appreciation by the multitude." "Many can read print & cannot read mezzotint," as Constable later remarked. Therefore the letter-press was added to "help, like spices & sweet sauce to get down bad venison." There would be, he said, as much in the way of "descriptions—quotations—poetic display—and principles of art, &c, &c . . . and as much moral feeling as possible."[2] His introduction was included in the final in-stallment of the series issued in July 1832, but almost immediately he revised it and wrote additional essays for the plates to accompany the second edition.

That *English Landscape* meant a great deal to Constable is plain from a reading of his letters to his engraver, David Lucas, and from the fact that he stopped work on the six-footers while launching the series. It should also be noticed that the project followed closely upon the death of Maria in 1828 and his election as Royal Academician in 1829. He must have felt this to be his final effort to vindicate himself as an artist and to make his point about specifically English landscape.

The series itself was conceived in the context of Claude's *Liber Veritatis* and Turner's *Liber Studiorum*. Constable owned a copy of Earlom's engravings of the *Liber Veritatis* (1777) and in his introduction takes up many of the same issues discussed by Earlom, assuming the opposite side of the argument. For example, his assertion that an English landscape can be so "embodied by highest principles as to become classical art" was a response to such state-ments as Earlom's, "We are, without doubt, far more obliged to those artists, who set before us such objects as our imagination cannot readily supply . . . who transport the scenes of distant countries to our own." Turner is the other opponent, whose *Liber Stupidorum* (as Constable called it) had presented academic landscape, with classical and pastoral staffage in dramatic and artificial poses, depicting ideal scenes, even when labeled a specific site.

Constable was reacting against these examples of idealized, academic landscapes arranged according to generic categories.[3] He must, however, have read as support for his own view of himself Earlom's curious opinion that Claude was too close to nature, that his style was "altogether the *rural* style of Landscape . . . he possessed, as it were, her [Nature's] genuine character at every hour of the day." And he must have read with interest Earlom's opening to his introduction: "There is too, sometimes, a close connection between the Life of the Artist, and his Performances. . . ." He began his *English Landscape* with the image of his own home in East Bergholt and included strongly autobiographical paintings, and he argued—to appropriate Earlom's words but not his sense—that "it is not, indeed, from the exactness of the imitation alone, but from the nature of the thing imitated also, that pleasure is derived." While Earlom meant distant and elevated subjects, Constable meant the area of his own "careless childhood," and a number of his statements show that he felt that "exactness of the imitation" was insufficient. Chiaroscuro, he wrote defending the choice of his own house as a subject, can give "an interest to a subject by no means attractive." To a lady who had called an engraving of a house "an ugly thing" he replied that "there is nothing ugly; I never saw an ugly thing in my life: for the form of an object be what it may,—light, shade, and perspective will always make it beautiful."[4]

What we notice in perusing the *English Landscape* mezzotints and letterpress are the many ways in which Constable emphasizes the personal, autobiographical aspect of his series, almost as if he were producing a graphic equivalent of Wordsworth's *Prelude*. The epigraph used in both the 1832 and 1833 versions of the title page is taken from Virgil's second *Georgic* (ll. 485–86):

Rura mihi: et rigui placeant in vallibus amnes,
Flumina amem, sylvasque, inglorius.

[Let my delight be the country; and the running streams
  amid the dells
May I love the waters and the woods, though fame be lost.]

The lines are appropriate, for he is producing georgic, not pastoral landscapes, but the particular lines he has chosen appear at the point where Virgil introduces the first-person singular ("Me vero . . .") in order to explain his purpose in writing georgic poetry. The epigraph indicates not only Constable's devotion to rural scenery but also his knowledge that in doing so he has personally sacrificed popularity and success (*inglorius*).[5]

Of the other epigraphs alongside the Virgil, the one from Ovid is particularly revealing if placed in its context in the *Tristia* (III. 10, 61–62):

> Vinctis post tergum capta lacertis
> *Respiciens* frustra *rura, laremque suum*

> [Some are driven into captivity with their arms bound behind them, looking
> back in vain at their countryside and their homes.]

The italicized words are Constable's epigraph: "Looking back at their countryside and homes." He has indicated a spiritual return home as the way to
discover rural landscape. These lines become, in the text to *Golding Constable's House,* "and he dwells on the retrospect of those happy days," with
"retrospect" recalling *respiciens.* He has, however, omitted the crucial word
frustra, and thus the context in which the men are driven into captivity and
their attempts to recall their homes are unsuccessful. The whole passage
describes the precise predicament out of which Constable produces his intense images of a lost idyllic past centered around his home.

The third epigraph also misquotes its source, in this case Wordsworth's
"Thanksgiving Ode" (ll. 140–44):

> "O England! dearer far than life is dear,
>   If I forget thy prowess, never more
> Be thy ungrateful son allowed to hear
>   Thy green leaves rustle, or thy torrents roar!"—

"England" should read "Britain," and the second line in Wordsworth's poem
reads:

>   If one there be
>   Of all thy progeny
> Who can forget thy prowess, . . .

The misquotation aligns the passage with Constable's own title, "*English*
Landscape," and the conflation of the three lines into one casts the speech
into the first person, a reinforcement of the Virgil passage, attributing the
love of the English landscape to himself and asserting once again that this is a
personal, indeed autobiographical work.

As we have seen, Constable begins the series with his own house in East
Bergholt: "a spot to which he [the artist] must naturally feel so attached; and
though to others it may be void of interest or any associations, to him it is
fraught with every endearing recollection." Then he takes up the subject of
chiaroscuro, which he had used to give "by richness of Light and Shadow, an
interest to a subject otherwise by no means attractive." He then gives the
house's history, quoting from *The Beauties of England and Wales* the rest of his
familiar cast of characters:

> 'South of the church is "Old Hall," the Manor House, the seat of Peter God-
> frey, Esq., which, with the residence of the rector, The Reverend Dr. Rhudde,

Mrs. Roberts, and Golding Constable, Esq., give this place an appearance far superior to that of most villages.'

A footnote brings in the other two paternal figures important to his personal and artistic development, Bishop Fisher and Sir George Beaumont.

Constable supports the personal validation, however, with every other sort of verbal element that can justify his visual images. "Spring," for example, allows him to take up "natural history" in describing his Stour Valley landscape precisely as he did Ruisdael's *Winter Landscape* in the lectures.[6] But then he also adds poetry for further validation. The skies, he begins by explaining, "are so particularly marked in the hail-squalls at this time of year" because "the clouds accumulate in very large and dense masses, and from their loftiness seem to move but slowly; immediately upon these large clouds appear numerous opaque patches, which, however, are only small clouds passing rapidly before them, and consisting of isolated pieces, detached probably from the larger cloud." But the passage ends: "The ploughman 'leaving o'er the shining share,' the sower 'stalking with measured step the neighbouring fields,' are conspicuous figures in the vernal landscape"—and we almost automatically substitute "verbal" for "vernal."

Every realistic, natural-science history of the weather has to be poeticized. As in the lectures, Constable says that painting is not a branch of literature, morality, or philosophy, but of science, and yet he fills the notes to his mezzotints with quotations from every relevant poem that said what he now thinks he is attempting (or had attempted) to represent in his landscape. The poems (including Wordsworth's) are imposed after the fact, based on similarities gleaned to support the status quo, in a final attempt (his double aim) to win a public for his and England's landscape.

The graphic, as opposed to the verbal, intensification is carried out through the use of chiaroscuro—which, however, he also feels he must verbalize. His aim, he writes in the introduction, is

> to arrest the more abrupt and transient appearances of the Chiar'oscuro in Nature; to shew its effect in the most striking manner, to give 'to one brief moment caught from fleeting time,' a lasting and sober existence, and to render permanent many of those splendid but evanescent Exhibitions, which are ever occurring in the changes of external Nature.

The mezzotints are, of course, percisely the graphic equivalents of his painting technique of building lights out of dark grounds, and his metaphor of the present emerging from the past (or freedom from occlusion or confinement) now takes the term *chiaroscuro*. But the effect in mezzotint is vastly intensified, the contrasts far more extreme, allowing him to take small oil sketches of years before, which are of fresh daylight scenes, and have them transformed by his engraver David Lucas into the later, more symbolic mode of *Hadleigh Castle* and *Salisbury Cathedral from the Meadows,* in which the reinforcing was conveyed by the ruins, agitated brushwork, whitewash, and rainbows. It is also a medium that recalls the isolated sunlit meadow of the six-footers. For, as he said of Rembrandt's chiaroscuro in his *Mill*, "a picture wholly made by chiaroscuro": "the *last ray of light* just gleams on the upper sail of the mill, and all other details are lost in large and simple masses of shade."[7] This quotation is related to his description of a Ruisdael sky of "large rolling clouds [which] scarcely permit a ray of sunlight to break the shades of the forest," and so to his use of "sudden and abrupt appearances of light" (p. 44) in the mezzotints.

Simultaneously with "to one brief moment caught from fleeting time" Constable's words slip from natural description to the topos of transience, which was to become the emblem of the rabbit juxtaposed to the ancient ruin of Stonehenge. "Chiaroscuro in Nature" is Constable's way of elevating nature, of giving it a "moral feeling," and endowing any place, even his own home in the Stour Valley, with deeper meaning and universal significance.[8]

The series of proofs, upon which Constable worked so hard with Lucas, show the various ways in which he intensified and added significance beyond purely formal considerations. As well as the darkening of skies and shadows ("I live by shadows," he wrote to Fisher, "to me shadows are realities"), he added rainbows, churning formations of clouds, and ruins of historical monuments. The introduction sets forth the distinction between scenes "of a particular neighbourhood" (the Stour Valley) and those others that "may be more generally interesting, as the scenes of many of the marked historical events of our middle ages." The latter consist in views of Old Sarum, Stonehenge, Hadleigh Castle, and ancient churches.

In *Old Sarum* (fig. 73) Constable evokes history, the English past, and ancient British settlements, further underlined ("to give additional interest," he writes) by the shepherd and flocks wandering over the once proud grounds, which thus become both an emblem of *Ubi Sunt* or *Sic Transit Gloria Mundi* and, in aesthetic terms, what Turner (in his *Liber Studiorum*) called Epic-Pastoral:

> '*Non enim hic habemus stabilem civitatem.*' The present appearance of Old Sarum—wild, desolate, and dreary—contrasts strongly with its former greatness. This proud and 'towering city,' once giving laws to the whole kingdom—for it was here our earliest parliaments on record were convened—can now be traced but by vast embankments and ditches, tracked only by sheep-walks: 'The plough has passed over it.'

But Old Sarum was also known in the 1830s and before as one of England's most "rotten boroughs," required by the 1832 Reform Act to give up its right to send two members to Parliament. Constable saw the Reform Act as a threat to the Constitution which gave the "government into the hands of the rabble and dregs of the people, and the devil's agents on earth—the agitators."[9] In the letterpress of the print, the words of Saint Paul, "Non enim hic habemus stabilem civitatem" ("Here we have no continuing city"), evoke the passage from Hebrews (13:14) which continues: ". . . but we seek one to come." In other words, Old Sarum is all that is left of *earthly* cities; we can now look only to heavenly ones.

The letterpress draws attention to the political and moral significance of the landscape, but we also know that Old Sarum was only a mile and a half north of Salisbury, where Constable's great friend John Fisher lived and where he repeatedly painted the cathedral. Constable had sketched Old Sarum before, but it seemed to have acquired added interest for him during his visit to the Fishers shortly after Maria's death in 1828. Constable's political conservatism explains something of the intensity of his feelings about this spot, but "reform" must also have been a particularly disturbing idea for him at a time when he needed the support of every external form of strength and authority to maintain himself in the face of the deaths and failures he was experiencing. Saint Paul's words, "Here we have no continuing city," connect the public and personal referents of Old Sarum.

Constable tells us, in his correspondence, that the ruins of man, the turbulent phenomena of nature, and the gleams of light in darkness are to be identified not only with English history but with his own states of mind. On ruins, for example, he wrote to Lucas (about the print of *The Glebe Farm*): "I have added a 'Ruin,' to the little Glebe Farm—for, *not* to have a symbol in the book of myself, and of the 'Work' which I have projected [i.e., the *English Landscape* series itself which was receiving an unenthusiastic reception], would be missing the opportunity."[10] Of the tendency to depict stormy weather, he writes to Leslie that "every gleam of sunshine is blighted to me in the art at least. Can it therefore be wondered at that I paint continual storms?" Just looking at Lucas's large prints of *The Lock* and *The Cornfield* in 1834, he applied the metaphor of the mezzotints to himself: "Now for some wise purpose is every bit of sunshine clouded over in me. I can never now look at these two lattering testimonies of the result of my singularly marked life . . . without the most painful emotions."[11]

Stoke by Nayland (fig. 74) begins as a simple oil sketch that does not rely upon the evocative public dimension of *Old Sarum*. The strong contrasts of light and shade in the oil sketch are greatly intensified in the mezzotint. The bright spot of the clearing, the dark woods, and the church tower in the distance stand out with intense concentration as a seemingly arbitrary concatenation of circumstances and details recalling the same sort of strange circumstances and details Wordsworth associated with what he called the "spots of time" of which memory is constructed.[12]

Then, however, Constable adds a rainbow, and in the letterpress he begins by noting the overall effect: "The solemn stillness . . . ," and from this launches into a disquisition on the nature of a rainbow, in which semiscientific observations are mixed with aesthetic and moral ones. The church itself is first introduced as another symbol (like Old Sarum) of past greatness, "the remains only of former opulence and comfort," and this leads to a short digression on the wool trade—interestingly, on the Flemings "who found here a refuge from the cruel persecutions of their own Country"—which recalls not only the epigraph from Ovid's *Tristia* but his lecture remarks about Titian and Saint Peter Martyr, which seem to have personal application. After this Constable ends with an element he has omitted altogether from the landscape itself: "In this church," he tells us, "are many interesting monuments, giving their frail memorial of departed worth and power: amongst them several of the noble family of the Edwards . . . [and so on]." He is describing what is *not* shown in the scene: the hearldry, the tombs, the human interest, the "Elegy in a Country Churchyard" allusion, that are to be seen inside the church—the depopulated dimension of the landscape which now (as in the lecture referred to above) he actually fills in with words.

The other thing to notice about *Stoke by Nayland* is that the paths to the horizon are now totally blocked; they lead nowhere. The full-scale painting (Chicago Art Institute) Constable developed from the small oil sketch shows how far he has come, by this time, from the accurate topographical spaces of the early Stour Valley views and the six-footers, to the heavy texture ("whitewash") but flat absence of depth in the late landscapes. The effect—very like the one we noticed in *The Cenotaph*—is of closing the surface, blocking off all the paths that lead anywhere, and pushing the surface out toward the viewer. The effect is, to say the least, claustrophobic.

The changes in the paintings were accompanied by a personal sense of loss and defeat and by a growing pessimism about the contemporary political situation. Constable was oppressed both by the deaths of wife and friends and by the continuing refusal of the artistic establishment to recognize his powers as a landscape painter. His election as Royal Academician *after* Maria's death ("it has been delayed," he told Fisher, "until I am solitary, and cannot impart it") was probably in part out of sympathy for his bereavement, and his final attempt at reaching a larger public in the *English Landscape* series was a failure. On the level of public events, the rick-burnings and farm riots of the mid-1820s, which had a direct impact on his beloved Suffolk, could be taken as objective correlatives of those personal oppressions. "My brother is uncomfortable about the state of things in Suffolk," he writes to Fisher. "They are as bad as Ireland—'never a night without seeing fires near or at a distance,'" and he adds that both rector and squire "have forsaken the village"—a significant statement for the author of those remarks and images of georgic order.[13] It is arguable that the effect of the riots began to show in Constable's work as early as the sinking viewpoint and agitated brushwork of *The Leaping Horse*.

CHAPTER 15 🍀
REPRESENTATION
AND SYMBOLIZATION

I see two issues raised by Constable's later paintings. One has to do with the increasing remoteness of the sunlit meadow and the other with the appending of verbal and public elements to the originally graphic representation. We might say that the first has to do with absence and the second with certain kinds of presence or addition.

We cannot fail to notice that at the time when Constable is finally reunited with Maria he' uses the first six-foot canvases as an expression of fulfillment. And yet as early as *The Hay Wain* he is also recreating images of absence, involving blockage of the way to the distant meadow. Perhaps the way to the meadow became increasingly difficult because Maria's health was failing, perhaps because of his failure year after year to be elected to the Royal Academy, perhaps because the political situation in England seemed to be worsening in step with his own career. Or was the absence, which began by being specifically associated with Maria, in time attached to these other subjects—or was it in fact a way of avoiding the deeper absence and loss of the Stour Valley he was depicting? In other words, was the absence never about Maria but about the loss of his childhood—or of something deeper still—for which the Maria situation served as a screen memory?

Barrell accepts the political explanation only. He argues that in the early works, up to the dramatic play of paint in *The Leaping Horse,* Constable excluded the laborers or pushed them into the background because he could not face the reality of the rural working poor in his idealizing recollection of the past/English landscape.[1] If one acknowledges that he simply was not much concerned with people as his subject, as opposed to the places—the houses, mills, trees, and above all the fields, where the people are indicated as part of the productive process—or that he subordinated the laborers to purely formal problems (particularizing them too much would have distracted from the painting as landscape), then one may have some sense of why figures are not prominent before 1822 or 1823.

But in light of the dramatic brushwork, into which Barrell thinks Constable translated his anxieties about the workers, and the obvious emotion with which the later landscapes are instilled, we can look back and say with equal justice that it was the meadow *without* Maria—without both himself and Maria—which obsessed him; and that he later rationalized this into his theory of the absent history figure (but with its effects remaining on the landscape). This Saint Peter Martyr or crucified Christ, especially now that Maria herself was dead, was simply a respectable, history-painting version of himself.

Speaking in aesthetic terms, we can say that in all of the late paintings the sublime is less that of Burke's *Philosophical Enquiry* than of his *Reflections on the Revolution in France* (1790). When I look at the late landscapes I am reminded of passages like this one in Burke's *Third Letter on a Regicide Peace*

(1797): "All the little quiet rivulets, that watered an humble, a contracted, but not an unfruitful field, are to be lost in the waste expanse, and boundless, barren ocean of the homicide philanthropy of France."[2] Burke sees himself as witness to the beautiful (in his own terminology of forty years earlier) being transformed into the sublime. Constable's landscape, in these terms, becomes the scene of egress from this male, threatening sublime foreground into the feminine, peaceful, restful, beautiful sunlit spot of meadow in the distance. Gothic towers and ruins as conventional signs may in fact explain the images of the earlier paintings. For the tower simply replaces the locks and eel-traps, the ambiguous and often phallic posts of the foreground, as a more traditional symbol of "the Doctor" denying access to Maria—the father and the mentor guarding the way to the mother, the threatening sublime (the French Revoluion, the rick-burnings, the Luddite activity, as well as Maria's death, and other deaths) blocking the way to the beautiful, the peaceful past, childhood, the maternal, infantile, gratifying, regressive associations to be found at the end of the rainbow, which are the alternatives to agon and strife and suffering in the present.[3]

From 1825 to 1834, as Constable was painting his six-footers, Samuel Palmer was depicting as small and particular a local English countryside in and around Shoreham, Kent. Palmer is useful as a foil to adduce at this point because his obviously visionary landscapes draw our attention to the visionary quality in the landscapes of both Constable and Turner. The only difference was that while Constable's were visionary in the sense of recapturing a personal memory of a lost time, and Turner's in the sense of raising to a cosmic philosophical level the landscape before him, Palmer's landscapes were visionary in the more conventional sense that they reflected a reading of the Bible, *Pilgrim's Progress,* Milton's *Paradise Lost,* and Blake's *Songs of Innocence and Experience.*

Palmer's most characteristic landscapes—in the sense of repeated, personal, and unlike anyone else's—are essentially depictions not of Shoreham but of Bunyan's Beulah or Blake's "Echoing Green." The light in its intensity is not of this world: not of the Campagna Romana or Venice, let alone of southern England. On the other hand, Palmer and Constable share a structure, the sunlit area which Palmer sees, however, in a much remoter, more storybook way than Constable: as Alice sees the garden through the keyhole when the key is out of her reach. Palmer shows these sunlit or moonlit areas through windows and frames of obstruction. They convey something of the sense one gets today walking through the tunnel-like paths around Shoreham, seeing at the end, often framed like Palmer's scenes by trees joining in Gothic arches (as Constable himself framed one of his views of Salisbury Cathedral), a sunlit area of rounded hills, not breastlike but comfortably humped like a hill in the *Très Riches Heures* of the Duc de Berry.

Ruth Returned from Gleaning (1828–29, fig. 75) has a confused, occluding foreground beyond which paradisal hills may be glimpsed in the distance, and, in this case, a pilgrim strides boldly from the foreground toward the area of stream, foliage, and hills. Some of these paintings (*The Sleeping Shepherd,* or the so-called *Magic Apple Tree* of 1830, or *The Shearers* of ca. 1832–33) employ a foreground frame, perhaps a reclining figure, past or through which is seen the glowing distant scene. The simplest form the structure takes (as in *Drawing for Landscape, Twilight,* and the finished *Landscape, Twilight* of ca. 1833–34) is the glimpse of a warm, lighted window in the distance of a dark evening landscape.[4] In almost every case, heavy coulisses frame the distant golden scene.

The area Palmer chooses to paint is, much more simply than in Constable's paintings, the traditional *locus amoenus,* an Edenic spot with one or more trees, a meadow, and a spring or brook, distanced from the rest of the wilderness.[5] The basic landscape pattern we are discussing is clearer in literature than in art. As the remote lighted window is the simplest form the *locus amoenus* takes in Palmer's landscapes, so in such literary sources as Milton's *Comus* the brothers, lost "in double night of darkness and of shades," pray for "som gentle taper / Though a rush Candle from a wicker hole / Of som clay habitation. . . ." (ll. 336–38). Here is one of Milton's similes from Book 2 of *Paradise Lost* (italics added):

> As when from mountain tops the dusky clouds
> Ascending, while the North Wind sleeps, o'erspread
> Heaven's cheerful face, the lowering element
> *Scowls o'er the darkened landscape snow, or shower;*
> If chance the *radiant sun* with farewell sweet
> Extend his evening beam, *the fields revive,*
> The birds their notes renew, and bleating herds
> Attest their joy, that hill and valley rings.
>
> [ll. 488–95]

The simile, however, is describing the fallen angels' response to their leader Satan. Again:

> as when a Scout
> *Through dark and desert wayes* with peril gone
> All night; *at last by break of chearful dawne*
> *Obtains the brow of some high-climbing Hill,*
> Which to his eye discovers unaware
> *The goodly prospect of some foreign land*
> First-seen, . . .
> Which now *the Rising Sun guilds with his beams.*
>
> [Bk. 3, ll. 543 ff.]

As James Turner has noticed, Satan's progress from Pandemonium to Eden "is marked by intense images such as these; it is impossible not to share their jubilance and relief."[6] The contrast between Satan's fallen world and the Eden to which he moves explains some of the feelings we sense behind Palmer's images: this is the way paradise looks to poor fallen man as pilgrim or shepherd.

In the later eighteenth century this sort of landscape is most intensely at work in Ann Radcliffe's gothic novels, which provide the sources and models for many of the preoccupations and fictions of the Romantic poets.[7] Near the beginning of her first novel, *The Castles of Athlin and Dunbayne* (1789), we find the clearest indication of a landscape structure that appears in many guises in her major novels. Osbert, the hero, wanders out of his path, "over hills covered with heath, from whence the eye was presented with only the bold outlines of uncultivated nature, rocks piled on rocks, cataracts and vast moors unmarked by the foot of traveller." In this sublime landscape he "lost the path which he himself made; he looked in vain for the objects which had directed him; and his heart, for the first time, felt the repulse of fear. No vestige of a human being was to be seen; and the dreadful silence of the place was interrupted only by the roar of distant torrents, and by the screams of the birds which flew over his head." In this situation, "He remained for some time in a silent dread not wholly unpleasing, but which was soon heightened to a degree of terror not to be endured" (p. 9). It is now that

> he came to a narrow pass, which he entered, overcome with fatigue and fruitless search: he had not advanced far, when an abrupt opening in the rock suddenly presented him with a view of the most beautiful romantic spot he had ever seen. It was a valley almost surrounded by a barrier of wild rocks, whose base was shaded with thick woods of pine and fir. A torrent which tumbled from the heights, and was seen through the woods, rushed with amazing impetuosity into a fine lake, which flowed through the vale, and was lost in the deep recesses of the mountains. Herds of cattle grazed in the bottom, and the delighted eyes of Osbert were once more blessed with the sight of human dwellings.

In "this Elysian vale" he has found his *locus amoenus,* and nearby is the threatening castle of Dunbayne, where he will be imprisoned and fight out his revenge with Baron Malcolm.

Radcliffe is broaching the structure that Wordsworth will develop in the final books of *The Prelude,* when he finds that he must progress beyond the sublime of, for example, political revolution to the beauty of retirement and poetry writing. Landscape painters avoid the "beautiful" pastoral landscape of Claude, and almost equally the "sublime" landscape that had developed in England in the work of J. R. Cozens and the early Turner, for a landscape that combines the two. In Turner's early *Buttermere Lake* (fig. 34) he places a *locus amoenus* of the sort Radcliffe describes in a setting of barriers and inaccessible mountains, lit up by a marvelous sunburst and emphasized by a rainbow. This is the reverse of the typical Turner landscape, in which the light suffuses the whole central part of the landscape space, leaving darkness on the periphery; or divides the landscape with darkness, or with a second source of light.

The closest parallel to Radcliffe's image is in the storybook pictures of Palmer, which give us access to the sun-drenched meadow through windows and frames of obstruction. Not the image of Alice looking through a keyhole, perhaps, but the basic gothic visual structure—at least as far as landscape is concerned—seems the appropriate one here: the prison cell with the outside world (the landscape) glimpsed through a small window. This image explains the landscape we associate with Palmer and also, in a way, that of Constable, who did look at the world around Bergholt from the windows of what he regarded (vis à vis the lost Maria) as a prison.[8]

If the *locus amoenus* carries some of this cultural baggage for Constable, then what does the thick, increasingly impenetrable wood mean to him—whether it is part of a landscape or, as in *The Cenotaph,* almost all of it? We have to return once again to *Paradise Lost,* this time to the "thickest wood" in Eden, to which Adam and Eve retreat after the Fall:

> and both together went
> Into the thickest Wood, there soon they chose
> The Figtree, not that kind for Fruit renown'd,
> But such as at this day to *Indians* known
> In *Malabar* or *Decan* spreads her Arms
> Branching so broad and long, that in the ground
> The bending Twigs take root, and Daughters grow
> About the Mother Tree, a pillar'd shade
> High overarch't, and echoing Walks between;
> There oft the *Indian* Herdsman shunning heat
> Shelters in cool, and tends his pasturing Herds
> At Loopholes cut through thickest shade.
>
> [Bk. 9, ll. 1099–1110]

While in unfallen Eden the tree flourishes, growing upward toward heaven, here in the scene of sin the figtree (from which Adam and Eve will take the coverings for their sexuality) spreads and branches down into the earth, rerooting itself. This is an image like Swift's spider, or Blake's Urizen, which continues to reproduce its own self-centered, self-rooting, self-enclosed world.

It is time now to address the second issue. There is no doubt that Constable added visual and verbal symbols to the landscape of his affections (without suppressing the personal image); the question is whether he has done so in order to draw the viewer's attention away from the personal or to draw his attention to it through stronger, perhaps more public, imagery.

It is arguable that he has to add towers, cenotaphs, rainbows, and dark skies—the chiaroscuro, whitewash, and agitated brushwork—to get at the meaning he can no longer express in his letters to Maria, who is now dead. Whereas before he had verbal structures to relate to the paintings, after 1828 he has only the paintings (the letters are silent because, perforce, communication with the object has ceased) and the events in the external world. One explanation is that the verbal structures of the letters to Maria, which we have traced, now find their way more readily into the paintings, or into the more public explanations in his letters to Fisher and Lucas. The many quotations used in *English Landscape* suggest that Constable found it difficult to express himself in his *own* words, or felt his own words less adequate than those of poets.

The basic problem raised by Constable's landscapes is the relationship between representation and symbolization. The "meaning" of the late paintings is in this sense simply the replacement of what Freud called "representation" (an attempt to recover primal scenes) by what he called "symbolization" or conventional structures, stereotypical images of meaning, in one way or another linguistic. But symbolization, as Paul Ricoeur says, "tends to denote any substitute formation in cases where resistance is exercised against the return of the repressed memory."[9] It is possible to conclude, then, that at the end of his career Constable uses symbolization (or words of the "other") much as I have proposed Turner did, to replace and repress (or merely make publicly acceptable) the personal content with a public, political "meaning" concerning such literary commonplaces as *vanitas* or *Ubi sunt,* or such contemporary political commonplaces as the spread of revolutionary ideas and the sad democratization of Englishmen.

But the difference between Turner and Constable is more striking than the similarity. Turner's procedure was to add peripheral superscription over a very particular, personal, and dynamic form; Constable's was—according to his lectures at least—to begin with a charged superscription that is not peripheral but central (not merely illustrative of a central prospect, whether as violent human action to a storm or as pastoral figures to springtime) and then remove it, leaving only the form/representation of the landscape, which still carries the same charge. It is a question of priority and precedence. Turner starts with a form and gradually adds (or makes fit) the landscape and then the history. Whereas Constable takes a history landscape by Titian or Poussin and removes the history, but (as in his lecture) tells us he is doing it.

I mean to suggest that Constable's experiments were more controversial, less easily acceptable by contemporaries then Turner's, because they were more radical. His symbols were literally (and merely) the detritus of history, not its fanciful reconstruction. What he kept was the remnant of historical images in contemporary ruins, and what he suppressed was precisely the Turnerian legend. These paintings, therefore (as opposed to his letterpress), have to be taken less as his attempt to turn a landscape into an acceptable

Royal Academy piece, a public and mythological subject, or to replace a private with a public significance, than his desire to interpret and understand the personal form and representation, or raise it to a higher level of intensity. The symbols, I believe, emphasize a new, more tragic meaning, which Constable can express only in this way.

Constable can be seen (contrasted with Turner) as an artist whose aim to regard nature as independent whole-object was the tenor of all his early theoretical statements:[10] thus his talk about dew, freshness, even tactility, and especially about truth. This desire is compromised or complicated, however we wish to regard it, by his ostensible desire to recapture the past, a Genius of the Place associated with painter and friends, and his complementary desire to come to terms with the primal scenes that took place there, of parental figures denying him the woman he loves and repudiating his work as an artist. In order to express his art—to poeticize, control, even render acceptable to those families and mentors (and even patrons and buyers)—he enlarges and monumentalizes, and he does this in forms that in effect transform nature into the part-objects of Titian's *St. Peter Martyr:* not into the body parts Stokes sees in Turner's landscapes, but into a unity in which the "dewy freshness" connects the subject and the object to give the viewer an intense empathy with what he sees or (literally) feels. We have noticed that the addition of "whitewash," the "chiaroscuro," and the turbulence of the brushwork only increase with the addition of symbolic ruins, as another way of turning natural phenomena into part-objects.[11]

If we now introduce Jacques Lacan's distinction between an imaginary and a symbolic realm, in which the symbolic is a way to control the imaginary, which remains essentially visual, we can see the tower and cenotaph as expressions of Constable's desire to understand his past through the stereotypic symbols of common use.[12] Maria's death only leads him to move further into the symbolic realm of literary and even verbal vocabulary. We have to think of his public utterances, in his *English Landscape* and his lectures, as the use of words or public symbolism to say something he could not say in the vocabulary he had so far constructed for himself. The painter now unburdens himself in words, his relief coming from having verbalized or in some way communicated what was before hidden: to himself, in order to learn what he was trying to say in the earlier landscapes, and to a larger audience whose understanding will corroborate his own. Or is he actually trying to *change* what he was trying to say in the earlier landscapes?

The issue of symbolism/representation can also be approached in cultural-aesthetic terms. Constable's *Hadleigh Castle* and *The Cenotaph* make some sense in the context of the English garden of the late eighteenth century. From the 1740s to the end of the century, from William Kent to Capability Brown to Humphry Repton, the garden of monuments, with statues of gods and sages, was transformed into a bare park of natural forms and human remnants. A garden in which the literary and historical imagination (aided by the statues) completed the visual structures was replaced by one in which "local accidents" were allowed to remain. The progression was from a garden filled with objects of association to a picturesque one of *objets trouvés,* and by the "picturesque" we mean the substitution of personal for public, historical associations.[13]

The picturesque demanded that nature be allowed to have its way (against the "dreadful havock too often made by injudiciously felling large trees," as Repton said).[14] Association is then reassigned to ruins—to the "remains of antiquity such as the ruin of a cloister or a castle," perhaps a Stonehenge, an Old Sarum, or even a Salisbury Cathedral. But these antiquities are no longer primarily objects of historical association; they are now important for their personal associations. The garden functions, as J. C. Loudon put it, by "personal attachment to long known objects such as a seat, tree, walk, or spot endeared by the remembrance of past events."[15] A Stonehenge or a Salisbury Cathedral is now subsumed under "personal attachment to long known objects."

The picturesque landscape was thus cut off from a historical and social context and given a personal one. The statues and other "readable" topography were removed, as to a large extent was reference to the outside world as a whole. We can see Constable justifying both a landscape of personal association and "local accidents" such as "remains of antiquity" as the proper corrective to the old emblematic landscape full of temples and statues or, in painting, of gods and goddesses, crucifixions and entombments.

Ancient remains offer an alternative to *istoria* or *poesia*. As Thomas Whately said, their "imperfections and obscurity are their properties; and to carry the imagination to something greater than is seen, their effect." Such objects can carry one's imagination back to the historical past and "certain sensations of regret, of veneration, or compassion, attend the recollection" of this pastness.[16] In fact, as Repton believed, we tend to remove association from the process of history and make the important consideration our own personal associations with the ruin. I think we can connect Repton's view of the garden—and Constable's of the landscape—with an avoidance of public language, the raising of the imagination to something more universal and greater than is seen, and turn it to a private expression of self.

The procedure of the 1820s six-foot landscapes of the Stour Valley was to divest a history painting of its history, but to invest it with Constable's personal structure of memory, which produces a landscape of the affections. But then from the later 1820s until his death the procedure was to add to the landscape of his affections stereotyped visual and verbal symbols—ruins and poetic inscriptions. These may have been, I am suggesting, simply assimilated to his original intention in *The Hay Wain* and *Stratford Mill*. At the same time, as he explained in his lectures of 1836, a landscape is (or can be) a divested history painting, as *Dedham Vale* may be a divested *Martyrdom of St. Peter Martyr;* and yet he has added a gypsy mother and child in the foreground. (If this had been a Turner, the *St. Peter Martyr* structure of the landscape would rather have supported the prolepsis of the crucifixion implicit in a madonna-child composition, as in his *Holy Family* of 1803.)

If we place Constable, as we have Turner, in the context of his contemporaries, the Romantic poets, we may wonder whether language did not carry the sort of power Constable was seeking. For though Jacques Lacan interprets the movement into the symbolic realm, the accession of language skills, as a direct break with the imaginary, and so an end to subjectivity (and an acquiescence before the Law of the Father), the Romantic poets saw language in a very different way. Wordsworth in the Blind Beggar passage—or Cole ridge or Shelley—elevated language and the capacity for fiction-making into an act of self-mastery. The ego is not so much exposed as exalted and given a satisfactory sense of control by its linguistic prowess.

It remains a question whether symbolization for Constable means the reinforcing of a private and demonic energy, or the broaching of an alternative discourse which is more public in its mythology and associated with codes of authority outside the self. We must remember that in terms of his own theory, expressed in all of his writings, symbolization in the paintings is an acknowledged regression to a historically earlier stage of art; just as, in terms of the revolutionary aspect of his career as painter, it is a retreat. We cannot dismiss the possibility that the symbolization is to some extent, as with Turner, a further repression.[17] Nevertheless, though Constable was putting the literature back into landscape, it was in order to reinforce a structure that had itself been strengthened formerly by the purging of literature. There is a sense in which he is both regressing (to history and symbolization) and summing up, reinforcing, reconceiving his brilliantly original Stour Valley paintings—working a synthesis—with this tension between presence and absence.

The question might be whether it is healthier, more mature, to move from part-objects to whole-objects, or to work out one's fantasies in symbols—the tower, Stonehenge, church spires—that are substitutes for objects. But this is only part of the larger question of whether Constable's paintings of the 1830s demonstrate that the acquisition of the symbolic order of language is in fact a precondition for a mastery of the imaginary—the verbal for full mastery of the visual. It can be argued that the artist first finds object-substitutes and then has to name them, and the art work consists of the tension between the conventional symbolic structure and its representational structures with their regressive, instinctual pull back to repressed memories. Verbalization also superimposed on the imaginary fantasy of the object-substitutes a symbolic relationship (inevitably a "meaning") which is different and modifying of that reality. Once the artist has the symbol (visual or verbal), which can only alienate the truth of the image, we have to ask whether his accession to speech and the symbolic is in fact accompanied by an increase, rather than a lessening, of anxiety.[18] For Constable all we have to go on are the letters and lectures themselves, and the paintings.

As early as 1825, when he exhibited his compromising attempt to win public approval, *The Cornfield* (fig. 48), Constable wrote to Fisher, who had referred to his "imaginary" ills:

> It is easy for a bye stander like you to watch one struggling in the water and then say your difficulties are only imaginary. . . . My master the publick is hard, cruel, & unrelenting, making no allowance for a backsliding. The publick is always more against than for us, in both our lots, but then there is this difference. Your own profession closes in and protects you, mine rejoices in the opportunity of ridding itself of a member who is sure to be in somebody's way or other.

In a metaphor of drowning, Constable singles out the two enemies who seek to destroy him—the public, "the rabble and dregs of the people,"[19] and the academicians, the members of his own profession.

In a gloomy letter of 1833, when he was in the midst of the work on *English Landscape,* he writes on the "notions" of painting of "picture admirers in general":

> I looked on *pictures* as things to be *avoided.* Connoisseurs looked on them as things to be *imitated,* & this too with a deference and humbleness of submission amounting to a total prostration of mind, & original feeling, that must obliterate all future attempts—and serve only to fill the world with abortions.

But he ends by despairingly acknowledging the impossible discrepancy between any painting and the painter's aspiration to recapture something that cannot be recaptured—perhaps whatever that sunlit meadow signified to him:

> Good God—what a sad thing it is that this lovely art—is so wrested to its own destruction—only used to blind our eyes and senses from seeing the sun shine, the feilds bloom, the trees blossom, & to hear the foliage rustle—and old black rubbed-out dirty bits of canvas, to take the place of God's own works.[20]

The subject of Constable's painting is, in this sense, painting: the agitation in the foreground, the dewy whitewash, is not only a replacement of the human element of history but also the material he both loved (to touch, experience, and represent) and felt to be an obstacle to overcome in order to reach the spot of beauty and repose in the distance, which after 1828 has become (as in his description of the *St. Peter Martyr*) an even more remote "vision of angels."

One has to conclude that Constable experienced not repression but the growing recognition—parallel in its way to Turner's—that however he tried he could not recapture or recreate, let alone convey to another person, the truth of landscape as he felt it—neither (like Toby Shandy) the particular "place where he was wounded" nor the general sense of "English Landscape"—and that this sense of incommensurability led to the frantic efforts at this, that, and the other subterfuge to make his point.

CHAPTER 16   ☙
HAMPSTEAD HEATH

Constable's solution in graphic terms, however, may have been found not in the Stour Valley landscapes but in the Hampstead landscapes he painted during the same years during which he was recreating his memories of the Stour. For Hampstead Heath is the other Constable milieu, the other subject he explored in something like the depth of the Stour Valley. He moved there with his family in 1819, and from that year onward he often exhibited Hampstead canvases alongside the six-foot Stour Valley landscapes.

The procedure was to paint in his Charlotte Street studio in central London but to sketch and live in the Hampstead landscape. He had taken his subjects and locales (in accurate, "true" sketches), in Suffolk in the period up to about 1815; then he painted them with his own personal vision of the Valley in the six-footers in Charlotte Street in the 1820s; and this involved revising the originally topographical sketches (and the whole topographical bent of his early years) in the light of the characteristic sketches of clouds and seasonal and atmospheric change he was making up in Hampstead.

Of course, Constable painted a series of accurate topographical views of Hampstead, as he had painted accurate versions of the vegetable garden and other spots observed from the windows of his East Bergholt house. He seems always to have felt that he must capture and record the places most immediately close to him—the house he lived in, the houses and gardens adjacent to it. His views of Hampstead Heath, however, are in some ways different. They began as yet another attempt to recapture the "careless boyhood" of the Stour Valley and then became an alternative to that vision, one unhampered by the specific and primal associations of that childhood.

What is remarkable about Constable's presence in Hampstead is that he sketched widely, produced most of his cloud studies there, but in fact only became deeply interested in working up one or two spots. It is easy to make a Constable tour of the Heath because the recognizable (identifiable) scenes can almost all be viewed from along the top of the Heath (just north of the village) looking north or northeast down into and across the Heath—much as he walked around the Stour Valley and looked down into and across it.

There are, however, differences. The famous cloud studies emerge at this time because, though the landscape itself was fairly similar to that of the Stour Valley, Hampstead had none of the human landmarks to which Constable was accustomed. Except for the Saltbox (and perhaps Jack Straw's Castle) there were no steeples or farms or vicarages unless he went all the way to the horizon or added them himself. Moreover, the fringe of trees only directs one's eyes upward to the clouds: there is nothing to hold them down in the valley except the flora and fauna at one's feet. In many spots on the Heath—and in many of Constable's sketches, with their attempt to capture the troughs and hollows of the flat landscape stretching to the horizon— there is the same play of horizontals which he explored in his sea studies. Both land and sky at Hampstead allowed Constable more scope for freedom of brushwork, and therefore of atmosphere—of the changing seasons—than had the Stour Valley.[1]

We can therefore imagine Constable going down to London to paint these landscapes from memory but retaining what he had learned up in Hampstead about the clouds and the seasons, as well as about the looser, freer brushwork needed to express these changing phenomena. (And also, of course, as the 1820s advanced, from Hampstead he brought with him awareness of Maria's deteriorating health and the anguish he could not show in her presence.) Constable's preoccupation in the Hampstead views was with a sight familiar on the Heath even today: broken earth, eroded by rain or dug out by laborers for the sand, as paths or as excavations, in contrast with wide expanses of grass.

The two spots on the Heath itself that held Constable's attention and led to exhibited paintings (though not to six-footers) were the Vale of Health Pond and Branch Hill Pond. The first of these was seen from above, roughly along the Whitestone Walk looking northeast toward Highgate, and only one or two worked-out canvases of it were produced. The other, Branch Hill Pond, which inspired a series of views, was a site that is now rendered somewhat difficult to judge by the fact that the pond dried up earlier in this century (though its shape can still be made out in the deeper green of the grass) and by the related fact that the other prominent feature besides the pond, the large sandbank that appears in all of Constable's views of it, no longer resembles the one Constable painted. It is quite possible that he exaggerated it, but it is also certain that it is now no longer the same shape; even in his paintings we see workmen digging out the sand or gravel and hauling it away in carts drawn by donkeys, for use in pathways, foundations (cement), and stuccowork. During the two world wars the Heath was used as a source for the filling of sandbags, and there is no telling how many hills were leveled.

Of the Vale of Health paintings (1819–20, fig. 76) what we need to notice is that, given all the possible views Constable could have painted, he chose the one that most closely resembled the Branch Hill Pond composition he settled on at roughly the same time. The components of this composition are the pond at lower left, the high bank of earth at the right, and the view to the horizon with tiny buildings along it. The complex cloud formations on the left balance the humped ground formation on the right.

In the earliest of the Branch Hill Pond compositions (1819–20, fig. 77) Constable paints from a position at the extreme westerly edge of Judges' Walk, a position to which he never returned. It gives him something not far from the composition of the Stour Valley pictures, but from a perspective that almost places the woods-vicarage grouping back in its larger context of *Golding Constable's Kitchen Garden* (fig. 65). Notice that his focus could have been on the middle-distance woods, but as usual they are merely broken paint in shadow. If this had been a topographical study of a house in the manner of Sandby, it would have been focused on the Saltbox, the house which gives the picture its name. But while the houses are important, they are only part of—equal to—the sunlit area of the intersection, which points the eye toward the Saltbox but also in a more general way into the distance toward the horizon line. This segment of the painting is close to the composition of the six-footers of the Stour Valley on which Constable was working in Charlotte Street. The trees along Branch Hill are in shadow, a blocking area that has to be gotten over or around in order to reach the sunlight on the road pointing northwest toward Harrow (and not the horizontal line of West Heath Road).

What we see, then, is the composition of the woods and vicarage "found" in the relationship of woods and houses. This is the reason, presumably, for the particular vantage point and composition; and also for the open meadows beyond this configuration.[2] Constable has not, however, yet found a role for Branch Hill Pond itself. The trees on the left are still the obstruction, and the sandbank is barely visible on the far right. The water merely contributes to the sense of openness to the right, anticipating the joining of water and sunlit meadow in *The Leaping Horse* and the eventual subsuming of meadow in the sheet of sunlit water seen in *Hadleigh Castle*.

For the composition he was to repeat and elaborate, Constable moved a little way to the east along Judges' Walk, placing the sandbank between him and the pond, and probably increasing its size, or at least exaggerating the lowness of his position behind it. The effect can be seen in the version in the Victoria and Albert Museum (dated 1819, fig. 78) which employs the sandbank and not the woods along Branch Hill Road as the agent of blockage. An art historian might first conclude that the sandbank in the foreground is employed as a repoussoir and/or to give the scene a picturesque composition (as well as texture). But rather than projecting depth, the sandbank becomes an obstruction the viewer has to get beyond to reach the far meadows and the Harrow Hills, and more immediately to reach the pond. It is certainly not the subject of the picture, despite its loving texture, any more than the woods on the left of the earlier landscapes are. (Even in the Vale of Health Pond composition Constable secured the humped effect of the sandbank by looking east and using the high path to the right.)

Later, when he needed a vignette for *English Landscape* to represent Hampstead Heath, and indeed to close the original series, Constable used the sandbank with an artist atop it sketching but with no letterpress to describe or symbolize the view.[3] It is probably significant that he used no letterpress for any of the Hampstead scenes he included in *English Landscape*. They have found their reinforcement in brushwork or in the emphatic shape of the composition itself and do not need verbalization in the way other scenes seem to. Perhaps because they were not his youthful haunts—and in that sense were neutral—they could be transformed with impunity in more literal ways. They allowed him to seek out other aspects.

To begin with, of course, these separate sketches of sandbanks show the characteristic view Constable took of the heath—a rim of horizon line, looking up, and the sky, which he was then free to paint as cloud studies. But the model we must assume is the Boston *Stour Valley and Dedham Church* (fig. 66) with the prominent muck heap in the foreground. Like it, the sandbank on the heath was being *used,* dug into, by laborers—only in this case it was carried off for urban rather than rural use.[4]

The compositions that follow alternate between a sandbank that breaks the horizon and one that runs below the skyline, presumably seen from a much higher viewpoint (indeed, one suspects it must have been seen from a tree; but it is also possible that this view was the normative, actual one and the horizon-breaking view the intensification). In this alternative composition (for example, 1825, fig. 79) our view of the horizon is unobstructed very much as in the Boston painting of the Stour Valley. In both, the muck heap is well below the horizon line, and the distant prospect is the important element. But this was the year when this particular *Branch Hill Pond* and *The Leaping Horse* (fig. 57) were exhibited at the Royal Academy. In both of these emphatically rectangular and planar compositions the water and the sunlit meadow beyond have joined in a *locus amoenus.* The difference is that in *Branch Hill Pond* the mound is on the right and the path to the *locus amoenus* leads around it to the left, but in this case the sunlit prospect extends to the right above the mound, closed only by a building (corresponding to the church tower in *The Leaping Horse*). Moreover, the barrier aspect is not emphasized.

Constable had the two versions of the *Branch Hill Pond* composition engraved in mezzotint for *English Landscape,* one from the higher and one from the lower viewpoint, and chose the lower with the hill breaking the horizon. This more dramatic version draws the spectator into the immediate landscape, breaks the horizon with the mound, reduces his overall sense of control and order that comes with the higher, more georgic prospect, and reintroduces the barrier aspect.

The 1828 Royal Academy painting (fig. 80) that was used for *English Landscape* was exhibited with *Dedham Vale* (fig. 69). The sandbank, breaking the horizon, has the same framing function as the bank and tree in *Dedham Vale,* revealing the area of pond, slope, and horsemen, as the other picture reveals the valley with mill, river, meadow, and church tower. But in the Branch Hill Pond landscape the high sandbank also reinforces the sunkenness of the pond, further emphasized by the digging down into the dark hole in its side by the sand-carters.

Besides the sandbank, other elements are repeated in the views with the broken horizon. One is the dark cloud in the left of the sky, which balances the dark, occluding mound at the lower right. Then there is the white house that appears to nestle at the left edge of the tip of the sandpile, but in fact sits on a distant hill (in roughly the position of Jack Straw's Castle, though moved west). The Tate version of 1825 replaces the building with a boy in a red jacket, and the version in which the sandbank is below the horizon moves the building far to the right to about the place where Jack Straw's Castle actually was situated. In other versions the building takes different shapes but remains part of the composition.

Now we return to the pond itself, the one element that is blocked in both versions of the Branch Hill Pond scene. The pond peeps out from behind the sandbank. A horseman and swimmers are in it, and carters are moving away from it, together with other scattered figures on the shore. This pond is in fact (especially because of the diagonal of the horizon-breaking sandbank) distinctly reminiscent of the typical Gainsborough composition in which gently sloping forms lead down to a pond into which animals and humans seem to be descending. I suspect that Constable in some way picked up this composition from Gainsborough (rather than, say, Rubens) and that it injects another kind of meaning into the Hampstead paintings. But it is important to notice the differences. First, Constable gives us a panoramic view, which in effect subordinates the Gainsborough composition to a larger landscape including Constable's distant meadows and church towers. Constable is still attempting history painting, and so he extends the context and scope of the scene, making the Gainsborough composition only one element in it. This also means that while Gainsborough habitually gave his viewer the sense of being inside the scene he painted, Constable places him outside, with a sense of perspective—whether of the horizon or of the spatial relationship between muck heap and distant meadows.

Second, one of the features of Gainsborough's ponds was the parallel of the movement down into the pond with the undifferentiation of color and texture as the merging takes place in the lower part of the canvas. Constable usually makes his demarcations very clear. And although in the Branch Hill Pond scenes he comes as close as he ever does to blurring distinctions, he paints the pond itself as a bright sheet of water. It derives, in all probability, from the gleaming meadow and the strip of bright ocean in *Hadleigh Castle,* just as the sandbank derived from the muck heap in the Boston *Dedham Vale* and the slimy, rotting shapes of the six-footer foregrounds.

It is perhaps necessary to remark that when I wrote about Gainsborough some years ago I concluded, on the evidence of his one mythological paint-ing, *Diana and Actaeon* (fig. 24), that he created in his landscapes a mythological scene of a certain sort—basically a Diana-Actaeon scene—and then removed the figures, leaving only the plunging banks, the pool, and the sense of metamorphosis and a magic spot. We have noticed that Constable, to judge by his own words, may be said to have taken the Crucifixion out of a history painting, leaving only the perturbed, divested landscape. But again, the difference is between the small, interior scene of Ovidian metamorphosis and the tragic scene of the Christian Passion. In the latter context the shining sheet of water as well as the distant meadow become important elements, in the same way that the sandbank or muck heap becomes both obstruction to the meadow and fertilizer of that richly productive haven in the distance. Constable's dark equivalent of Gainsborough's lower reaches (including the pond area) is the side of the sandbank that is turned toward the viewer in those scenes in which it breaks the horizon; there the dark excavated areas, the grottos into which the workers are mining for sand, contrast with the gleaming light of the pond on the other side.

In the late 1820s, however, he develops a kind of landscape we have seen thus far in *The Cenotaph,* but which is perhaps better represented by *The Dell in Helmingham Park* (R.A. 1830, fig. 82), *The Glebe Farm* (1827–30, Tate), and other paintings that draw on both *Branch Hill Pond* and Gainsborough's self-enclosed landscapes. The first version of *The Glebe Farm* (ca. 1827) is a Gainsboroughized landscape with two exits up, away and into the sky, and the pond downward. *Helmingham Park* is another Gainsborough landscape, quite different from the Stour Valley landscapes. But notice what has hap-pened: whereas in the Hampstead pictures the Gainsborough pond has be-come one element in a larger, epic landscape structure, in the late *Helming-ham Park* paintings it has become the whole picture, as it was for Gains-borough himself.[5]

So Constable moves in both directions: from the early river-canals to the Branch Hill Pond subordinated to a larger landscape, and to the late dell paintings where the pond is the whole, inside view. The refuge aspect of the water-wood relationship in *The Hay Wain* is simply intensified and then isolated in these late landscapes. Of the first four *English Landscape* mezzo-tints issued, *A Dell, Helmingham Park* can be taken to be a sign of this composition Constable has been drawn into by the Hampstead Branch Hill Pond paintings—essentially an enclosed, interior scene that is a close-up of Branch Hill Pond without the prospect, a strong response to Gainsborough's ponds.

Water in the form of a pond can have equal validity as a symbol of living or of dying; it can suggest experience or serve as a boundary; immersion in it can be rebirth or drowning. In any case, its function is very different from that of a river or canal, which has a direction, a goal, and implies a journey, if only of a horse and barge. Along with the sky, the pond, for Constable, is the other exit from the late, occluded landscapes. Pointing us toward that strange pond in *The Cenotaph* out of which the stag seems to be stepping, initially Branch Hill Pond served to produce an alternative image to the lock, canal, and river of the Stour Valley pictures. What began as an edge-of-the-river (and edge-of-the-forest) phenomenon became another transitional state closer to that of the Gainsborough pond. In *The Cenotaph* the river has become the mysterious, rejuvenating, mythic pond; and in the Hampstead pictures this sense of rejuvenation associated with the muck heap and the sandbank somehow gets transferred to the pond. We might recall the refugelike effect of the pond as it merges with the darkness near Willy Lott's cottage in *The Hay Wain,* and there is already some sense of the Gainsborough pond in the horse and cart standing indecisively in the midst of the body of water. But in *View on the Stour, The Leaping Horse,* and *Salisbury Cathedral from the Meadows,* the canal or river seems to lead—to offer a gently turning channel—into the distant sunlit meadow; and then in *Hadleigh Castle* it becomes the sheet of sunlit water on the horizon.

In the Hampstead pictures, as we might expect in the later 1820s, the blocked version of the sheet of water takes precedence, as the scene grows darker and the texture more striking, until finally the building that appears at the edge of the sandbank is replaced by a windmill and a rainbow is added for further emphasis (1836, fig. 81). This version—the very dark, textural, occluding heap dominating the composition—is the Hampstead parallel to *Salisbury Cathedral from the Meadows.* The sky is fretted with birds as well as with the rainbow. The donkeys for carting sand are present, but no miners or diggers. A tiny shepherd appears near the top of the sandbank. This is also the one version in which the dark clouds on the left, which balance the sandbank on the right, are moved directly above the sandbank in overwhelming and lopsided reinforcement.

On Hampstead Heath Constable first educed the vicarage structure and then the compost heap and the idea of renewal. But now renewal is associated not only with the fields beyond, as in the Stour Valley, but with a sunken pool in the middle distance—cut off, almost private (though peopled with swimmers and cart-horses), and narrowly delimited. He begins to darken the sky and make the muck heap more emphatic, blocking, threatening—a wall or barrier. The pond was originally a transitional element linking the muck heap to the fields beyond; it could go either way, becoming part of the *locus amoenus* or part of the muck heap. In the 1828 Royal Academy painting (fig. 80), the pond is part of the sunlit area stretching beyond it. In the 1836 painting (fig. 81), it is part of the foreground sandbank—whereas now the rainbow descends upon the windmill and the fields beyond as a separate phenomenon.

Straight through those dark clouds curves the rainbow, which, with the pond below, defines the final range of meaning in "dewy freshness." Constable loved Rubens's rainbow landscapes, he said, for "the rainbow itself, I mean dewy light and freshness, the departing shower, with the exhilaration of the returning sun."[6] The rainbow contained it all: the cycle of rebirth, the joining of muck heap and cultivated fields, the concord of sky and earth (an earlier version was the waterwheel); and at the end of the rainbow, as Constable's final reinforcement of his meaning, was the windmill, a symbol he associated with his first introduction to the landscapes of clouds and "dewy freshness" as a child in East Bergholt.

The sandbank is as dark and opaque as the cloud above it. The sunken pond is absorbed as part of its shape: one rises, the other sinks down into the earth. The fructifying aspect of the muck heap supports the pond; its blocking aspect remains in the near side, which draws ever closer and becomes more wall-like, seemingly moved up to the picture plane, an impenetrable screen of foliage, sandbank, and paint. The pond—though part of it is still in the sunlight—seems to be merging in a Gainsborough-like metamorphosis into the shape and texture of the sandbank. Looking back, we see that the mucky foreground has always been as seductive in its way as the distant meadow, serving in one sense as a cause of the meadow's georgic fertility; in another, as a paradoxical contrast or blockage to it; and in yet another, as an independent alternative. It is this solution that Constable seems to have arrived at in these last paintings.

A recently identified landscape (fig. 83, authenticated by Charles Rhyne and tentatively dated circa 1835) shows the sunlit water in the distance, the woods and high foreground on the right rather like a simplified version of *Dedham Vale* or a reversal of *Hadleigh Castle*. But the high foreground area in this case is crowned by a mound of earth in the shape of a natural altar on which an open book rests. The muck heap or sand pile is authenticating the regenerative aspect of the pond. This is Constable's most explicit statement of a covenant of the sort Thomas Cole painted in the foreground of *Sunny Morning on the Hudson River* (fig. 3). It reminds us that a covenant in one of its various forms—as altar or rainbow—may be the central clue to the meaning of these late paintings.

CHAPTER 17 ❦
CONCLUSION:
GEOLOGICAL
AND PSYCHOANALYTIC
MODELS

I have tried to explain Constable's particular landscape forms in terms of cultural-moral, aesthetic, prospect-refuge, and psychosexual categories. The last has perhaps received a disproportionate amount of emphasis. To restore the balance, therefore, I would like to turn to the larger issue of the whole range of Constable's landscapes—sketches as well as finished landscapes, Stour Valley as well as Hampstead Heath—and ask whether there is any intrinsic reason for his having been drawn to paint the two areas he made his own, and indeed the particular places outside these areas (for example, Hadleigh Castle).

One of the explanations for the opening to the right in some of the Stour Valley landscapes could be the presence (as in *Stratford Mill*) of a tow-track on one side of the canal. This is an explanation that can be put alongside the composition of the Raphael Cartoons or the model of the landscape Constable saw looking toward Dr. Rhudde's vicarage from the window of his home in East Bergholt while thinking of Maria. Because of Constable's primary attention to the facts of the ground, the matter of external reference is an appropriate question to ask. With a landscapist like Gainsborough it is less so. For example, Gainsborough was capable of painting a typical Gainsborough landscape that was made to end in the usual Gainsborough pond, and then adding an ocean shore, rather like the seacoast of Bohemia in Shakespeare's *Winter's Tale*.[1] The ocean on the right is geologically impossible given the left half of his landscape. But this ocean rises to the right, leaving the declivity down the middle into the foreground that we expect of a Gainsborough landscape. Other Gainsborough landscapes leave us with the uneasy feeling that they are a compilation of different pieces from different Dutch or Italian landscapes, different conventions; and when, in one of the landscapes of the last decade in London, we see the occasional recognizable Lake District mountain, one recorded fairly accurately in a pencil sketch, we notice how he alters its shape to fit the formal demands of his composition. Constable, by contrast, always begins with and returns to the recalcitrance, not the fluidity, of nature.

The two areas that Constable painted do, as Jay Appleton has shown, share certain basic geological similarities.[2] Most of London is built over the so-called London Clay, a stiff blue-gray clay which turns brownish-red when exposed to the air. On the high ground of Hampstead Heath there is a capping on this clay of what are called Bagshot Beds, a surface of fine, whitish sand mixed with flint-pebble gravel, and below that (for about 50 feet) Claygate Beds, alternations of sand and clay. This is the area that Constable shows being mined in many of his Hampstead landscapes. But the general "cap-rock" situation means that there is a covering of the easily eroded clay by protective layers of sands, sandstones, and gravels. The result is a hill formation characterized by a sharp convex edge, while the lower slope, of clay more easily eroded, tends to be concave.

The arrangement in the Stour Valley is not very different, and in fact must have set up the expectations fulfilled in the Hampstead landscape that was in his mind as he painted his six-foot canvases of the Stour Valley. The underlying stratum of the Stour Valley is the same London Clay. The sandy deposits, which form the plateau edge along much, though not all, of the plateau flanking the valley on both sides, are described as "glacial sands and gravels," and they differ in detail from the Bagshot/Claygate series but not much in the function they perform in providing the convex slope or "lip." The actual valley floor, where it is not occupied by water, usually consists of alluvium, material deposited by the river.

The soils developed on the sandy series along the ridges around the Stour Valley are generally less fertile and therefore less likely to have been ploughed. Only in exceptional cases are Constable's foregrounds ploughed, cultivated fields, as they are, for example, so often in Claude's landscapes. Constable finds more interesting the combination of contrasting features in uncultivated, even "waste" or "dead ground," roads, paths, and tracks of various sorts, with trees, shrubs and scrublike vegetation, occasionally including vertically standing banks on the side of roads, sand-pits, and the like. The cultivated, alluvial area of the valley proper is in the middle distance.

A second implication is that the convex change of slope at the "lip" of the plateau-edge, and the sudden cut-off of "dead ground" from the visible foreground are used by Constable as the technical devices by which he is able to separate his foreground from his middle ground with an exaggerated, almost melodramatic emphasis. We have noted that as this area becomes larger, more emphatic, Constable is (in aesthetic terms) developing a picturesque landscape. But we have also noted the contrast, which we now see built into the geology of the area, between the barren, blocking area in the foreground and the fertile area, the *locus amoenus*. This "dead ground" is, we have noticed, emphasized by a refuse or muck heap which is being carted down into the fertile alluvium, connecting the two areas. The canal paintings are situated down in the valley, and yet Constable sets them up so that the towpath and canal bank or lock are seen as a ridge beyond which we glimpse the stretch of valley. The ridge serves the double (or ambiguous) function of lock and compost heap, and like both it grows ever larger and more emphatic.

What Constable had in the Stour Valley, and what he found in Hampstead, is the separation of foreground and middleground by breaks of slope which are formed directly by the junction of the overlying sands with the London Clay. There is no doubt that in both areas this kind of convex "lip" occurs with great frequency in precisely such a geological situation. It also allows for the contrast between the textures of the cultivated and uncultivated, the grass and the broken clay.

Dedham Vale (fig. 69) and one of the *Branch Hill Pond* paintings in which the sandbank breaks the horizon (fig. 80) are both views over ridges, a fertile valley lying beyond with river and all the signs of an alluvium. The tree of the one serves the purpose of the sandbank of the other. The difference is that the meandering stream becomes in Hampstead the more focused area of the sunken pond. The form can, therefore, be regarded geologically as well as in terms of georgic poetry, Gainsborough forms, and personal metaphors of death and rebirth. But the composition we have described in fact applies to a great variety of Constable's paintings of the Stour Valley, as early as the watercolor *Dedham Church and Vale* of 1800 (Manchester, Whitworth) and the oil *Dedham Vale: Evening of 1802* (V & A)—and even a view of the Stour Estuary (1804, Beecroft Art Gallery).[3]

There are similar paintings of Hampstead, not with the sand heap but with the ridge as the foreground "lip" overlooking the alluvial plain.[4] *The "Salt Box"* (fig. 77), *The Vale of Health Pond* (fig. 76), and the various views across the heath (for example, in the Fitzwilliam) show the bare ridgeline to which we are most accustomed in the Hampstead pictures. But there are also ridges with trees along them which are much closer to the Stour Valley views. In all of these cases the fertile valley is visible beyond, though sometimes there is only the merest glimpse of it.[5]

In short, the Hampstead pictures and the Stour Valley ones, and the sketches as well as the six-footers, come around to the same general configuration. The difference lies in the dramatic or melodramatic emphasis of the addition to the ridgeline—the sand or muck heap—and so of the opposite feature, the sunken pond.

Some of the other landscapes Constable painted also have the convex slope—for example, *Hadleigh Castle* (fig. 59). The castle is perched on a tiny fragment of the most easterly outcrop of the Claygate Beds, resting on the London Clay, exactly as at Hampstead, in which it has preserved such a steep slope that the geological map marks a landslip at this point. The great tract of low-lying land on the right of the picture is formed by alluvium which bears exactly the same relationship to the London Clay slopes as in the Stour Valley. We could argue that, although the bank is on the left rather than the right and is surmounted by the ruins of a castle, the composition is much the same as the Branch Hill Pond views in which the sandbank breaks the horizon.

Salisbury Cathedral from the Meadows (fig. 60) operates in only a slightly different way, with the "dead ground," mere blockage of shrubs and scrub-like vegetation and man-made posts, separating us from the rich, green, watery meadows of the title. Even *The Chain Pier, Brighton* (fig. 61), follows the structure, though it gives us pure water instead of fertile fields or a pond.

The geological approach is salutary, as it forces us to balance nature with culture, choice with opportunity; but it seems to me that the facts of the Stour Valley and Hampstead Heath have brought us back to the presuppositions of the painter. With his choice of terrain as of painterly models, we return to the workings of his mind as they are reflected in the landscape he paints. I am sure the reader has noticed that behind my discussion is a model of the "work of art" based on Freud's "dream-work" as outlined in his *Interpretation of Dreams*. My inference is that the work of art must be taken as the totality of the symptomatic scene in which desire, meaning, and dream come together, in the sense of their joining as a shared social experience (faute de mieux in words). The work of art does not end with the marks on canvas any more than the "dream" does with the fugitive, essentially lost experience of the dream itself. This model includes, therefore, the phases of creation and revision, as well as analysis, but without losing sight of the intense concentration and enigmatic beauty of the original marks on the canvas.

The model is based on the Freudian assumptions that primary-process thinking (characteristic of the unconscious, marked by condensation, displacement, and representation) tends to be pictorial rather than verbal and is governed by the pleasure principle, that is by the tendency to reduce tension by hallucinatory wish-fulfillment. Secondary-process thinking, on the other hand, obeys the laws of verbal grammar and logic and is governed by a reality principle which seeks to reduce tension through adaptive behavior. The question then is whether these processes are complementary or stand in opposition to each other. We might, for example, associate the primary processes with neurosis and the secondary with the ego and healthy adaptation; or associate the primary with truth and the secondary with repression and censorship. Or we might (like the English object-relations theorists) see both processes as coexisting and complementing each other. In any case, an ontological series replaces a stable object as the "work of art":

(1) The dream-thoughts, or day residues, which precede the dream, we might say, include the primal scenes, as well as the observed landscape and literary and graphic genres such as georgic and ideal landscape, that willy-nilly contribute to the dream itself, the visual image. The actual spot of nature which is the referent of the landscape painting has no particular priority among the dream-thoughts, though it may be given more by some painters than by others (more by Constable than by Gainsborough).

(2) The dream-work, or the artist's attempt to understand his dream, then follows in written texts. In Constable's case the dream-work includes his revisions, his lectures, his letterpress, and all of the texts in which he imposes meaning on the energy of desire manifest in the painting itself. His letters to Maria Bicknell or John Fisher can fall into either category, sometimes

dream-thoughts before the fact, sometimes dream-work recreating after the fact the experience that has been represented in the painting. The addition of symbolic objects in the painting itself is even more problematic: this can be either part of the hallucinatory formulation of the dream-thoughts into the dream or a *re*formulation, a secondary revision that accompanies the retelling of the dream in the dream-work.

(3) The phase of analysis then introduces the critic's attempt to uncover and work out the relationships between meaning and desire, symbolization and representation, repression and regression. The critic may uncover, or work back toward, the trauma of the primal scene, and analyse the substitute-formation (or projective identification) in which various kinds of love objects are found to serve as equivalents of the original presence. His role is not very different from that of Panofsky's iconologist, one of whose tools is iconography (conventional images or symbolization), but the materials with which the analyst works are, I think, more refined than Panofsky's "pre-iconographical description, iconographical analysis, and iconological interpretation."[6]

(4) The crucial difference between dream and landscape painting, of course, is that the dream is irrecoverable, and indeed the most striking revelations of the dream are often to be found in the dreamer's reconstruction of his lost dream. By "dream" then I mean the painting as primary process—Turner's original marks on canvas, the image Gowing and many others (myself included) see as the essential Turner—before the painting has suffered or benefited from the secondary-revision of the artist on the canvas, off the canvas, and in his critics' interpretations. The painting is (unlike the dream) concretely present, and yet there is much that is only recoverable in the dream-work that follows upon, and helps to create, the image itself. The painting is a case in which a seemingly subordinate supplement—a revision or a remark in a letter—may introduce considerations that are implicit or repressed in the image itself. We are never unaware that this is a periphery of meaning surrounding a core of concentrated indeterminacy. We can nevertheless get some fix upon the image, without explaining it, by examining Constable's (or Turner's) symbolizations, their own verbal interpretations of their landscape paintings.

At the very least, the dream analogy attests to the crucial fact "that we constantly mean something other than what we say," that there is always (as in any symbol) doubleness of meaning. It forces us to face the interplay of conscious and unconscious, so that we must examine both what the artist thought he was saying and what he did not quite know he was saying, as well as what others thought he was saying as they tried to understand him. It forces us to see that we are dealing not so much with a relation of meaning to thing as of meaning to meaning—one meaning either disguising or revealing the next. An unintelligible text is replaced first by the artist and then by the analyst/critic with a more intelligible one, as a translator carries his text from one language into another.

But whatever the importance of "meaning" and interpretation, we begin with the energetics of the visual image itself, which apparently antedates meaning. Freud's two models, as Paul Ricoeur shows us, are of psychoanalysis as "an explanation of physical phenomena through conflicts of forces, hence as an energetics," and "as an exegesis of apparent meaning through a latent meaning, hence as a hermeneutics." The question remains whether the first, the sheer energy of the paint on the canvas, is "irreducible to any other by reason of what we will call the unsurpassable character of desire"—that is, has priority over any meaning or interpretation. But even the energetics of the dream/landscape itself consists of mixed elements of representation and symbolization as well as the purely formal elements of the paint applied to canvas. It is quite possible that we can reach a point at which "the positing or emergence of desire manifests itself in and through a process of symbolization," and not in any real sense through itself, either those mere marks on canvas or the mere likeness.[7]

Regression is, of course, a movement in the direction of the pictorial, beginning as desire and then being transformed into the perceptual images in which the dream is experienced—and then made conscious by the secondary revision of the waking moment, which is a process of repression. This is not to deny that the original impetus, the desire, may be preceptual or conceptual, rather than perceptual, and that the analysis is in a sense a recovery of an original previsual precept. But the aim of the dream-work itself is regressive, seeking to work from words back to pictorial representation, and yet it does so in the medium of words. It has to begin with secondary revision, the verbalizing reconstruction (or repression) by the dream-work of the dream-thoughts, followed by its analysis.

Certainly the point seems to be that in a landscape like either Turner's or Constable's we are drawn apart by the opposite pressures of the painter's medium, on the one hand toward regression, Freud's "representation" of primal materials, energy, process, the visual and the unformulable; and, on the other hand, toward repression in the form of meaning, unity, organization, symbolization, writing, secondary revision—and eventually the history of its reception and of contemporary taste. Both must be accounted for in the total comprehension of a painting. But meaning is ultimately any formulation or ordering of the raw materials (and experience is something we have already, at this point, left far behind).

This is a model that may apply only to graphic art, and perhaps most precisely to certain landscapes. Landscape painting offers, even more than still-life, a fluidity and flexibility of shapes, colors, and representations that allow for a much greater pull toward regression on the one hand, and toward its opposite, repression, on the other—toward private and public polarities that are not necessary in the more restrictive genre of history or subject painting. Landscape painting—this is another way of saying—offered the means for the great breakthrough from objective to subjective art. By contrast, the earlier model we saw in Hogarth (and still find operative in some Turners) uses the process of symbolization to elucidate meanings the artist has planted, and so although there is undoubtedly also a secondary tension between a regressive and repressive antinomy (as in Hogarth's *Industry and Idleness*), in general the symbolization develops a manifest, not a latent, meaning.

The basic transformation we have traced in the construction of visual images is from the optative "I wish" to the present indicative "It is"; but then the "It is" is given the hallucinatory visual representation of a dream. The wish is pushed back to condensed or displaced pictorial images, and this is followed by a tendency or need to change the "It is" to the imperative "You shall" or "You should" of history painting, even in so subtle and ambiguous a form as Hogarth's "modern moral subjects."

Landscape painting offers an opportunity to cover the whole spectrum of the "work of art" as process, as it originates in desire and, made visual, is modified by formal considerations, and then is transferred (in some sense) into a "history" or "subject" painting and then decoded into its original constituents by the critic or by a determined artist. In the cases of Turner and Constable we have come down to the question of whether the gradual verbalizing that takes place as the symbolic order is imposed on the landscape makes clear to the painter (and to the world) his trauma, or only a displaced or public problem, or only masks desire with a stereotypical meaning, the "I wish" with an "It is" or even a "You should"? Is the process of landscape painting (to use Ricoeur's terms) one of revelation or of masking?

This is the general question I have asked about Turner and Constable. The questions that first started me were: Why did Turner add that rabbit in *Rain, Steam, and Speed?* How can I explain to myself the feeling I have before an "unreadable" Constable landscape like *The Leaping Horse?* Why, when I had spent hours in the Turner exhibition of 1975 (Royal Academy), did I go to the Victoria and Albert Museum for relief and stand in front of Constable's *Leaping Horse?* Why did I feel that this painting was more dearly won by the artist than anything in the admittedly impressive Turner exhibition? Why did I feel that Constable had produced a landscape that was in a more tense and powerful way than Turner's "historical landscapes" comparable to the great history paintings of the continental tradition?

From my initial questions has emerged a rough model—one I did not start with but one that at the end has served as a formulation into which my findings about Turner and Constable seem to fit. Like any model it radically oversimplifies the reality of their practice and my explication of their practice. I therefore leave with the reader yet another of the formulations that may bring us a little closer to the obviously unformulable "dream" of the image itself. It may help us to see something of how landscape painting operated at the crossroads when it still carried the literary baggage of the eighteenth-century doctrine of *ut pictura poesis* but was opening up modern landscape, offering access to a passage at the other end of which are the water lilies of Monet and the landscape-like skeins of Pollock.

NOTES

PREFACE

1 A. Richard Turner, *The Vision of Landscape in Renaissance Italy* (Princeton, 1966), p. 212.
2 I use Claude's *Narcissus and Echo* as an example because it was a painting Constable knew and admired. It belonged to Sir George Beaumont (who gave it to the National Gallery, London, where it now hangs). Constable wrote to his wife, Maria: "I am now going to breakfast—before the Narcissus of Claude. How enchanting and lovely it is, far very far surpassing any other landscape I ever yet beheld." *John Constable's Correspondence,* ed. R. B. Beckett 6 vols. (Ipswich, Suffolk, 1962–68), 2: 294). Hereafter referred to as *JCC*.

INTRODUCTION

1 The "Blind Beggar" passage has recently been analyzed by both Frances Ferguson and Neil Hertz. My remarks follow from Hertz's, but Ferguson makes interesting points that substantiate my argument: that the "written paper" is obviously not written by the blind man himself; that it is a form of writing he is unable to read himself, either to affirm or deny; and yet that it is nevertheless his only connection with the world—it is all he has and all we have. His hope, Ferguson says, is that the external form of these written words "will arouse an imagination of his inward existence, a pity which can only be communicated through the giving of alms, another excursion into outward form. . . . Thus, the 'Blind Beggar' episode operates both as an insight into the alienness of external form and as a testimony to the power of external form for creating the very possibility of internality" (*Wordsworth: Language as Counter-Spirit* [New Haven, 1977], pp. 143, 145). For Hertz, see "The Notion of Blockage in the Literature of the Sublime," in *Psychoanalysis and the Question of the Text: Selected Papers from the English Institute, 1976–77,* ed. Geoffrey Hartman (Baltimore, 1978), pp. 62–85.
2 E. H. Gombrich, "Talking of Michelangelo" (an attack on Leo Steinberg's *Michelangelo's Last Paintings*), *New York Review of Books,* 20 January 1977, pp. 17–20. Cf. Steinberg's reply in *Critical Enquiry* 6 (1980): 411–54.
3 Letter, 16 February 1919, in Virginia Woolf, *Letters,* ed. Nigel Nicolson (New York, 1976), 2: 331.
4 Robert R. Wark, *Ten British Pictures, 1740–1840* (San Marino, Calif., 1971), pp. 18–23.
5 I am, of course, oversimplifying, especially in the case of David. But for a brilliant phenomenological analysis that argues against the verbal dimension of much ordinarily moralized North European art, see Edward A. Snow, *A Study of Vermeer* (Berkeley and Los Angeles, 1979), and his *Re-thinking Bruegel: A Tour of "Children's Games"* (Berkeley and Los Angeles, forthcoming).
6 Ronald Paulson, *Emblem and Expression: Meaning in English Art of the Eighteenth Century* (London and Cambridge, Mass., 1975).
7 Martin Price, *Sewanee Review* 85 (1977): 68, and, in general, 646–51.
8 Bernard Berenson, *Italian Painters of the Renaissance* (New York, 1964), pp. 171–72.
9 Jay Appleton, *The Experience of Landscape* (London and New York, 1975), pp. 73–74.
10 *Landscapes: Paintings and Drawings from the Royal Collection* (London, 1975–76), no. 46.
11 Appleton, *The Experience of Landscape,* pp. 83, 79, and 125.
12 John Berger, *Ways of Seeing* (London, 1972), p. 105.
13 See Melanie Klein, *Love, Guilt and Reparation and Other Works, 1921–45* (New York, 1977), pp. 85, 96, 98. In psychological terminology, parts of the landscape are either directly connected to one's own body (part-objects) or separated from it (whole-objects), and thus carry either the calm balance of mature relationships (the beautiful), the threat

of a male force that is keeping one from his object of desire (sublime), or the object of desire itself embodied above all in points of intersection that recall the genital area of the female body. As Melanie Klein explains the phenomenon, first there is something like identification: "at an early stage of its development the child tries to rediscover its bodily organs and their activities [their functioning] in every object which it encounters." Then "when repression begins to operate," the child moves from identification to symbolism, displacing the libido onto other objects. Klein's exemplary case is of the boy whose great "pleasure in roads," "his love of exploring roads and streets (which formed the basis of his sense of orientation) developed with the release of the sexual curiosity which had likewise been repressed owing to the fear of castration." In its crudest form, the urge to explore, according to Klein, corresponds "to the desire for coitus with the mother." Closer to the sense of emotional involvement one feels in landscape exploration is another Kleinian formulation: the strong "sense of orientation" is "determined by the desire to penetrate the mother's body and to investigate its inside, with the passages leading in and out and the processes of impregnation and birth." But always nearby is the counterobject, the threatening hazard symbol (as Appleton would call it) of the father, which in the period under consideration sometimes takes the form of unapproachable, snow-capped mountains—a masculinity which Burke saw as embodying the sublime, keeping us away from the beautiful, sunlit meadow.

14 Turner, *The Vision of Landscape in Renaissance Italy*, pp. 104–05.
15 Thomson, "Spring," ll. 506–07; Alexander Pope, *Windsor Forest*, ll. 17–20. See Carole Fabricant, "Binding and Dressing Nature's Loose Tresses: The Ideology of Augustan Landscape Design," in *Studies in Eighteenth-Century Culture*, ed. Roseann Runte (Madison, Wis., 1979), 8: 109–35.
16 See Milan Kundera, *The Book of Laughter and Forgetting*, trans. Michael Henry Heim (New York, 1980), in which a widow observes that "the only person who had ever really interrogated her was her husband, and that was because love is a constant interrogation." The narrator agrees: "in fact, I don't know a better definition of love . . . which means that no one loves us better than the police."
17 See Berger, *Ways of Seeing*, but also Fabricant, "Augustan Landscape Design," and John Barrell, *The Idea of Landscape and the Sense of Place 1730–1840: An Approach to the Poetry of John Clare* (Cambridge, 1972), passim.
18 Laurence Sterne, *A Sentimental Journey* (1768), ed. Gardner D. Stout (Berkeley and Los Angeles, 1967), p. 217.
19 See James Turner, *The Politics of Landscape* (Cambridge, Mass., 1979).
20 Appleton, *The Experience of Landscape*, pp. 124–25.
21 Bryan Wolf, "Thomas Cole and the Creation of a Romantic Sublime," chap. 5 of *Romantic Re-Vision: Essays on American Painting of the Nineteenth Century* (Chicago, 1982). For the adumbration of this structure, see Thomas Weiskel, *The Romantic Sublime: Studies in the Structure and Psychology of Transcendence* (Baltimore, 1976), which shows its literary origins and application; and Paulson, "Toward the Constable Bicentenary: Thoughts on Landscape Theory," *ECS* 10 (1976–77): 254–61, which applies it to landscape painting.
22 See below, chap. 15, n. 8.
23 Ann Radcliffe, *Mysteries of Udolpho*, ed. Bonamy Dobrée (Oxford, 1966), p. 424.
24 See, for example, Norman N. Holland and Leona F. Sherman, "Gothic Possibilities," *New Literary History* 8 (1977): 279–94.
25 See Ronald Paulson, *Popular and Polite Art in the Age of Hogarth and Fielding* (Notre Dame, Ind., 1979), pp. 115–33. Horace Walpole, in *The Castle of Otranto* (1765), regarded his novel as something of a play, dividing it into five acts and referring as his model to Shakespeare. His characters are "actors," and the readers "the public [who] have

applauded the attempt." And "yet if the new route he [i.e., Walpole] has struck out shall have paved a road for men of brighter talents," he says he will be happy.

26 Jerrold Lanes, "Romantic Art in England," *Artforum* 6 (1968): 28.

27 John Barrell, *The Dark Side of the Landscape: The Rural Poor in English Painting 1730–1840* (Cambridge, 1980), pp. 89–130.

28 See Steinberg's article, referred to in Introduction, note 2 above.

29 Richard Wollheim, *Art and its Object* (New York, 1971), pp. 76, 103.

1. ANTI-LANDSCAPE

1 Carl O. Sauer, "The Morphology of Landscape," in *University of California Publications in Geography* 2, no. 2 (Los Angeles, 1925): 29–39; in general, 19–53.

2 See Lawrence Gowing, "Hogarth, Hayman, and the Vauxhall Decorations," *Burlington Magazine* 95 (1953): 4–19, and Brian Allen's work-in-progress on Hayman and the Vauxhall decorations, which has uncovered much new information; also Ronald Paulson, *Hogarth: His Life, Art, and Times* (New Haven and London, 1971), 1:347–48.

3 See J. Richard Judson, *Dirck Barendsz 1534–1592* (Amsterdam, 1970), pls. 49–52 (*Times of the Day*), 53–56 (*Seasons*), and 57–60 (*Saints*). See also Egbert van Panderen's engravings after Tobias Verhaecht (F. W. H. Hollstein, *Dutch and Flemish Etchings, Engravings, and Woodcuts ca. 1450–1700* [Amsterdam, 1949–60], 1: 102; 15: 101). The work of Crispijn de Passe de Oude (e.g., his *Times of the Day* after Gerard van der Horst; Hollstein, 9: 147) was probably known to Hogarth and English artists, since Oude's sons and daughters all worked in England.

4 Kenneth Clark, *Landscape into Art*, rev. ed. (London, 1976), p. 22.

5 That Hogarth's *Times of the Day* are the urban relict of an emblematic landscape, drawing on the *points du jour* tradition, has been shown by Sean Shesgreen, on whose research I gratefully draw for some of the examples and generalizations in the following pages: *William Hogarth's "Four Times of the Day" and the Points du Jour Tradition* (Ithaca, forthcoming).

6 See Ronald Paulson, *Hogarth's Graphic Works* (New Haven, 1965; rev. ed., 1970), cat. nos. 152–56, and *Hogarth: His Life, Art, and Times*, 1: 394–404. Although he probably wrote the "Britophil" essay to help explain himself on the matter of his new series, he had actually begun to advertise the series as early as the issue of 10–12 May 1737.

7 Hogarth, *The Analysis of Beauty* (1753), ed. Joseph Burke (Oxford, 1955), p. 82.

8 Shesgreen argues that the old woman (not the sky) is the principal center of light in the engraving. Her goldenness is stressed in the painting, but in the engraving the light seems to shine upon her, not out of her—originating from the pretty girls and their lovers; which may also be significant as a displacement of Aurora's function from her dried-up surrogate to these sensuous young people.

9 See *Hogarth: His Life, Art, and Times*, 1: 401–02.

10 Walter Sickert, "The Study of Drawing," in *New Age*, 16 June 1910; reprinted in *A Free House*, ed. Osbert Sitwell (London, 1947), pp. 315–16.

11 Paulson, *Hogarth: His Life, Art, and Times*, 1: 403.

12 Jonathan Swift, *Poems*, ed. Harold Williams, rev. ed. (Oxford, 1958), 3: 1035; and for the interpretation of Swift's poems, see Carole Fabricant, "The Garden as City: Swift's Landscape of Alienation," *ELH* 42 (1975): 531–55.

13 See Ronald Paulson, *Book and Painting: Shakespeare, Milton, and the Bible* (Knoxville, Tenn., 1982), for an account of the impact of Shakespeare on the emergence of English painting in the eighteenth century.

14 Barrell, *Dark Side of the Landscape*.

15 See James Turner, *Politics of Landscape*, p. 4.

2. FIGURES IN THE LANDSCAPE

1   John Berger, *About Looking,* p. 77; A. Richard Turner, *The Vision of Landscape in Renaissance Italy,* where he remarks suggestively that "the landscapes are the soft echoes of the figures' unarticulated thoughts" (p. 105). He places at one extreme the peace of Bellini's *Madonna of the Meadow* or the Dresden *Sleeping Venus,* and at the other the tempestuous terror of Titian's *St. Peter Martyr.* Landscapes, he argues of Italian Renaissance paintings, "have meaning insofar as they echo and magnify the actions and thoughts of their inhabitants" (p. 112). He divides the Venetian genre into the literary pastoral, "a landscape either peopled with mythological beings, or the shepherds, nymphs, and fauns of Arcadia," and the local, "the observed world of the Venetian mainland where dwells a hardy stock of peasants" (p. 125). "A landscape painting *per se* had little interest for the Italian, for he expected landscape in a painting to be either a pleasantly incidental view, or to have rich human associations." And "he enjoyed nature most when it was controlled, when its accidents were purged by the order of art," which often took the form of the figures in the landscape (p. 129).
2   Elizabeth Einberg, *George Lambert (1700–1765)* (London, Kenwood exhibition, 1970), cat. nos. 5, 6, p. 14. Barrell believes the paintings are paired as Summer and Autumn (see *Dark Side of the Landscape,* pp. 42–48, where he analyzes them). He also claims (p. 44) that the remarkable composition derives from Knyff's *View from Richmond Hill,* a drawing in Luke Hermann, *British Landscape Painting of the Eighteenth Century* (New York, 1974), pl. 2c.
3   Einberg thinks that "Rather than representing just a country picnic idyll, as has been generally thought, they might also be engaged in a land survey" (p. 14); but no instruments, papers, or other indications of such activity are visible.
4   Barrell, *Dark Side of the Landscape,* p. 52. What Barrell objects to is the absence of a social awareness in the landscape painters. They precisely do not see rich and poor in "an appropriate place within an area which can only be articulated, can only become a painting, a 'landscape' at all, by being translated into a structure by which that area is automatically and necessarily perceived as unified, orderly, harmonious" (p. 46). When he objects to a passage from Gay's *Rural Sports* (ll. 269–80) on the ground that it assumes a harmonious relationship between rural sports and rural labor as "but various aspects of one unified life in nature" (p. 47), when in fact no such unity existed, he is asking that Gay's georgic become one of Hogarth's "modern moral subjects," in which the disunity of industry and idleness or diversions and labor is the subject. He is probably right in thinking that he can explain the unity or disunity of a composition as a reflection of the artist's attitude toward the assumptions of his society: Gay chooses a georgic, Hogarth something else again.
5   Collection of Sidney Sabin, London.
6   Sir John Denham, *Cooper's Hill* (1655), ll. 191–92.
7   Gilbert White, *The Natural History of Selborne,* ed. Richard Kearton (Bristol, n.d.), Letters 7, 9, pp. 31, 36.
8   Ibid., p. 36.
9   Cobbett, *Rural Rides,* ed. G. D. H. Cole and Margaret Cole (London, 1930), 1: 189.

3. CITYSCAPE AND LANDSCAPE-ENCLOSURE

1   See. W. G. Constable, *Canaletto,* 2d ed., rev. J. G. Links (Oxford, 1976), chap. 14; Paulson, *Emblem and Expression,* pp. 115–19; and Paulson, "Types of Demarcation: Townscape and Landscape Painting," *Eighteenth-Century Studies* 8 (1974/5): 337–54.
2   *Letters of Thomas Gainsborough,* ed. Mary Woodall (Greenwich, Conn., 1963), pp. 87–88; Constable is quoted by Jack Lindsay, *Turner: His Life and Work* (New York, 1966), p. 46.

3   Mark Girouard, *Life in the English Country House* (New Haven, 1978).
4   See Irene Scouloudi, *Panoramic Views of London, 1600–1666* (London, 1953); and Ida Darlington and J. L. Howgego, *Printed Maps of London c. 1553–1850* (London, 1964).
5   See Joann Hackos, "Metaphor of the Garden in Defoe's 'A Tour thro' the Whole Island of Great Britain,'" in *Papers on Language and Literature,* vol. 15 (Spring 1979); and Paulson, *Popular and Polite Art in the Age of Hogarth and Fielding,* pp. 109–12.
6   Joseph Rykwert, *The Idea of a Town* (London, 1976), pp. 51–58.
7   Ibid., p. 62.
8   Fabricant, "Binding and Dressing Nature's Loose Tresses."
9   "An Epistolary Description of the Late Mr. Pope's House and Garden," in *The Monthly Intelligency,* January 1748, in *The Genius of the Place: The English Landscape Garden 1620–1820,* ed. John Dixon Hunt and Peter Willis (London, 1975), pp. 250–51.
10 Stephen Switzer, *Oconographica Rustica* (1718; 2d ed., London, 1742), 1: xxxvi; Sir Thomas Whately, *Observations of Modern Gardening* (2d ed., 1770), pp. 213–15.
11 See Barrell, *Idea of Landscape and the Sense of Place,* pp. 1–2.

4. THE HOUSE IN THE LANDSCAPE

1   John Harris, *The Artist and the Country House* (New York, 1979), p. 250.
2   Quoted in Lindsay, *Turner,* p. 47.
3   Horace Walpole, *Anecdotes of Painting in England,* ed. R. W. Warnum (1862), 2: 717–18.
4   William Marshall, *Planting and Rural Ornament* (1772), 1: 270–71.
5   Hogarth, *Analysis,* p. 36. Cf. Ronald Paulson, "The Pictorial Circuit and Related Structures in Eighteenth-Century England," in *The Varied Pattern: Studies in the Eighteenth Century,* ed. Peter Hughes and David Williams (Toronto, 1971), pp. 165–88.
6   David Solkin, "Richard Wilson and the British Landscape: A Thematic Study in Early English Landscape Painting" (Ph.D. diss., Yale University, 1978). The basic work on Wilson is W. G. Constable, *Richard Wilson* (London, 1953), but Adrian Bury's *Richard Wilson, R.A.: The Grand Classic* (Leigh-on-Sea, 1947) and Brinsley Ford's *The Drawings of Richard Wilson* (London, 1951) are also useful.
7   See J. S. Howson, "The Dee: Its Aspect and History," *Art Journal* 12 (1873): 161.
8   Joseph Warton, *Essay on the Genius and Writings of Pope* (1756), p. 7.
9   Daniel Defoe, *Tour* (1761 ed.), pp. 346–47.
10 See Evan Evans, *Some Specimens of the Poetry of the Antient Welsh Bards* (London, 1764), p. 22; Thomas Warton's note to his poem "The Grave of King Arthur," in *Poems. A New Edition, with Additions* (1777), p. 62.
11 See Evans, *Antient Welsh Bards,* p. 15. Cf. Shenstone's Elegy 21 (ca. 1746), "Taking a View of the Country from his retirement, he is led to meditate on the character of the ancient Britons":

>   Yet for those mountains, clad with lasting snow,
>   The freeborn Briton left his greenest mead;
>   Receding sullen from his mightier foe,
>   For here he saw fair liberty recede.

[*Works in Verse and Prose,* 1764, p. 78] See also James Thomson, "On Liberty" (1735–35), and Richard Rolt, *Cambria, A Poem, in Three Books* (1749). The latter praises the Welsh as people who take refuge in their rough mountain fastnesses rather than submit to the rule of England, and therefore now live in harmony with nature.
12 T. M. [Thomas Morgan], "Account of a Remarkable New Bridge in Glamorganshire," *Gentleman's Magazine* 34 (1764): 564–65; slightly abbreviated in the *Annual Register* 7 (1764): 147–48.

13 Wilson's politics seem confused. During the heated controversies of 1761–63, when artists took sides with Bute and the new George III or with William Pitt, Wilson supported the former, but in aesthetic rather than political terms. He exhibited views of Kew Gardens at precisely the time in 1762 when William Chambers and his garden architecture were being ridiculed as "Butefying." Coincidentally, Chambers, Kew, and its Chinese pagoda were all symbols of obloquy for the Pittites. It is possible that Wilson was most impressed by the analogy between Bute's Scottish roots, the subject of many attacks on him, and his own Welsh ones.

5. POETIC LANDSCAPE

1 J. H. Fuseli, *Lectures on Painting* (1820), p. 179. For the importance of Fuseli's theory on landscape painting, see Paulson, *Book and Painting,* chap. 4, pt. 4.
2 *The Works of James Barry* (1809), 1: 405–06.
3 Sir Joshua Reynolds, *Discourses,* ed. R. R. Wark (New Haven, 1975), p. 70.
4 See Barrell, *The Idea of Landscape and the Sense of Place,* pp. 7–11. "This distance is the goal of the imaginary traveller in Claude's landscapes," writes Michael Kitson, "and is the point on which the whole composition depends" (Introduction, *The Art of Claude Lorrain* [catalogue of the 1969 Arts Council Exhibition, Newcastle upon Tyne and London], p. 7).
5 Recounted by Sir William Beechey (W. T. Whitley, *Artists and Their Friends in England 1700–1799* (London, 1928), 1: 380. My remarks on Wilson in this chapter first appeared in "Types of Demarcation: Townscape and Landscape Painting," *Eighteenth-Century Studies* 8 (1974/5): 344–48.
6 Constable recognized the two aspects of Wilson: "He is now walking arm in arm with Milton—& Linnaeus. He was one of the great appointments to shew to the world the hidden stores and beauties of Nature" (*Journals of John Constable,* 6: 117).
7 Ovid *Metamorphoses* 10. 9–11 (trans. Rolfe Humphries).
8 Turner, *Politics of Landscape,* p. 42.
9 Ibid., passim.
10 Appleton, *The Experience of Landscape,* p. 164.
11 Luke Hermann, *British Landscape Painting of the Eighteenth Century* (New York: Oxford University Press, 1974), p. 54.
12 Discourse 14 in Reynolds, *Discourses,* p. 255.
13 Bury, *Richard Wilson, R.A.,* p. 14, pl. 41.
14 Bury, p. 33, leaves open whether the picture is "a comment on ascetism [*sic*] or, on the other hand, a reminder that the physical beauty of the universe is not the whole purpose of life." I think the prominence of the young folk, sometimes lovers, makes it clear that the monk is the comment and not the subject. Various versions of *The White Monk* are in Cardiff, the National Museum of Wales, the Detroit Institute of Arts, the Montreal Museum of Fine Art, the Lady Lever Art Gallery, and several private collections (see Constable, *Richard Wilson,* p. 270).
15 See Linda Cabe, "Sir Richard Colt Hoare, Italy, and Turner," in *Classic Ground: British Artists and the Landscape of Italy, 1740–1830,* ed. Duncan Bull (New Haven, 1981), pp. 17–22.
16 See Paulson, "Gainsborough: Form and Representation," in his *Emblem and Expression.* Jack Lindsay, in his recent *Thomas Gainsborough: His Life and Art* (London, 1981), argues that the pattern of the roads winding down, often to the bottom left of the canvas, and ending in a pool or stream, was impressed on the artist by his childhood views of Stour Croft, a common at the back of his father's house in Sudbury. According to Lindsay's Marxist view, this was a structure of landscape that represented for Gainsborough, ever after, an image of "a satisfying world which denied, and was in turn denied by, the world

of property-values dominant in the gentry whose portraits he painted." The closest Wilson comes to a Gainsborough composition is a painting like *The River Dee* (1762?, Late Lord Tollemarche). Marcia Pointon attempts to explain the Gainsborough landscapes and fancy pictures by the literary conventions of the Shenstone circle (and Gainsborough's intermediary, Richard Graves). She believes that they are probably less the escape from his portraiture Gainsborough claimed they were than complementary aspects of an ethos adopted by himself and by his patrons. His patrons were city men who spent the "season" in Bath and craved an image of rural retirement in picturesque cottages. Gainsborough was a country man himself, and although he might have imbibed some fashionable notions about melancholy from the Shenstone circle, these ideas were in the air and (as Chauncey Tinker suggested long ago, and Joseph Burke more recently) could have been the result of reading Gray's "Elegy in a Country Churchyard." See Pointon, "Gainsborough and the Landscape of Retirement," *Art History* 2 (1979): 441–55; Tinker, *Painter and Poet* (Cambridge, Mass., 1938); Burke, *English Art 1714– 1800*, pp. 218–19; and Kenneth Clark, *English Romantic Poets and Landscape Painting* (privately printed, Curwen Press, 1945), p. 3.

17   Compare Alberti's claim that Narcissus was the inventor of painting; for "what else can you call painting but a similar embracing with art of what is presented on the surface of the water in the fountain?" (*On Painting,* trans. John R. Spencer [New Haven: Yale University Press, 1956], p. 64). Writers went on to point out that from this fable it is obvious that the subject of art is man—a theory which Wilson spent his career disproving.

18   See James Heffernan, "Reflections on Reflections in English Romantic Poetry and Painting," *Bucknell Review* (Fall 1978), pp. 15–37.

19   See *The Inspection,* in *The Amorous Illustrations of Thomas Rowlandson* (New York, 1969), pl. 25.

6. THE VERBAL ASPECT

1   Lawrence Gowing, *Turner: Imagination and Reality* (London, 1966), and John Gage, *Colour in Turner: Poetry and Truth* (London, 1969). For confirmation of Gowing's view, see Jack Lindsay, *J. M. W. Turner: A Critical Biography* (London, 1966), p. 169; and, more recently, Kenneth Clark, *The Romantic Rebellion: Romantic versus Classic Art* (New York, 1973), pp. 2–3.

2   G. D. Leslie, *Inner Life of the Royal Academy* (1914), pp. 144–45. See John Gage, *Turner: "Rain, Steam and Speed,"* in the "Art in Context" series (London, 1972).

3   The fact is that the two Claudes, *Embarcation of the Queen of Sheba* and *Marriage of Isaac and Rebecca* (known to Turner simply as "The Mill"), were painted as pendants, and so Turner had no choice but to accept the second if he wanted the first, the seaport scene. His *Sun Rising through Vapours* was, I suspect, chosen because it illustrated the Dutch or more natively English side of his landscape-painting practice, and because it used a body of water in a way similar to that in *Isaac and Rebecca,* but once again open rather than closed. Turner's painting also has the same sense of foreboding as his *Dido,* though muted: he placed his grotesque Dutch figures (out of Ostade) in an unsustainable position. The beach on which they are cleaning fish and drinking will be covered at high tide, forcing them to the higher pier at the right. He emphasizes the state of low tide by showing one of the fishing boats on the beach being unloaded and by painting the pier, which is land level at high tide. Thus we realize that the tide will come in soon, ending the party and the cleaning of fish now taking place on the shore, floating the grounded boat away, and beginning another cycle of the fishing activity.

4   John McCoubrey, one of the sharpest-eyed and most acute explicators of Turner, points out these details. His analysis of *War, the Exile and the Rock Limpet* sees—probably quite

correctly—the Napoleon figure as a way of contrasting not only the internments of Wilkie and Napoleon (roughly contemporary), but the figures of the artists Wilkie and Robert Benjamin Haydon, who associated himself with Napoleon (and painted an interminable series of Napoleon on St. Helena). I do not, however, agree with McCoubrey's admiring evaluation of these intellectual structures, which I am arguing Turner imposed on his essentially graphic materials. See McCoubrey, *Poetry, Painting and the Contemporary World in Some Late Works of J. M. W. Turner* (forthcoming).

5   E. V. Rippingille, *The Art Journal* (1860), p. 100; quoted, A. J. Finberg, *The Life of J. M. W. Turner, R.A.,* 2d ed. (Oxford, 1961), p. 351; Gowing, *Turner: Imagination and Reality,* p. 38. Cf. W. Fawkes, quoted by Thornbury, *Life,* 2d ed. (1904), 2: 52: "he began by pouring wet paint onto the paper till it was saturated, he tore, he scratched, he scrubbed at it in a kind of frenzy and the whole thing was chaos—but gradually and as if by magic the lovely ship, with all its exquisite minutiae came into being."

6   Gage, *Colour in Turner,* pp. 163, 263n., 125; Walter Thornbury, *Life and Correspondence of J. M. W. Turner* (London, 1877), pp. 625–28; and Finberg, *Life of J. M. W. Turner,* p. 444, n. 1. For a concentrated argument against the independent status of the "unfinished" works, see Gage, "The Distinctness of Turner," *Journal of the Royal Society of Arts,* July 1975, pp. 448–57.

7   Sir Thomas Monnington, in response to Gage, "Distinctness of Turner," p. 457.

8   For the quotation, which was formerly misread as "Indistinctness is my forte," see Gage, "Distinctness of Turner," p. 448.

9   Lecture by Jerrold Ziff, "Turner's First Quotations of Poetry: An Examination of Intentions," delivered at the Yale Center for British Art, February 1981. The verse is taken from Thomson's "Spring," ll. 189–205. Turner accompanied 53 of his paintings with verses, 26 of which he composed himself. He used six by Thomson, three by Milton and Byron, and others from Gray, Mallet, Rogers, Langhorne, Gisbourne, Callimachus, Shakespeare, and Pope's Homer. Fifty other paintings, over half of those he exhibited, were related to literature by their titles or subject matter. His literary taste was formed by his copy of Robert Anderson's *Works of the British Poets with Prefaces Biographical and Critical* (1795). See Mordechai Omer, *Turner and the Poets* (London: Greater London Council, n.d. [1975]).

10 In the "Tweed and Lakes" sketchbook (pl 35, p. 84; reproduced in G. Wilkinson, *Turner's Early Sketchbooks,* New York, 1972, pl. 84).

11 Adrian Stokes, "The Art of Turner," in *Painting and the Inner World* (1963), vol. 3 of *The Critical Writings of Adrian Stokes* (London, 1978), pp. 236–60.

12 Blake does something similar with the little pictographs appearing between or filling out his lines of poetry, which are a direct extension of the meaning of the words. His pages tend to dramatize the reversal of the process of language, starting with alphabet arranged into words and going off into visual shorthand and hieroglyph, a semantics of his own which we learn as we gain familiarity with a great many pages. Turner, however, without any doubt demonstrates the opposite process: from undifferentiation or, in the artist's terms, the totally gestural image, he moves toward the reassuring difference of language and ego control.

13 See Roy Park, "'Ut Pictura Poesis': The Nineteenth Century Aftermath," *Journal of Aesthetics and Art Criticism* 28 (1969): 155–64.

14 Coleridge, *Shakespearean Criticism,* ed. T. M. Raysor (London, 1930), 2: 138.

15 Lecture, Yale Center for British Art, 8 December 1977.

16 Kenneth Clark, *The Romantic Rebellion* (New York, 1973), pp. 236–37; W. J. T. Mitchell, "Metamorphoses of the Vortex: Vision and Pictorial Space in Hogarth, Blake, and Turner," forthcoming.

17 A drawing in Turner's "Calais Pier" notebook (reproduced by Gage, *Turner and Colour,*

pl. 63); see discussion, *Turner 1775–1851* (Tate Catalogue, London, 1975), cat. no. 77, p. 51.

18 See Paulson, *Hogarth: His Life, Art, and Times*, 1:265 ff.

19 On the snake—according to Ruskin, Turner's emblem of evil—and a possible connection with Jacob Boehme, see Gage, *Turner and Colour*, p. 140.

20 I owe this point to Mitchell's essay "Metamorphoses of the Vortex" (n. 16 above).

7. THE CONVENTIONAL ASPECT

1 John Pye, Turner's engraver on occasion, tried to interpret P. as representing "the more prosaic realities of English life," whereas the feeling pervading the E.P. is that of repose: "Under P. he shows us the rustic landscape of Gainsborough and under E.P. he conforms to the ideal of Claude, as exhibited in the Liber Veritatis" (J. L. Roget and J. Pye, *Notes and Memoranda respecting the Liber Studiorum of J. M. W. Turner* [London, 1879], p. 25).

2 Dugald Stewart, "On the Sublime," *Philosophical Essays* (Edinburgh, 1819), p. 422; Hugh Blair, *Lectures on Rhetoric and Belles Lettres*, 3d ed. (London, 1787), p. 58; both cited in Andrew Wilton, *Turner and the Sublime* (Toronto and New Haven, 1980), p. 46.

3 For example, Wilton, *Turner and the Sublime*, p. 79.

4 John Gilbert Cooper, *Letters concerning Taste* (London, 1755), p. 13.

5 Edmund Burke, *Philosophical Enquiry into the Origin of our Ideas of the Sublime and Beautiful* (1756), ed. J. T. Boulton (London, 1958), p. 40.

6 Ibid., p. 62.

7 Cf. John Berger, who observes that Turner's landscape "precludes the outside spectator." A traditional landscape was built on the assumption that "a landscape is something which unfolds before you"; whereas in Turner's *Snowstorm* (Tate) "one is in the centre of a maelstrom: there is no longer a near and a far" (*About Looking*, pp. 147–48). Among other things, the foreground, middle distance, and far distance—and the problems of their representation—have been disposed of.

8 See Paulson, *Book and Painting*, chap. 2, pt. 1.

9 Ruskin reports Turner's account of the incident to the Reverend William Kingsley. *Modern Painters*, 5th ed., in *Works*, ed. Cook and Wedderburn (1903–12), 3: 569–71; 13: 161–63.

8. THE REVOLUTIONARY ASPECT: THE SUN

1 Sir John Gilbert to Sir George Sharf, quoted in Gage, *Colour in Turner*, p. 169.

2 Turner's source for his account of Regulus's blinding was probably G. Adams, *An Essay on Vision* (1789), p. 9. See Gage, *Colour in Turner*, p. 143, and Andrew Wilton's rejoinder, *J. M. W. Turner: His Art and Life* (New York, 1979), pp. 220–21. Noting that an engraving of *Regulus* was published during Turner's lifetime, entitled *Ancient Carthage—The Embarcation of Regulus* (engraved in 1840 by D. Wilson), Wilton argues that Regulus himself appears at the top of the flight of steps leading down to the water at the right in both engraving and painting. Turner may, as Wilton thinks, have had Horace's *Ode* 3. 5 in mind, with its vivid description of Regulus's embarcation from Rome with his family and friends around him. But if we assume that Turner influenced the engraving and its title, the subject seems to be his embarcation *from* Carthage to Rome. The barrel and carpenters at left then become proleptic of Regulus's fate on his return from this doomed mission: they are already preparing in case of his failure. The subject of Benjamin West's *Regulus* (R.A. 1769), suggested by George III, was, according to its title, "the final departure of Regulus for Rome," though the painting itself is ambiguous. This painting, in the Royal Collection, may have been the picture Turner set out to surpass with his own *Regulus*.

3   For an analysis of *Juliet and Her Nurse* in these terms, see Paulson, *Book and Painting,* chap. 4, pt. 4.

4   See Gage, *Colour in Turner,* p. 131.

5   John Ruskin, *Works,* ed. Cook and Wedderburn (1903–12), 36: 543. For the sun as god, see, for example, Jacob Bryant, *A New System: Or, An Analysis of Ancient Mythology,* 3 vols. (1774–76), where he argues that all religions were originally one: "I have mentioned that the nations of the east acknowledged originally but one deity, the Sun" (1:306). He believes that monotheistic sun-worship degenerated into polytheism because borrowers misunderstood the different attributes of the sun-god and made them into separate gods.

6   Exodus 33 : 20; cf. Revelation 1 : 16, where at the Last Judgment God's "countenance was as the sun shineth in his strength."

7   William Hazlitt, "On Imitation," in "Round Table," *Examiner,* 18 February 1816, in *Collected Works,* ed. A. R. Waller and Arnold Glover (London, 1902), 1: 76n.

8   Dugald Stewart, "On the Sublime," *Philosophical Essays* (Edinburgh, 1819), p. 384.

9   As an example of the royal sun, we can recall Lord Pomfret, on the City's Remonstrance to George III in May 1770: "However swaggering and impudent the behaviour of the low Citizens in their own dunghill, when they came into the Royal Presence, their heads hung down like bulrushes and they blinked with their eyes like owls at the rays of the sun" (cited in W. P. Treloar, *Wilkes and the City* [London, 1917], p. 99). For the second sense of *sun,* as the human enlightenment that disperses the darkness of church and state, see the frontispiece of the *Encyclopédie* (1764) showing Truth unveiled, emitting rays of sunlight—pure light or enlightenment—with a separate ray directed down from heaven onto Theology, a woman with a Bible and a pious expression. Two other women, variously identified as Reason and Philosophy, or Reason and Imagination, are lifting the veil and pulling it away from Truth. Although the printed explanation that accompanies the frontispiece says the woman pulling the veil away from Truth is Philosophy, Diderot's explanation, in his *Salon of 1765,* that it is Imagination fits with the image in Ripa (1757 ed.). See Georges May, "Observations on an Allegory: The Frontispiece of the *Encyclopédie,*" *Ventures* (Fall 1969), pp. 53–64. At the other extreme, compare Goya's *Capricho* no. 43 and *Desastres* nos. 79–80.

10 J. Tiersot, *Les Fêtes et les chants de la révolution française* (Paris, 1908), p. 40; Sir Samuel Romilly, *Thoughts on the Probable Influence of the French Revolution on Great-Britain* (1790), pp. 203; James Mackintosh, *Vindiciae Gallicae* (1791), p. 345; William Hazlitt, from *The Memoirs of Thomas Holcroft,* in *Collected Works,* 2: 155.

11 William Hazlitt, *Winterslow* (1850), pp. 73–74. A different version, published in *The Monthly Magazine,* March 1827 (unsigned), introduced double suns: "the sun of Liberty rose upon the sun of Life in the same day, and both were proud to run their race together." See *Complete Works of William Hazlitt* (London, 1930–34), ed. P. P. Howe, 17: 197.

12 Burke, *Philosophical Enquiry,* ed. Boulton, p. 80.

13 Burke, *Reflections on the Revolution in France,* ed. W. B. Todd (New York, 1959), p. 73. For Burke's comments connecting the sun with the stripping off of clothing, see pp. 92–93, 105–06, 110. See Ronald Paulson, "Burke's Sublime and the Representation of Revolution," in *Culture and Politics from Puritanism to the Enlightenment,* ed. Perez Zagorin (Berkeley and Los Angeles, 1980), pp. 241–70.

14 Cf. T. R. Malthus's summation of his times, looking back from 1798 as "the new and extraordinary lights that have been thrown on political subjects, which dazzle, and astonish the understanding; and particularly that tremendous phenomenon in the political horizon the French revolution, which, like a blazing comet, seems destined either to inspire with fresh life and vigour, or to scorch up and destroy the shrinking inhabitants

of the earth. . . ." *Essay on the Principles of Population,* ed. Philip Appleman (New York, 1976), p. 16.

15 Burke, House of Commons speech, 18 February 1793, in *Speeches* (1816), 4:120.

16 Richard Price, Sermon, 4 November 1789, to the Society for the Commemoration of the Glorious Revolution, published as *A Discourse on the Love of Our Country* (1789).

17 Thomas Paine, *Rights of Man,* ed. Henry Collins (London, 1969), pp. 232, 294–95.

18 On the splendor of fires, see William Gilpin, *Observations on the Western Parts of England,* 2d ed. (London, 1808), pp. 205–14, where he constructs a scale upward from campfires to shipyard fires, the burning of houses, and erupting volcanoes. Ships burning are, for example, "more productive of greater ideas, and more picturesque circumstances than the burning of houses. The very reflections from the water add great Beauty." Lindsay comments on Turner's growing interest in fires and other conflagrations within the political context of the 1830s (pp. 179–81). These were the years when fire expressed unrest and terror in the rural provinces. The ways of protesting or seeking relief from social pressures ranged from the theft of potatoes or turnips to incendiarism or threats of it and the destroying of machines—the very basis of unemployment (the thresher took away the worker's winter labor). For Constable's response, see above, p. 146. Some of this imagery also relates to the notorious illuminati, castigated by the Abbé Barruel as originators of the French Revolution. *Memoirs, Illustrating the History of Jacobinism,* trans. Robert Clifford, 2d ed. (London, 1798).

19 Keats's myth of overthrow and rebellion, of the sublime replaced by the beautiful, also employs two suns or sun-gods, Hyperion who is replaced by Apollo. The sun myths popular in the Romantic period began with the Promethean (Napoleon, for one example) who steals fire for men and is punished by the source of fire/light, Zeus; but also popular were Icarus, who flies too close to the sun and is thus destroyed, and Phaeton—both stories which involve fathers: Daedalus who invents the wings and advises Icarus not to fly so high, and Helios, whose advice to Phaeton concerns the sun chariot. The real sun-father-god punishes the son's hybris.

20 Samuel Taylor Coleridge, *Rime of the Ancient Mariner* (New York, 1946), p. 93.

21 See above, p. 66 and n. 5.

22 Of course, in one sense, Turner is simply applying a technique learned from watercolor painting to oil painting. But its significance is too great to be explained only as a technical consideration.

23 Appleton, *The Experience of Landscape,* pp. 109–10, 77.

24 Ibid., pp. 109, 77.

25 Ibid., p. 110. "Never during the whole process does it lose its essence. It is just as much 'sun' at every stage of the cycle. But in terms of the terrestrial environment it becomes for a time manageable, assimilable, comprehensible."

26 John Dennis, "The Grounds of Criticism in Poetry," in *Works,* ed. E. N. Hooker (Baltimore, 1939), 1: 339, 356, 359. Dennis contrasts the sun in ordinary conversation, "a round flat shining Body, of about two foot diameter," with the sun in meditation, "a vast and glorious Body, and the top of all the visible Creation, and the brightest material Image of the Divinity"—which expresses the ambiguity of Turner's feelings as well as explaining Blake's remark that he saw in a sun the size of a guinea all of the heavenly host.

27 Though not in German. See Sigmund Freud, *Complete Psychological Works,* Standard Edition, 12: 53–54.

28 *Spectator* No. 412. It is useful to contrast the "vagueness" or undifferentiation of a Turner landscape with that of a Gainsborough in its effect on the viewer. Gainsborough, too, builds around a vortical form, but his vortex is a plunging diagonal, represented in riverbanks and slopes which draw the viewer down into a watery, womblike rest; whereas

Turner's vortex forces the viewer to search in the undifferentiation for the slightest detail of difference—an emergent sea monster or landscape shapes, or the detail of a rabbit or snake. I believe that Gainsborough is thinking in terms of the beautiful, associated by both Addison and Burke with regression and return to a womblike peace; Turner, thinking in terms of the sublime, repels or pushes his viewer back from the vortex, and accompanies this thrust with attempts to coerce him.

29   Freud, *Works,* 12: 80–81.

30   To transfer the discussion from Turner's works to his life, we would have to note that he consciously identified with his father against his mother, with the superego against the undifferentiation that was, however, the chief defining force of his art. He referred to the Royal Academy as a mother rather than a father (as in the famous story in which he said Haydon "stabbed his mother, he stabbed his mother"), and he took on the role of father in relation to his own father in later years.

31   Lindsay, p. 213; but also Gowing, *Turner: Imagination and Reality,* p. 31.

32   It is also true that Turner is consciously obscure in some of his later work, i.e., he seems to be concealing, not making public, his meaning. There are stories of his puzzling Ruskin over the meaning of *The Exile and the Rock Limpet,* and David Roberts's remark to Thornbury: "Nothing seems so much to please him as to try to puzzle you, or make you think so; for if he began to explain or tell you anything he was sure to break off in the middle, look very mysterious, nod, and wink his eye, saying to himself 'make of it what you can'" (Walter Thornbury, *The Life of J. M. W. Turner, R.A.,* 2d ed. [1877], p. 229; for Ruskin's story, see *Works,* ed. Cook and Wedderburn, 7: 435n., also pp. 434, 452). However, hermetic or not, this is still "meaning"—even if, as is sometimes the case, we can only come at it (as contemporaries could) through research into the poet's mind. This is also, I would argue, public meaning, because Turner is using it at least partly to rationalize and justify himself.

33   See Millard Meiss, "Light as Form and Symbol in Some Fifteenth-Century Paintings," *Art Bulletin* 27 (1945): 175–81; idem, *Giovanni Bellini's St. Francis in the Frick Collection* (Princeton, 1964), pp. 29–33. The kind of engrossment employed by Turner echoes such biblical images as the sun at the center of the whirlwind in Ezekiel, to which is added the fact that "Also out of the midst thereof came the likeness of four living creatures" with men's faces, wings, and so on (Ezek. 1:4–5).

34   Ruskin, *Works,* 3:254n.; *Blackwood's Edinburgh Magazine* 54 (October 1843): 492. See Graham Reynolds, *Turner* (London, 1969), pp. 200–01, for a contrary opinion; and for a supporting one, Lindsay, *Turner,* p. 213. For a discussion of Ruskin's later suppression of the passage, see George Landow, "Ruskin's Revisions of the Third Edition of *Modern Painters,* Volume I," *Victorian Newsletter* 33 (1968): 12–16.

9. THE OTHER SUN

1   The rabbit/hare was identified by Turner as a "hare" to Leslie (*Inner Life of the Royal Academy,* pp. 144–47). See M. E. Tilley, *A Dictionary of the Proverbs of England* (London, 1966), and *OED,* under "Hare.".

2   *George Cruikshank's Omnibus* (1840), p. 202.

3   The Maidenhead area has been identified by Martin Davies in the *National Gallery Catalogue: The British School* (London, 1959), pp. 99–100. This countryside was described as especially beautiful by William Gilpin and others in guidebooks to the area, and it was a spot often painted by Turner. See, for example, Gilpin, *Observations Relative Chiefly to Picturesque Beauty* . . . (1786), 1: 20; also the guidebook issued by the Great Western Railway (1839), J. C. Thorne's *The Thames* (1847), and illustrated views in W. B. Cooke's *Description of Views of the Thames* (1822), to which Turner himself contributed a drawing of the Thames.

4   See Kathleen Raine, *Blake and Tradition* (Princeton, 1968), 1: 117–19, 197–99. Cf. Turner's verses for *Apollo and Python* from the "Hymn to Callimachus."

5   The image of Venice on the sail was first noted by Sidney Colvin in *The Portfolio* (1874), pp. 75–76, who observed that the sail "represents Venice herself, with the sun rising gloriously just above the horizon."

6   Turner's first Venetian painting, *Bridge of Sighs, Ducal Palace and Custom House, Venice: Canaletto Painting* (1833, Tate) introduces the interpretation he was to perpetuate in his later paintings. The title asks us to remember Byron's well-known opening lines to *Childe Harold,* canto 4: "I stood in Venice on the Bridge of Sighs / A palace and a prison on each hand." Turner's interest in Venice probably dated back to the illustrations he made between 1823 and 1833 for John Murray's edition of Byron, followed by his visit to Venice in 1833. The England-Venice parallel is also made in pendants of 1834–35, *Keelmen Heaving in Coals by Moonlight* (on the River Tyne) and *Venice* (both in National Gallery, Washington). But Byron is Turner's chief source for the association of Venice with decline, and of England with Venice. For example, Byron thus addresses Venice in *Childe Harold:*

> and thy lot
> Is shamefull to the nations, most of all
> Albion! to thee; the Ocean queen should not
> Abandon Ocean's children; in the fall
> Of Venice think of thine, despite thy watery wall.
>
>   [4:xvii]

7   James Heffernan, "The English Romantic Perception of Color," in *Images of Romanticism,* ed. Kroeber, p. 142. See also Gage, *Colour in Turner,* pp. 180–87.

8   Hazlitt, "Round Table," *Examiner* (1816), in *Complete Works of William Hazlitt,* 4:76. Cf. for example, John Harris's view that "the destruction Turner was to wreak upon the normalised topographical view" (on the order of Wilson's, to which we have already referred) followed from his "becoming increasingly conscious of the atmospheric potentialities of a view." In fact, Harris sees the corollary of atmospherics as "the dissolution of the classical composition or picture in the frame."

9   David Bindman, *Blake as an Artist* (London, 1977), p. 83. Painters other than Wright of Derby tried, according to Charles Stuckey, to evoke eternity by representing both sun and moon in the same scene. (See "Temporal Imagery in the Early Romantic Landscape," Ph.D. diss., University of Pennsylvania, University Microfilms, 1972). One could mention other versions of the two suns: for example, that of Dante in *De Monarchia*—one the secular, the other the divine (the emperor and the pope, the earthly and heavenly paradises), his argument being that the path to the heavenly paradise lay through earthly peace and justice. For this and much about the use of light imagery in revolutionary affairs, see Melvin J. Lasky, *Utopia and Revolution* (London, 1976), in this case, pp. 25–26.

10   I am indebted throughout this section to my colleague J. Hillis Miller, with whom I have talked about Turner, and whose colloquium at the Yale Center for British Art (Spring 1980), a reply to my essay "Turner's Graffiti," clarified certain issues for me. Miller believes that *words* about "turning" from the passage about Ulysses and Polyphemus in the *Odyssey* may have, in some sense, preceded the visual image: "The passage describes both a kind of hideous sexual penetration and at the same time a displaced act of castration, the unmanning of the Cyclops by blinding him. Could it be possible that Turner saw a figure for his own name and his own equivocal power in the two figures Homer uses—the turning of the shipwright's drill and the hissing of the white hot metal when it is plunged in water by the smith?" This suggestive view must be

complemented by the alternative explanation—namely, that the painting may have a totally independent chain of *graphic* sources, which Turner adapts to illustrate the text, and which have precedence over the verbal text which explicates them.

   Miller's association of Turner with Polyphemus as human creators has also to be complemented by the identification Turner himself must have felt with Ulysses. As W. J. T. Mitchell points out, "Turner's mythic prototype is Ulysses, the rugged, wily seafarer, the secretive 'man of many turns' who would, at the age of sixty-five, expose himself to the fury of a Channel snowstorm in mid-January, . . . in an attempt to explore the boundary between form and chaos." Again: "Turner's insistence on facing the 'one-eyed monster' in nature is all of a piece with his self-dramatization as Ulysses, who faced just such a challenge in Polyphemus, the one-eyed giant. In Turner's painting of 'Ulysses deriding Polyphemus' we see the giant in his 'natural' form, as the smoky peak of an erupting volcano. Ulysses stands on the deck of his ship hurling his defiance or perhaps, like Turner himself, simply observing with fascinated delight 'what such a scene was like.' The contrast is between the smokey obscurity of Polyphemus' realm and the dazzling sun-rise on the right" ("Metamorphoses of the Vortex," forthcoming). In short, we can regard Polyphemus with his forge as the challenger of nature, or Ulysses as the man challenging and momentarily defeating nature in the form of Polyphemus the volcano. It is in any case a very rich image.

11   Cited in Martin Butlin and Evelyn Joll, *The Paintings of J. M. W. Turner*, (London and New Haven, 1977), p. 157.

12   See Gage, "The Distinctness of Turner," *Journal of the Royal Society of Arts* (July 1975), p. 449: "for the Cave we are led to expect from his title is nowhere in sight; it is indeed at the opposite, south-east, side of the island." Gage is simply wrong.

13   Gage, "The Distinctness of Turner," pp. 453–54. See William Daniell, *Illustrations of the Island of Staffa* (1818).

14   Gage, "The Distinctness of Turner," p. 454.

15   *Fraser's Magazine*, July 1832; cited in *Turner* (R.A. catalogue), no. 490.

10. THE VORTEX: REPRESSION OR REINFORCEMENT

 1   Jack Lindsay, *Turner: His Life and Work*, p. 163. It is possible that the late circular pictures, such as *The Morning after the Deluge* and even perhaps *The Angel of the Sun*, may owe something of their composition to baroque ceilings that Turner would have seen in Italy.

 2   Charles Stuckey, "Turner, Masaniello, and the Angel," *Das Jahrbuch der Berliner Museen* (1976), pp. 155–75.

 3   Peter Cunningham, "Memoir," in John Burnet, *Turner and His Works* (1852), p. 33.

 4   Walter Thornbury, *The Life of J. M. W. Turner, R.A.*, 2d ed. rev. (1872), p. 237; quoted in *Turner in Yorkshire* (exhibition catalogue; York, 1980), p. 7.

 5   12 November 1798, *The Diary of Joseph Farington*, ed. Kenneth Garlick and Angus Macintyre (New Haven, 1979), 3: 1090; also Finberg, *The Life of J. M. W. Turner, R.A.*, 2d ed. (Oxford, 1961), p. 55. The barber's pole came into existence through the barber-surgeon's habit of giving his patient a pole to grasp during the blood-letting—the equivalent of "making a fist" today—"in order to make the blood flow more freely. . . . As the pole was of course liable to be stained with blood, it was painted red; when not in use, barbers were in the habit of suspending it ouside the door with the white linen swathingbands twisted around it." By the end of the eighteenth century, barbers were using the pole alone, surgeons, adding a gallipot and red flag. See Jacob Larwood and J. C. Hotten, *The History of Signboards* (London, 1908), pp. 341–42, and, for an example, Hogarth's *Four Times of the Day: Night* (1738).

 6   John Berger has speculated provocatively about the origins of Turner's landscapes in the

external world of his childhood surroundings and in the way he would have seen things as
a child. He groups these around "the visual elements of a barber's shop": "water, froth,
steam, gleaming metal, clouded mirrors, white bowls or basins in which soapy liquid is
agitated by the barber's brush and detritus deposited." Berger goes on to see analogies of
a more Freudian sort between the father's razor and Turner's own palette knife, and
between the blood and water of the barbershop and his apocalyptic paintings, as the
milieu extends from the barbershop to the surrounding world in which blood and steam
become the fire of furnaces and the productive energy of machines (*About Looking,* p.
143–44). Many more prosaic, and more elemental, examples come to mind. The Ferrer
arms consist of a shield vaire, and some families of the name adopted the horseshoes of a
farrier. Fletcher employs an arrow (*flèche,* or *flécher*), referring to the employment of a
fletcher, an arrow-maker. Fox arms carry foxes and foxes' heads, Lyons carry lions,
Trotter a horse, and Oakes, acorns: "in fact," says Fox-Davies, "by far the larger proportion of the older coats of arms, where they can be traced to their real origin, exhibit some
such derivation."

7 See Ambrose Heal, *The Signboards of Old London Shops* (London, 1947), pp. 173–74,
passim; and Arthur Charles Fox-Davies, *A Complete Guide to Heraldry* (London, 1949),
pp. 301–02, fig. 556, also pp. 5, 80.
8 Thornbury, *Life of J. M. W. Turner, R.A.,* p. 620.
9 Alain Grosrichard, "Gravité de Rousseau," in *Cahiers pour l'analyse,* 8: 64; quoted in
Paul de Man, "Theory of Metaphor in Rousseau's *Second Discourse,*" in *Romanticism:
Vistas, Instances, Continuities,* ed. David Thornburn and Geoffrey Hartman (Ithaca and
London, 1973), p. 98.
10 De Man, "Theory of Metaphor," p. 101; see Rousseau, *Essai sur l'origine des langues*
(published 1817).
11 Quoted in Lasky, *Utopia and Revolution,* p. 279. And compare with the quotation from
Ward, above p. 86.
12 See E. H. Gombrich, *Symbolic Images: Studies in the Art of the Renaissance* (London, 1972),
pp. 18, 159, 182; and my critique of Gombrich, which builds on the argument of the
present essay, in "Iconography Revisited," *MLN* 112 (1977): 1052–66.
13 I am indebted for this analogy and the remarks on Coleridge to Peter Mileur. For the
aesthetic background, see Roy Park, "'Ut Pictura Poesis': The Nineteenth-Century
Aftermath," *Journal of Aesthetics and Art Criticism* 28 (1969): 155–64.
14 This is Miller's argument; see above, chap. 9, n. 10. John Dixon Hunt has recently
argued that the "empty center" of the Turner landscape has to be seen as a response to
Burke's "stress upon the advantages that poetry possesses over painting as a sublime
structure." Turner shows that a painter can be just as indefinite and suggestive in his
representations as a poet can be with his words. There is truth in this; but my own
evidence suggests that Turner's intention cannot be described as offering us "the opportunity to participate ourselves in creating its final meaning." "Wondrous Deep and
Dark: Turner and the Sublime," *Georgia Review* 30 (1976): 141, 144, 153.
15 In *The Angel Standing in the Sun,* for instance, his glosses draw attention away from the
ultimate association of himself with God or the Avenging Angel itself. For we have to
ask whether Turner is accepting Ruskin's, let alone Eagles's, version of him as the angel,
or is in reality claiming as sanctuary the structure of Revelation, in which his role is only
that of Saint John, the prophet who writes: "And I saw another mighty angel come down
from heaven, clothed with a cloud: and the rainbow was upon his head, and his face was
as it were the sun, and his feet as pillars of fire: And he had in his hand a little book
open. . . ." The "I" is told to go and take this scroll, eat it, and "utter prophecies over
peoples and nations and languages and many kings"—as Turner is doing in this painting. Thus, in the Revelation fiction he is evoking, we find the sun-God, and standing

before him the angel—both witnessed by the figure of Saint John, who is told to transmit the vision as prophecy—in Turner's case, through his painting.

16 "This Son of Man must be lifted up as the serpent was lifted up by Moses in the wilderness, so that everyone who has faith in him may in him possess eternal life" (John 3 : 14–15). One literary source for the rainbow as hope is the passage in *Paradise Lost,* Book 11, where Adam watches Noah looking toward heaven and sees:

> A dewy Cloud, and in the Cloud a Bow
> Conspicuous with three listed colors gay,
> Betok'ning peace from God, and Cov'nant new.

[ll. 865–67]

11. THE STOUR VALLEY

1 *Table Talk and Omniana of Samuel Taylor Coleridge,* ed. T. Ashe (London, 1909), p. 103.
2 *John Constable's Discourses,* ed. R. B. Beckett (Ipswich, 1970), p. 60.
3 *Complete Works of Hazlitt,* ed. Howe, 8: 43–44; 4: 120 (or again, 11: 88).
4 *Poetical Works of William Wordsworth,* ed. Ernest de Selincourt and Helen Darbishire (Oxford, 1940–49; rev., 1952–59), 2: 383, 386. The question of the Constable-Wordsworth relationship is not relevant to this study of Constable. It might be, if any direct influence could be traced from one to the other at an early date (a letter from Constable to Wordsworth survives from 1836). They knew each other through their common friend, Sir George Beaumont; they were coincidentally seeking roughly the same ends in their earlier works and the same sorts of reinforcement and intensification in their later ones. The analogies are thoroughly discussed by a number of writers. See, for example, Morse Peckham, "Constable and Wordsworth," *College Art Journal* 12 (1952): 196–209; Karl Kroeber, *Romantic Landscape Vision: Constable and Wordsworth* (Madison, Wis., 1975); and James A. W. Heffernan's forthcoming book on the subject.
5 *Complete Works of Hazlitt,* 16:265.
6 Ibid., 4:76n.
7 JC to John Fisher, August 1824; *John Constable's Correspondence,* ed. R. B. Beckett, 7 vols. (Ipswich, 1958–62), 6: 172. Hereafter cited as *JCC.*
8 JC to Dunthorne, 29 May 1802, *JCC,* 2: 32.
9 JC to Fisher, August 1824, *JCC,* 6: 172.
10 See Kroeber's analysis, in *Romantic Landscape Vision,* p. 31.
11 The inscription on the stretcher makes it clear that *Winter Landscape in the Minories* (Coll. Sir Robert Peele, Colchester), is an authentic Constable copied from a Ruisdael in 1832. There is no way to be absolutely certain that this is the painting Constable showed in his third lecture (although Beckett assumes it is in his annotation to *John Constable's Discourses,* p. 64). However, among the known copies of Ruisdael by Constable, it is the only one that fits the evidence closely enough to be the painting used. Presumably, the few strokes of pigment behind the feet of the largest figure toward the left represents the dog which Lucas said was added by Constable (*John Constable: Further Documents and Correspondence,* pp. 61–62), and the windmill we see from the back "has the canvas on the poles." The painting was included in the 1976 Tate bicentenary exhibition (no. 292). I am indebted to Charles Rhyne for this identification.
12 *John Constable's Discourses,* p. 64.
13 *Constable Paintings, Watercolours and Drawings* (London: Tate Gallery Exhibition, 1976), no. 207.
14 See Paulson, *Hogarth: His Life, Art, and Times,* 1:264–65, 274.
15 John Eagles, *The Sketcher* (1856), p. 79. The remarks originally appeared in a series of articles published in *Blackwood's Magazine* in 1833–35.

16 *JCC,* 6: 98.

17 Harris, *The Artist and the Country House,* p. 347. As Nicolaus Pevsner has said in *The Englishness of English Art* (London, 1956; 1964 ed.), "it was England in the Romantic Age that led Europe away from the landscape arranged of carefully disposed masses and towards the atmospheric landscape." Or put differently: "the intensity of feeling for nature combined with an unreal coherence of the surface, independent of the corporeal shapes lying as it were behind" (pp. 166, 167). This was one aspect of the landscape "revolution."

18 January 1842, in *The Letters of Edward Fitzgerald,* ed. Alfred M. Terhune and Annabelle B. Terhune (Princeton, 1980), 1: 295. Recall that Turner's own paintings were said to look like "soapsuds and whitewash" (Lindsay, *Turner,* p. 191).

19 *JCC,* 6: 200. I suspect that Constable got the word *dew* from the Frenchman whose remark on his paintings in the Louvre was reported to him in 1824: "look at these English pictures—the dew is upon the ground" (6: 185). Thereafter he was quick to pick up such remarks: that the engraver Reynolds has told him "my 'freshness' exceeds the freshness of any painter that ever lived—for to my zest of 'color' I have added 'light' " (6: 181); and Lady Morley's comment on one of his paintings: "how fresh—how dewy—how exhilarating!" of which Constable says, "half of it, if true, was worth all the cant & talk of pictures in the world" (JC to Leslie, 3: 98). There is also the story of Chantrey "passing a strong glazing of asphaltum" over Hadleigh Castle in the Royal Academy, and Constable's response: "there goes all my dew" (3: 177). He refers to Rubens's "dewy light and freshness" in the *Discourses* (p. 61) and kept talking about "freshness" throughout his career (6: 198, 211, 258); but it is one of the earliest words he found to describe the effect of his own landscapes.

20 23 October 1821, *JCC,* 6: 77.

21 Ibid., p. 78.

22 It is this tension that Basil Taylor described (which turned away some patrons) as the defiance of the principles of "unity of notation" and "unity of touch or handling"— namely, the accepted practice of making brushwork correspond to conventional and regular notations for leaves, grass, rivers, and so on, and the consistent, regular handling of the paint. *Constable,* 2d ed. (London, 1975), p. 40.

23 *JCC,* 6: 198. He also remarks to Fisher on some "Claude" sketches that "looked just like papers used and otherwise mauled, & purloined from a Water Closet" (6: 150). I do not mean to suggest that Constable himself thought of his foreground as a cow-turd, or that his aesthetic theory included the old Addisonian problem of painting a dunghill.

24 Constable did, of course, make sketches into the sun at sunrise and sunset. He exhibited the picture as "Landscape: Noon" but referred to it in his correspondence with Fisher as "Hay-Wain"; the associations are not specifically with harvest ("Bring in the harvest," etc.) but merely with haymaking, producing fodder for the animals. In the Royal Academy, 1821, and the British Institute, 1822, it was entitled "Landscape: Noon"; only at the Paris Salon of 1824 was it called "une charrette à foin traversant une gué au pied d'une ferme; paysage". See Fisher's letter of 14 February 1821, *JCC,* 6: 62).

25 Constable tells the story; *JCC,* 4: 387.

26 William Marshall, *Rural Economy of Norfolk* (1787), quoted in S. G. Hoskins, *The Making of the English Landscape* (London, 1955), p. 184.

27 Hoskins, p. 187. On enclosed versus common ground in seventeenth-century topo-graphical poetry, see Turner, *Politics of Landscape,* pp. 124–29.

28 Ibid., pp. 146, 179.

29 Lines 71–80. See Barrell, *The Idea of Landscape and the Sense of Place 1730–1840,* pp. 62, 75 (my italics).

30 The Victoria and Albert version of *Cottage in a Cornfield,* though completed (and exhib-

ited) in 1833, probably goes back to 1817, when another version (recently identified in a private collection) was exhibited. The V & A painting is closer to Constable's pencil sketch of August-September 1815. See Ian Fleming-Williams, "The Venables *Cottage in a Cornfield," Connoisseur* 198 (1978): 234–37.

31 C. R. Leslie, *Memoirs of the Life of John Constable* (1843), 2d ed. (1845; London, 1951), p. 18.

32 John Barrell, *Dark Side of the Landscape,* pp. 131–64.

33 See Paulson, "Types of Demarcation: Townscape and Landscape Painting," pp. 337–41, and, on Guardi, pp. 341–43.

34 There are a few drawings and watercolors in which Constable is looking along the rise of the valley, outward, standing above Flatford and looking away from Flatford. Of course, in these there still is a church or some such landmark in the distance. Even in major six-foot canvases, such as the *Hay Wain,* once we get into the distance, we are looking out of the valley, though this is, of course, a minor part of the entire view.

35 This is Meyer Abrams's description of the "greater Romantic lyric." "Structure and Style in the Greater Romantic Lyric," in *From Sensibility to Romanticism,* ed. F. W. Hilles and Harold Bloom (Oxford, 1965), p. 533.

12. THE SIX-FOOTERS

1 See C. R. Leslie, *Memoirs of the Life of John Constable* (1843), pp. 285–86. Alastair Smart doubts whether there was a view to the meadows from this point, but the ever-optimistic Attfield Brooks, who would like for Constable to be the "natural painter," supposes that in the period that elapsed between the sketches and the six-footer the undergrowth on the right might actually have been cut. Since Constable's *Hay Wain* was painted in London, presumably from the surviving sketches, this seems a weak argument. Brooks would have to produce a sketch that showed the riverbank without trees. (See Smart and Brooks, *Constable and His Country* [London, 1976], pp. 88, 136.) What Constable did to remove trees from nature is best demonstrated by a sketch of ca. 1812–13 published for the first time in Robert Hoozee's *L'Opera completa di Constable* (Milan, 1979), illustration and catalogue number 117. In painting *The Hay Wain,* Constable stood far to the right of his position in this sketch so that the trees at the right would be behind the mill (the building at the right). The trees at the left of this sketch, however, would be in full view, roughly behind the projecting wall, which just shows at the right in both the sketch and *The Hay Wain.* I am indebted to Charles Rhyne for drawing my attention to this photo and the facts.

　Although the Ipswich *Mill Stream* is not a sketch, it could have been painted mostly from nature. One can account for every tree except the one whose limbs project into the painting from out of the picture on the right. One might also notice that the roof of Willy Lott's cottage in *The Mill Stream* is exactly as it is in sketches from nature and as it can be caught in a photograph today, whereas in *The Hay Wain* it is severely compressed on the left and opened up and stretched out on the right.

2 Alastair Smart, in Smart and Brooks, *Constable and His Country,* p. 75.

3 *JCC,* 6: 89.

4 JC to Fisher, 23 January 1835, *JCC,* 6: 191.

5 Ibid., p. 198.

6 *JCC,* 4: 97. Leslie Parris and Conal Shields, *Tate Catalogue,* interpret *elibray* as "eel trap."

7 C. R. Leslie, *Memoirs of the Life of John Constable,* p. 142.

8 Constable had first included two lines from Robert Bloomfield's *The Farmer's Boy* in the Royal Academy catalogue entry for *A Summerland* in 1814; also in 1817 (*The Harvest Field* at the B.I.), 1827 (*The Cornfield,* B.I.), and after *Hadleigh Castle,* in 1831 (*Salisbury Cathedral from the Meadows,* R.A.).

9   It is of interest that the house at the end of the rainbow is the rectory where the
    Constables stayed with the Fishers—a parallel to the East Bergholt rectory, with which
    Constable also associated rainbows represented in a similar configuration.

10 Barrell, *The Idea of Landscape and the Sense of Place 1730–1840;* see Thomson, "Summer,"
    ll. 701–03.

11 I first sketched out these ideas in "Toward the Constable Bicentenary: Thoughts on
    Landscape Theory," *Eighteenth-Century Studies* 10 (1976–77): 245–61. I am happy to see
    confirmation of the structure I am outlining in Barrell's *Dark Side of the Landscape*
    (1980), where he writes: "As in the Claude [landscape structure], the objects are ar-
    ranged so as to facilitate the eye's flight, not to one but two areas of light just below the
    horizon, this time at the center and on the right of the composition—one either side,
    that is, of the tree in the middle distance, which thus complicates the design in a way
    that the trees at the centre of Claude's painting do not. The composition is complicated
    further by the fact that the position of the central group does not allow it to be a
    secondary object of attention, as the figures seem to be in Claude's painting. But still
    that bright penultimate band is what enables us to grasp how the three-dimensional
    space of the Stour Valley has been articulated in two dimensions, and to that extent it is
    on that alluring light that the organisation and the harmony of the landscape depend."
    Having made this formulation of the Constable composition in relation to the Claude,
    Barrell then adds: "What we discover in that band are more tiny figures, little more than
    blobs of white, apparently hay-making, yet curiously hard to make out, though they are
    the brightest objects in the gleaming tract of sunlight on the right" (p. 147). My own
    view is that the figures are subsidiary. See above, p. 147.

12 Appleton, *The Experience of Landscape,* p. 135.

13 There are two versions in the National Gallery, London. The contrast is starker, more
    intense in no. 2561, *View near Haarlem,* with church and foreground ruined castle and
    moat as hazard and, in the distance, the sunlit meadow this side of the church. The same
    elements appear in the larger, more finished version, which has a windmill in the sunlit
    space and an extra church tower on the horizon (no. 990, *Landscape with Ruined Castle and
    a Village Church,* Wynn Ellis Bequest, 1876). Another painting that creates a similar
    effect, though without the ruin in the foreground but with the same distant sunlit field,
    is *View of Haarlem from the Dunes* (Boston Museum of Fine Arts, no. 39.794). Also in the
    Thyssen Collection are a small similar version (no. 271) and another that derives the same
    effect from a different composition (esp. 269, with two areas of light; but also no. 270).
    In the Metropolitan Museum, New York, there is a *View of Haarlem and Grainfields.* In
    other words, this is a scene that was much repeated.

14 *Discourses,* p. 63.

15 There is no reason not to take seriously Alastair Smart's suggestion that the experience of
    living on Hampstead Heath, that "sombre landscape, illuminated here and there by
    flashes of sunlight," while down in the Charlotte Street studio he painted his Stour
    Valley scenes, may also have recalled the image of the Ruisdael landscapes (Smart and
    Brooks, *Constable and His Country,* p. 77).

16 Rhyne first presented this part of his thesis in "Constable's Views of East Bergholt
    Common," at the annual meeting of the College Art Association, Washington, D.C.,
    January 1970; an expanded version was delivered at the Tate Gallery and at Yale
    University in March and April 1976.

17 *Discourses,* p. 12.

18 JC to Maria, *JCC,* 18 September 1814, 2: 78; 2: 132.

19 I must mention the painting of 1802 (?), the first of such views, seen from the lower
    window of the Constable house, in which the field beyond the vicarage is cut down to
    almost nothing, and the emphasis falls on the large sunlit field *this* side of the vicarage
    (Downing College, Cambridge). It is only in the finished representation of the kitchen

garden that Constable chooses the upper window for the definitive composition, with its emphasis on the field to the right of the vicarage.

An early view of the rectory group is dated 1808, before Constable's meeting with Maria (Fitzwilliam, *Tate Catalogue*, no. 83). One is inscribed "30 Sept. 1810 E. Bergholt Common" (John G. Johnson Coll., Philadelphia, *Tate Catalogue*, no. 93); one dated "18 Augst 1813" (Private Coll., *Tate Catalogue*, no. 120; 19 August 1813 (Mellon Coll.). Above all, *Golding Constable's Kitchen Garden* can be reliably dated 1815 (*Tate Catalogue*, no. 135). For that matter, there was apparently a significant day, to which Constable refers more than once, when Maria did some sketching with him at Flatford Mill (*JCC*, 2: 54, 80). Salisbury Cathedral, of course, he associated with the Fishers, but the reason for the great version of 1831, when Fisher was still living, was probably the associations he carried from his honeymoon in Oxmington.

20   Though I doubt whether it ought to be described in terms of the Romantic Window, "Keats' magic casements," as described by Lorenz Eitner, "The Open Window and the Storm-Tossed Boat: An Essay in the Iconography of Romanticism," *Art Bulletin* 37 (1955): 281–90.

21   *JCC*, 6: 142; see also Taylor, *Constable*, p. 38, who discusses the passage and, I think, misunderstands it. Since Kurt Badt's *John Constable's Clouds*, it has become conventional to say that the full-scale oil sketches were the recreation of the experience itself, whereas the finished academy piece was the "emotion recollected in tranquility" (*John Constable's Clouds* [London, 1950], p. 86). Obviously Constable painted with as much emotion in the "finished" version as in the sketches. And yet the passage in Constable's letter to Fisher makes me wonder whether "more than one state of mind" is not in fact what Wordsworth meant. It is largely a result of seeing the subject from different points of view that is embodied in the final versions; and this means somewhat more detachment, a diffusion of the energy that is concentrated in the sketch, and then something more.

22   *JCC*, 2: 78, 79, 80, 80–81.

23   Ibid., p. 81.

24   Ibid., p. 90.

25   Barrell, *The Idea of Landscape*, p. 50.

26   There is a remarkable small picture by Richard Wilson in Wilton House, called *Ariccia: Fallen Tree*, which shows the sun illuminating a strangely twisted and broken tree in the foreground and, separately, an opening in the woods far back to the left.

27   See Ian Fleming-Williams, "A Runover Dungle and a Possible Date for 'Spring,'" *Burlington Magazine* 114 (1972): 386–93. Cf. the oil sketch in the Leeds City Art Galleries in which "Harvest is still going on in the fields in the middle distance, while in the foreground two men are digging out a dunghill in preparation for the muck-spreading which preceded the winter ploughing" (*Tate Catalogue*, no. 127; related drawing, 1814 sketchbook, *Tate Catalogue*, no. 126). In the Boston painting (*Tate Catalogue*, no. 133) "the harvest is over and ploughing is beginning."

28   Barrell has written: "There was an almost universal tendency among landscape-poets—until the growth of the picturesque school—to evaluate the beauty of a landscape partly in terms of the expectation it aroused of a good harvest" (*The Idea of Landscape*, p. 61). For the equation of the beautiful and the useful, see ibid., pp. 73–75. Hugh Honour writes of Constable's landscapes: "The dung which fertilized the fields, no less than the rain that watered them, the mills in which the grain was ground, the boats on which it was transported by canal to the city—all played a part in his vision of the universal harmony" (*Romanticism* [New York, 1979], p. 89).

29   JC to Maria, 2 October 1814; *JCC*, 2: 133.

30   25 October 1814, ibid., p. 135. In his next letter of 12 November, he refers to his "wounded spirit" and his "mind (unfortunately perhaps) of the most excruciating sensibility" (p. 135).

31 JC to Maria, 9 May 1819, *JCC*, 2: 246.

32 Karl Kroeber has remarked "the obtrusiveness of all vertical forms" in *The Leaping Horse*, and the conflict or tension between the "temporarily rising verticals," such as the piles and the horse, and the "enduring horizontals" of nature, the water and the plain (*Romantic Landscape Vision,* pp. 113, 114).

33 *Salisbury Cathedral from the Meadows* (V & A) leads us back to the view of 1823, which is framed by a Gothic archway of trees. Churches seem to have activated Constable's latent need for conventional symbols; or perhaps we should say churches were the easiest symbols within his reach when he needed reinforcement.

34 Cf. Constable to Fisher: "In the dark recesses of these gardens, and at the end of one of the walks, I saw an urn—& bust of Sir Joshua Reynolds—& under it some beautiful verses, by Wordsworth" (2 November 1823, *JCC,* 6: 143).

13. ADDITION AND SUBTRACTION

1 *Discourses,* p. 40.

2 On Turner's use of the *St. Peter Martyr* composition, see above, p. 72.

3 *Discourses,* pp. 46–47.

4 Another example he takes is Domenichino's *St. Jerome,* in which the history is also an area of violent energy in the foreground, over and beyond which we see a peaceful landscape: "The placid aspect of this simple landscape seems like a requiem to soothe the departing spirit: its effect is like that of solemn music heard from an adjoining apartment" (p. 50)—another telling verbal account of the visual effect in Constable's own six-foot convases. As he says, turning to the example of Poussin's *Deluge* (Louvre): "the most awful subjects may be made far more affecting than by overloading them with imagery"—i.e., by removing or displacing the imagery (p. 60).

5 Ibid, p. 41.

6 Reynolds's foreground, by contrast, he notes to have been "rich masses of colour, or light and shade, which, when examined, mean nothing. In Titian there is equal breadth, equal subordination of the parts to the whole, but the spectator finds, on approaching the picture, that every touch is the representation of a reality"—and this, of course, is a description of Constable's own paintings climaxing in *The Leaping Horse* (p. 48).

7 JC to Maria, 2: 125.

8 *Discourses,* p. 47.

9 Ibid., p. 48. When he turns to Domenichino's *St. Jerome,* he makes the painter into the martyr: "It is mournful to reflect that neither age, worth, nor transcendent talents— could screen the virtuous Domenichino from the bad passions of intriguing contemporaries" (p. 50). Compare with a sentence from that most useful and knowledgeable of Constable scholars, R. B. Beckett. He is referring to the way in which Constable clung "to his trio of elderly monitors, Sir George Beaumont, Dr. Fisher, and Mr. Farington, in whom he could at least respect their sincere belief in the values of a great tradition, even though it might be a tradition from which he was already seeking to break away" (2: 5).

10 Tate, *Constable Catalogue,* no. 330.

11 The whole speech: "O Placidas, why pursuest thou me? I have come for thy sake to appear to thee in this animal. I am Christ Whom thou worshippest unbeknownst to thyself." See Erwin Panofsky, "Dürer's 'St. Eustace,'" *Record of the Art Museum, Princeton University* 9, no. 1 (1950): 2–10.

12 It would be nice to think that Constable could have seen Pisanello's *St. Eustace,* but it was not acquired by the National Gallery until 1895 (National Gallery Catalogue, 1929, no. 1436).

13 Constable made a large watercolor of the subject, apparently derived from a painting by Beaumont. It was shown at Colnaghi's in 1828 and exhibited at the Royal Academy in 1832 (now in the British Museum). He also contemplated an oil painting of the subject.

When it was returned from Colnaghi's, he had it engraved by Lucas in the *English Landscape* format. (The oil painting may have been the one sold in 1839; *JCC,* 4: 132, 157.) The entry in the Royal Academy Catalogue of 1832, under *Jaques and the Wounded Stag,* included the verses:

> The melancholy feeling Jacques, whose mind
> Griev'd o'er the wounded weeping hind.

See 'The Social Day' a poem by Peter Cose, Esq.

In 1797 Constable had attempted an illustration of "Romeo's account of an apothecary's shop"; in 1815 he painted the background for a painting of Miss O'Neill as Juliet (Garrick Club), and at Coleorton he joined the family in listening to readings from Shakespeare: "on Saturday evening it was 'As You Like It', and the Seven Ages I never so heard before" (*JJC,* 2: 292; also C. R. Leslie, *Memoirs,* pp. 27, 75, 129). The "Seven Ages" speech is, of course, Jaques's most famous one. From all the evidence I conclude that Constable associated himself with the misanthrope Jaques, and that he naturally focused on Jaques's response to the human incursions on nature.

If one looks closely at the clearing in *The Cenotaph,* it looks as if Constable had at some point included a huntsman—or some such figure—in the clearing and then partially obliterated him. Charles Rhyne, examining the painting as early as 1963, took this semifigure to be a little girl. See the 1946 edition of the *National Gallery Catalogue of the British School,* no. 1272.

14   We cannot rule out the possibility that the Wordsworth inscription on the monument led Constable to connect it with the stag of Wordsworth's "Hart-leap Well" (1800): "And, gallant Stag! to make thy praises known/ Another monument shall here be raised"—i.e., in memory of the stag's death. If so, the implication is much the same as in the other interpretations: the result was that this "jolly place . . . in time of old" is now in ruins: "the spot is curst."

15   The subject of the Reynolds *Cenotaph* is relevant here, because while Constable admired Reynolds as a painter, his representation of the memorial to him in a dense thicket on Sir George Beaumont's estate is full of ambivalence. In fact, this is the one explicit expression in his painting of the ambivalence his letters show to Beaumont and his other elderly mentors (Archbishop Fisher and Farington) in relation to the opposition advanced by academic opinion to the development of his landscape painting; they were his patrons and friends but utterly uncomprehending of what he was trying to do. And we see this in the letters directly concerned with his ambivalence toward the Bicknells in relation to his love for Maria. The issue of landscape painting was, of course, involved as the cause of the separation from Maria; it was the more lasting of the problems; and, indeed, was probably finalized with his feelings during Maria's decline and death when he was elected, too late, to the Academy.

16   *Discourses,* pp. 9–10; *Constable* (Tate Exhibition Catalogue, 1976), no. 3, *Christ's Charge to Peter (Feed My Sheep).* He copies at least two others, *The Death of Ananias* and *The Blinding of Elymas (Paul and the Proconsul).*

17   Sydney Freedberg, *Painting of the High Renaissance in Rome and Florence* (Cambridge, Mass., 1961), 1: 265.

14. ENGLISH LANDSCAPE

1   *English Landscape* appeared in five parts between 1830 and 1832; the first four contained four prints each, the fifth, six, making twenty-two altogether. The second edition of May 1833 contained the same plates but in different order. A new series, referred to as the "Appendix," was projected but incomplete at Constable's death in 1837. Some of these appeared among a further six plates published by Moon in 1838, and another

fourteen by Lucas himself in 1845. Besides the *English Landscape* series, Lucas also mezzotinted some large copies of Constable landscapes (e.g., *The Cornfield* and *The Lock,* 1834). See Andrew Shirley, *The Published Mezzotints of David Lucas after John Constable* (London, 1930), and Andrew Wilton, *Constable's 'English Landscape Scenery'* (London, 1979).

2 *JCC,* 3: 108; 4: 383.

3 C. R. Leslie, *Memoirs of the Life of John Constable,* p. 280. Leslie remarks "how very little Constable cared for the usual classifications of art" (p. 284), but at some point he seems to have attempted a system of categories similar to Turner's, and he sought variety in his series. The final result, however, leaned toward the "pastoral," and he insisted that the emphasis should be on this genre (*JCC,* 6: 335). One example will suffice. He omitted *Salisbury Cathedral, Stonehenge,* and *Castle Acre Priory* because they were too dominated by large, monumental architectural structures. *Hadleigh Castle* and *Old Sarum,* by contrast, showed a castle or city which had been transformed into a landscape (in the manner of the "muck heap"). *Waterloo Bridge,* on the other hand, was rejected because it depicted a specific historic event in London, and so worked against the timeless rural character of the "pastoral."

4 Earlom contrasts Claude's "rural" style of landscape with Poussin's heroic: "It must be confessed, that in the relation of his [Claude's] stories, they are often made too subservient to the Landscape, are composed on too small a scale, and want perhaps that dignity which the subject [i.e., the history? or the landscape?] requires" (*Liber Veritatis* p. 8). This could explain something of Constable's radical enlargement of the human signs in his landscapes. Although Earlom stresses Claude's truth to nature ("They exhibit a perfect Model of Truth and may serve to shew completely how the real disposition of the objects of Nature is to be imitated," p. 8), he attributes to him the "most laborious imitation" we usually associate with the Dutch landscapists. He says Claude lacks invention but offers a "happy combination" of materials: "It must be acknowledged, indeed that his combinations are mostly arbitrary, that the *unity of place* is often violated, and that the parts of his Picture do not always constitute a perfect whole" (p. 7)—the exception being his seaports.

5 Pope had used the same lines at the head of his *Pastorals* (1709).

6 I suspect that he printed the closing lines of the epigraph from James Thomson because they present a scientific description of nature, supporting his belief in the empirical observation of natural phenomena (also to draw attention to their similarity to the lines by Virgil).

7 *Discourses,* p. 62 (italics added for emphasis). When I say that Constable's painting technique involved building lights out of dark grounds, I mean in a general way. In fact, of course, Constable sometimes used as many as three different grounds in one painting, building both ways, into light and into dark.

8 The term "moral landscape" appears in Constable's correspondence, though not in *English Landscape.* It was probably taken from Robert Bromley's *A Philosophical and Critical History of the Fine Arts* (1793–95), which Constable owned, one of the first books to suggest that landscape, were it poetic and didactic, might be the equal of history. Bromley writes: "moral painting, under which term we include all that is historical or poetical, all that conveys a lesson, is [art's] noblest display." (See *John Constable: Further Documents and Correspondence,* ed. Leslie Parris, Conal Shields, and Ian Fleming-Williams (Ipswich, 1975), p. 28.

9 *JCC,* 3: 49.

10 *JCC,* 4: 382.

11 *JCC,* 3: 122.

12 See Hugh Honour, *Romanticism,* p. 89: "Often it is something unexpected if not, at first

sight, untoward—the haywain is not on dry land but splashing through water; the lumbering cart-horse prepares to leap over a barrier on the tow-path; the white horse is not drawing a barge but standing on one. It seems likely that these and many of Constable's other paintings are pictorial equivalents to the 'spots of time' of *The Prelude*. . . ." He does not explain why, but it is presumably the strange concatenation of things—Wordsworth's gibbet-trace, the Penrith beacon, the girl in the wind with a pitcher on her head. The pattern of crime-guilt-punishment-sublime expression, which is Wordsworth's version of the "spot of time" needs to be compared with Constable's. The oedipal situation which Wordsworth adumbrates is a more public and general one than Constable's, perhaps—and than Turner's ultimately enigmatic return to a primal confrontation without any public overtones. Or should we accept Wordsworth's love-betrayal of Annette Vallon, which he equated with his reaction to the French Revolution, as finding a counterpart in Constable's equation of Maria with his more public problems?

13   13 April 1822, *JCC,* 6: 88. Michael Rosenthal (in a forthcoming article) argues for the powerful effect on Constable's painting of the 1822 agricultural unrest—the Ludditism, riots, barn-burnings, and rick-burnings in the Stour Valley. He believes that before this time Constable's landscapes had been painted in a georgic mode, and afterward in an antigeorgic one—that is, they were no longer topographical descriptions of landscape or of agricultural activities (seasonal planting, reaping, and so on) but expressions of political upheavals. Of course, Constable had also moved away from home, and was not a Suffolk landowner but a Londoner. But his art does reflect what was happening in the world from his conservative point of view, and so it expresses anxiety. Machine-breaking and incendiarism began in the mid-1790s, then spread to the eastern counties in 1816, to East Anglia in 1822, and all over the east and south in the autumn and winter of 1830, when the double stimulus of the French and Belgian rebellions was felt as well. See E. J. Hobsbawm and George Rudé, *Captain Swing* (London, 1969), esp. pp. 83–84 and 152; J. L. Hammond and Barbara Hammond, *The Village Labourer* (London, 1911); and A. J. Peacock, *Bread or Blood* (London, 1965).

15. REPRESENTATION AND SYMBOLIZATION

1   John Barrell, *Dark Side of the Landscape,* chap. 3.

2   Edmund Burke, *Works* (London, 1893), 5: 268. As to the sublime, Constable tells Maria he prefers Allison's *Principles of Taste* to Burke's *Enquiry* because Allison "considers us as endowed with minds capable of comprehending the 'beauty and sublimity of the material world' only as the means of leading us to *religious sentiment*" (28 August 1814, *JCC,* 2: 131). This is once again the public, religious Constable writing to Maria.

3   As his letters to Lucas show, he sought variety in the *English Landscape* scenes, and his representation of ruins after Maria's death may have had utilitarian as well as personal significance: he may have needed to include a proportionate number of historical entries in his series.

4   See James Sellars, *Samuel Palmer* (New York, 1974), pls. 57, 120, 72, 91, 93.

5   The "minimum ingredients" of the *locus amoenus,* as E. R. Curtius writes, "comprise a tree (or several trees), a meadow, and a spring or brook" (*European Literature and the Latin Middle Ages,* trans. Willard R. Trask [New York, 1953], p. 195; also pp. 183–202). Palmer, incidentally, shared with Constable the same political pessimism; see Geoffrey Grigson, *Samuel Palmer: The Visionary Years* (London, 1947), pp. 104–07.

6   James Turner, *Politics of Landscape,* p. 23 (also pp. 21–23). Another verbal expression of the graphic structure Constable develops is offered us by C. R. Leslie: "Speaking of the taste for the *prodigious* and the *astounding,* a taste very contrary to his own, he made use of a quotation from the 1st Book of Kings. 'A great and strong wind rent the mountains, and brake in pieces the rocks before the Lord; but the Lord was not in the wind; and after

the wind an earthquake; but the Lord was not in the earthquake: and after the earthquake a fire; but the Lord was not in the fire; and after the fire *a still small voice*' " (*Memoirs of the Life of John Constable*, p. 280). What I see in this passage is the agitation of the foreground and middle ground of the Constable landscape (wind, earthquake, and fire), beyond which we make out the *locus amoenus* of the "still small voice."

7   See above, Introduction, pp. 11–15.

8   Quite independently, around 1827–28 in America, Thomas Cole was producing a series of paintings, beginning with *Landscape: The Blasted Tree* (Museum of Art, Rhode Island School of Design), which gives a simple equivalent of what Constable seems to have been working toward in the Stour Valley landscapes and the symbolized landscapes that followed. As Bryan Wolf has shown (see above, p. 174, n. 21), Cole employs a structure that involves a foreground promontory, a main mountain mass in the middle distance, and a peaceful stretch of scenery in the distance. Sometimes the foreground promontory merges, or seems to merge, with the mountain, in what Wolf regards as a single assertion of a narcissistic, mirror-image self; and sometimes there is an impassable chasm separating the promontory from the far larger and more threatening male shape of the mountain. In this case, the distant stretch of peaceful, horizontal, "beautiful" scenery shows a rearrangement of the vertical and threatening forms of the mountains—a "reaction formation" or escape from the sublime to the beautiful.

9   Paul Ricoeur, *Freud and Philosophy: An Essay on Interpretation,* trans. Denis Savage (New Haven, 1970), p. 97, n. 15. The Freud text is *The Interpretation of Dreams* (1900), trans. James Strachey (1958), *Standard Edition,* 5: 339–49.

10 It is useful to bring together Appleton's prospect-refuge theory with the distinctions made by Adrian Stokes (in his Turner essay) and Melanie Klein between modeling/ carving and regarding nature as part-objects or as whole-objects. See Stokes, for example, *Stones of Rimini* (1934) and his Turner essay in *Painting and the Inner World* (1963); Klein, *Love, Guilt and Reparation and Other Works 1921–1945* (New York, 1975), especially "The Importance of Symbol-Formation in the Development of the Ego" (1930).

11 Constable himself became aware of the self-reflexive quality of what others called "whitewash" and he called "dewy freshness." In 1830 he admitted to Fisher: "and you are quite right, I have filled my head with certain notions of *freshness—sparkle—* brightness—till it has influenced my practice in no small degree, & is in fact taking the place of truth so invidious [or insidious?] in manner, in all things" (24 May 1830, *JCC,* 6: 258). It is, he adds, "a species of self worship," when "we have nature (another word for moral feeling) always in our reach." And yet he also attaches public meaning to the whitewash through the principle of chiaroscuro, as he explains in the introduction to *English Landscape.*

12 I would refer the reader here to Fredric Jameson's excellent exposition of Lacan, "Imaginary and Symbolic in Lacan: Marxism, Psychoanalytic Criticism, and the Problem of the Subject," in *Literature and Psychoanalysis: The Question of Reading: Otherwise* (New Haven: Yale French Studies, 1977), pp. 338–95.

13 H. F. Clark, "Eighteenth-Century Elysiums: The Role of 'Association' in the Landscape Movement," *Journal of the Warburg and Courtauld Institutes* 6 (1943): 165–89. Constable's turning to ruins and to monuments like the cenotaph to Reynolds at Coleorton is the same memorializing phenomenon as the creation of visual epigraphs—"symbolic structures which bond together past and present, death and life" (see Lawrence Goldstein, *Ruins and Empire: The Evolution of a Theme in Augustan and Romantic Literature* [Pittsburgh, 1977], p. 178). Goldstein relates Constable's and Wordsworth's conservatism: both possessing, in Goldstein's words about Wordsworth, a "fear of change . . . based on his identification of self with landscape and landscape with nation" (p. 182).

14 Humphry Repton, *Observations on the Theory and Practice of Landscape Gardening* (1803), pp. 32–33.

15 J. C. Loudon, ed., *The Landscape Gardening and Landscape Architecture of the Late Humphry Repton* (1840), p. 243.

16 Thomas Whatley, *Observations on Modern Gardening,* 3d ed. (1771), p. 131.

17 I suspect that repression is one explanation for the full-size sketches that preceded and survived each six-foot Royal Academy canvas (although I am aware that each bears a different relationship to the exhibited painting). Constable kept them in his studio even after the final version had found a buyer. The doubling allowed for repetition in the Wordsworthian sense of "recollection in tranquility"; but it also ensured that Constable did not lose the large shape—the sheer energy, force, tonalities, and powerful feel he had to go some way toward consciously repressing in the "meaning" of the finished painting. The undisguised energy of desire shows in the unfinished sketch, while it is order and meaning that is relatively imposed in the finished six-footer, where Constable revises, moves things around, adds a church tower, and brings the picture to an acceptable level of finish—and then continues to order it in his letters and lectures. He had to repress and control, but the only way he could be sure that in the process he did not lost contact with the original conception was to keep it intact alongside. (Also, on a more practical level, if necessary he could always duplicate the finished painting, producing other versions for patrons; and he could, in this way, both sell the painting and keep it. He had difficulty parting with *The Hay Wain* and other six-footers.) I wonder, incidentally, what the significance may be, in the full-size sketch of *The Hay Wain,* of the fact that the sunlight is between the trees to the left and in the foreground of the meadow, rather than in the distance as in the final painting.

18 See above, p. 173, n. 13.

19 *JCC,* 6: 210.

20 *JCC,* 3: 94–95.

16. HAMPSTEAD HEATH

1 See Graham Reynolds, *Constable the Natural Painter* (London, 1965), p. 79; also Alastair Smart, who suggests that the experience of the Heath may explain the later six-footers. He refers to "this sombre landscape, illuminated here and there by flashes of sunlight" (*Constable's Country,* p. 77).

2 The Admiral's House may have recommended itself as a subject to Constable in so far as it resembled the vicarage/woods configuration of his Stour Valley experience—but without the prospect beyond which offers escape.

3 Versions are in both the Victoria and Albert and the Tate.

4 Compare George Morland's *The Sand Cart,* dated 1792 (on loan to Kenwood House), as it relates to Constable's sand-carters. Another kind of painting, Linnell's *Kensington Gravel Pits* of 1811–12 (Tate) also shows excavations of this sort. One view of Branch Hill Pond, presumably from the Whitestone Pond area, shows the other side of the sand bank; see *Hampstead Heath with Harrow in the Distance* (ca. 1820–23, Tate no. 1237).

5 Compare Constable's *Trees near Hampstead Church* (ca. 1829, Tate no. 2659), with cattle in a pond, which is very close to a Gainsborough with cattle, though flatter; also the two versions of *The Glebe Farm* (Tate).

6 *Discourses,* p. 61.

17. CONCLUSION

1 *Coastal Scene with Shipping* (Private Collection), in *Thomas Gainsborough,* ed. John Hayes (London: Tate Gallery Exhibition, 1980), no. 90.

2 I am indebted to Jay Appleton for the facts of London and Stour Valley geography in these pages (conveyed in personal correspondence).

3 See *Constable, Tate Catalogue,* nos. 22, 32, 41; also nos. 34, 43, 46, 47, 50, 55, and so on.

4   *Tate Catalogue,* nos. 186, 187, 188.
5   *Tate Catalogue,* nos. 194, 195, 196, 271, 283. Of the ridge only, without the indication of what is on the other side, see no. 204, and the vignette of the sand bank, no. 281.
6   "Iconography and Iconology," in *Meaning in the Visual Arts* (New York, 1955), p. 33.
7   Ricoeur, *Freud and Philosophy,* pp. 62–65.

ILLUSTRATIONS

1. Giorgione, *Sleeping Venus.*

2. Claude Lorrain, *Narcissus and Ecbo*.

3. Thomas Cole, *Sunny Morning on the Hudson River* (1827).

5. William Hogarth, *Four Times of the Day: Noon* (1738). Engraving.

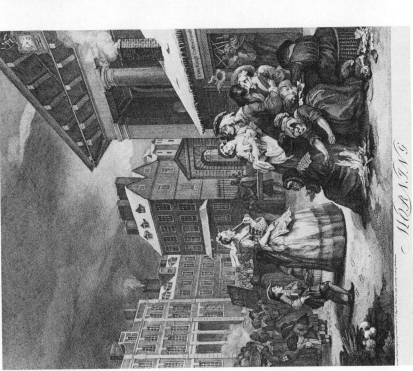

4. William Hogarth, *Four Times of the Day: Morning* (1738). Engraving.

7. William Hogarth, *Four Times of the Day: Night* (1738). Engraving.

6. William Hogarth, *Four Times of the Day: Evening* (1738). Engraving.

8. William Hogarth, *Strolling Actresses Dressing in a Barn* (1738). Engraving.

9. Dirck Barendtsz, *Times of the Day: Morning.* Engraving by Jan Sadeler.

10. Dirck Barendtsz, *Times of the Day: Evening.* Engraving by Jan Sadeler.

11. George Lambert, *Hilly Landscape with Cornfield* (1732).

11a. Detail of figure 11.

11b. Detail of figure 11.

12. George Lambert, *Extensive Landscape with Four Gentlemen on a Hillside* (1732).

12a. Detail of figure 12.

12b. Detail of figure 12.

13. Richard Wilson, *Dinas Bran near Llangollen* (1771).

14. Richard Wilson, *View near Wynnstay, Llangollen* (1771).

15. Richard Wilson, *Carnarvon Castle* (1762).

16. Samuel Scott, *An Arch of Westminster Bridge* (1748).

17. Canaletto, *The Thames from the Terrace of Somerset House, Westminster Bridge in the Distance* (ca. 1750–51).

18. Richard Wilson, *Syon House from Richmond Gardens* (1761?).

19. Gaspar Dughet, *Ideal Landscape*.

20. Gaspar Dughet, *Eurydice*.

21. Richard Wilson, *Destruction of Niobe's Children* (1760).

22. Richard Wilson, *The White Monk* (undated).

23. Thomas Gainsborough, *Classical Landscape: Rocky Mountain Valley with Shepherd, Stream, and Goats* (1780s).

24. Thomas Gainsborough, *Diana and Actaeon* (1789).

25. Thomas Gainsborough, *Hounds Coursing a Fox* (ca. 1789).

26. Thomas Rowlandson, *Landscape with Two Men* (ca. 1800). Drawing.

27. Thomas Rowlandson, *A Timber Wagon, ca. 1790*. Drawing.

28. Thomas Rowlandson, *Shipyard Scene* (ca. 1800). Drawing.

29. Thomas Rowlandson, *The Man of Letters* (ca. 1800). Drawing.

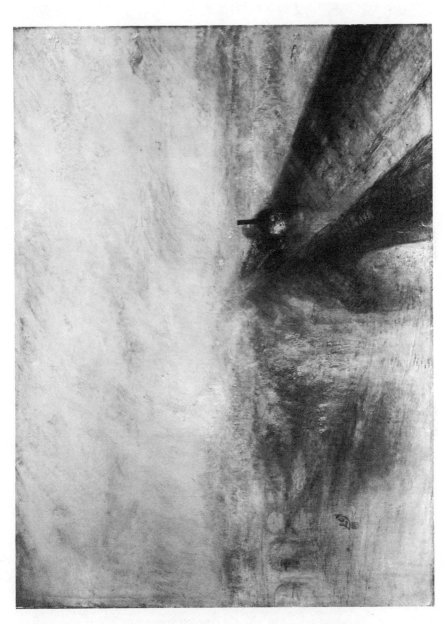

30. J. M. W. Turner, *Rain, Steam, and Speed: Great Western Railway* (1844).

31. J. M. W. Turner, *Dido Building Carthage* (1815).

32. Claude Lorrain, *Embarcation of the Queen of Sheba*.

33. J. M. W. Turner, *The Bay of Baiae: with Apollo and Sibyl* (1823).

34. J. M. W. Turner, *Buttermere Lake* (1798).

35. J. M. W. Turner, *Dolbadern Castle, North Wales* (1800).

36. J. M. W. Turner, *Palestrina—a Composition* (1828?).

37. J. M. W. Turner, *Calais Pier* (1803).

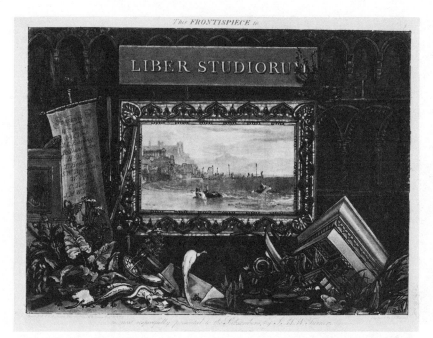

38. J. M. W. Turner, *Liber Studiorum: Frontispiece* (1812). Etching and aquatint.

39. J. M. W. Turner, *Liber Studiorum: The Fall of the Clyde.* Etching and aquatint.

40. Philippe de Loutherbourg, *An Avalanche in the Alps* (1804).

41. J. M. W. Turner, *The Fall of an Avalanche in the Grisons* (1810).

42. J. M. W. Turner, *View of Pope's Villa* (actually Lady Howe's villa under construction) (1808).

43. J. M. W. Turner, *Regulus* (1828–29, reworked 1837).

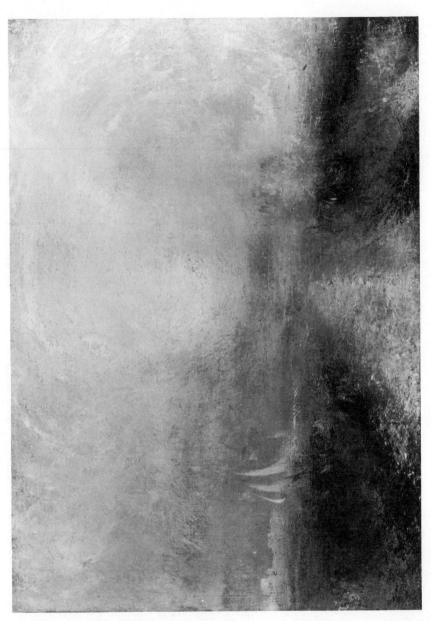

44. J. M. W. Turner, *Yacht Approaching Coast* (ca. 1835–50).

45. J. M. W. Turner, *Angel Standing in the Sun* (1846).

46. J. M. W. Turner, *The Sun of Venice Going to Sea* (1843).

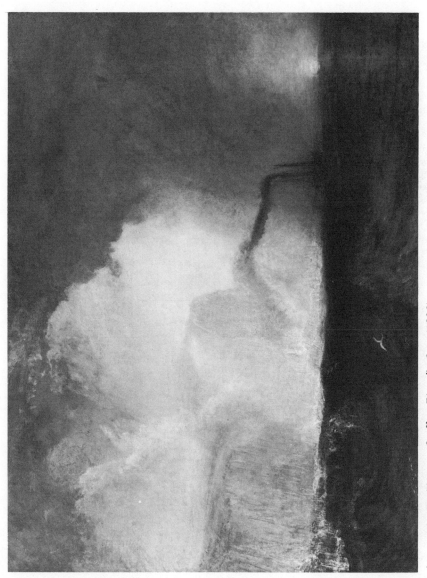

47. J. M. W. Turner, *Staffa—Fingal's Cave* (1832).

48. John Constable, *The Cornfield* (1826).

49. John Constable, *The Cornfield*. Sketch (1825).

50. John Constable, *Stonehenge* (1836).

51. John Constable, *Dedham Lock and Mill* (1820).

52. John Constable, *Cottage in a Cornfield* (1833; originally 1818?).

53. John Constable, *The Mill Stream* (1814).

54. John Constable, *The Hay Wain* (1821).

55. John Constable, *View on the Stour* (1822).

56. John Constable, *A Boat Passing a Lock* (1824).

57. John Constable, *The Leaping Horse* (1825).

58. John Constable, *The Leaping Horse*. Full-sized sketch (1825).

59. John Constable, *Hadleigh Castle* (1829).

60. John Constable, *Salisbury Cathedral from the Meadows* (1831).

61. John Constable, *The Chain Pier, Brighton* (1827).

62. J. M. W. Turner, *The Chain Pier, Brighton.*

63. Peter Paul Rubens, *Landscape with a View of the Chateau de Steen.*

64. Jacob Ruisdael, *View near Haarlem.*

65. John Constable, *Golding Constable's Kitchen Garden* (ca. 1812–16).

65a. Detail of figure 65.

66. John Constable, *The Stour Valley and Dedham Church* (1815?).

67. John Constable, *The Cenotaph to Sir Joshua Reynolds at Coleorton* (1836).

68. Titian, *Martyrdom of St. Peter Martyr* (1520–83). Woodcut by Martin Rota.

69. John Constable, *Dedham Vale* (1828).

70. Albrecht Dürer, *St. Eustace* (ca. 1500–01). Engraving.

71. John Constable, *Jaques and the Wounded Stag from "As You Like It"* (*English Landscape*, 1835).

72. John Constable, copy of Raphael, *"Feed My Sheep"* (engraving by Dorigny) (1795). Pen and wash drawing.

73. John Constable, *English Landscape: Old Sarum* (1833). Mezzotint by Lucas.

74. John Constable, *English Landscape: Stoke by Nayland* (1833). Mezzotint by Lucas.

75. Samuel Palmer, *Ruth Returned from Gleaning* (1828–29).

76. John Constable, *Hampstead Heath* (Vale of Health Pond) (ca. 1820).

77. John Constable, *Hampstead Heath: The House Called "The Salt Box" in the Distance* (ca. 1820).

78. John Constable, *Branch Hill Pond* (1819).

79. John Constable, *Branch Hill Pond* (1825).

80. John Constable, *Branch Hill Pond* (1828).

81. John Constable, *Branch Hill Pond* (1836).

82. John Constable, *The Dell in Helmingham Park* (1830).

83. John Constable, *Scene of Woods and Water* (ca. 1835?).

INDEX

Italicized numbers indicate figures.